THE CONVENTION ON THE
RIGHTS OF THE CHILD

The CONVENTION *on the* RIGHTS *of the* CHILD

United Nations Lawmaking
on Human Rights

LAWRENCE J. LeBLANC

≈

University of Nebraska Press
Lincoln and London

The paper in this book meets the minimum requirements of American National
Standard for Information Sciences–Permanence of Paper for
Printed Library Materials, ANSI z39.48-1984.

Library of Congress Cataloging in Publication Data
LeBlanc, Lawrence J.
The convention on the rights of the child: United Nations
Lawmaking on Human Rights / by Lawrence J. LeBlanc
p. cm. —(Human rights in international perspective; v. 3)
Includes bibliographical references and index.
ISBN 0-8032-2909-7 (cl)
1. Children (International law)   I. Title.   II. Series.
K639.A41989L43   1995
341.4'81—dc20   94-11887

For my mother and Charley

~

CONTENTS

LIST OF TABLES

viii

ACKNOWLEDGMENTS

I BEGAN MY RESEARCH on the Convention on the Rights of the Child, the focus of this book, during my sabbatical year 1990–91, and I am grateful for the help that I have received from a number of individuals and institutions in bringing the project to a close. To begin with, I had the very good fortune of spending the year as a visiting scholar at the Netherlands Institute of Human Rights (SIM) at the University of Utrecht. It was one of the most productive years of my professional life, and I am especially grateful to Peter Baehr, director of SIM, and to his colleagues Leo Zwaak, Jacqueline Smith, and Ineke Boerefijn for their intellectual stimulation and gracious hospitality and assistance during my stay. Moreover, many friends at the Netherlands Institute for Economic and Social Research (NISER) were very helpful in many ways. I also owe a special debt of gratitude to Fred Steenbergen, formerly director of the international organizations documentation section at the Netherlands Foreign Ministry in The Hague, for helping me gain access to many United Nations documents that were vitally important to my research.

Numerous people who represented organizations or governments in the open-ended working group that drafted the Convention on the Rights of the Child were also very helpful, granting me interviews in Geneva, London, and The Hague in which they shared their insight and observations about the drafting process. I especially wish to thank Nigel Cantwell and David Johnson (Defense for Children International), Cynthia Price Cohen (Human Rights Internet), Florence Bruce (International Catholic Child Bureau), Leah Levin (Anti-Slavery Society), Mashid Fatio (Bahai International), Shep Harder (International Save the Children Alliance), Toine van Dongen (Netherlands Mission to the United Nations in Geneva), and Jacques Jansen (Netherlands Ministry of Justice) for their help.

ix

Vernon Van Dyke, Peter Baehr, David Forsythe, Arthur Blaser, Conway Henderson, Cynthia Price Cohen, James Marlin, Minkyu Cho, Howard Tolley, Jr., and Michiel van Emmerik read the manuscript in whole or in part and offered many helpful suggestions for improving the final product. I hope that they will all be pleased with the results, even though I did not adopt all of their suggestions.

Despite all the good help that I have received from individuals who either read the manuscript or granted interviews, I alone am responsible for any errors of fact or interpretation that remain in the book.

My research was supported financially by several institutions. The Netherlands America Commission for Educational Exchange granted me a Fulbright research grant during 1990–91. In addition to the financial support, Joanna Wind, executive director of the commission, and her staff did much to help me and my family to settle in Utrecht and to enjoy the cultural and social life of the Netherlands. The John D. and Catherine T. MacArthur Foundation (Program in Peace and International Cooperation) awarded me a generous research grant that financed travel and living expenses during my sabbatical. I am also grateful for the faculty fellowships and research grants that I received from the Marquette University Committee on Research, and in particular, I am grateful to Thaddeus J. Burch, S.J., chair of the Committee on Research and dean of the Marquette University Graduate School, for faculty development awards during 1990–93 which facilitated work on the manuscript and its final preparation for publication.

Finally, I am, once again, grateful to my wife, Mary, my friendliest critic, for reading the manuscript and making many suggestions on matters of style and substance.

INTRODUCTION

THE UNITED NATIONS GENERAL ASSEMBLY adopted the Convention on the Rights of the Child in November 1989, bringing to a close ten years of debate and discussion over the merits of the project and the content of its main provisions. Although some delegates expressed misgivings about several articles of the convention, or treaty, it was adopted by a broad consensus among the member states of the United Nations (see appendix C). By September 1990, less than one year after it was adopted, the convention had been ratified by 20 countries, the threshold figure required for it to enter into force. This set in motion the first election of the ten-member Committee on the Rights of the Child (CRC), the body that is charged with monitoring the implementation of the convention among the states that have ratified it, in February 1991. The convention continued to gain wide acceptance, and by the end of December 1992, it had been ratified by 127 countries and signed by 27 others (UN LS, 1993:187–88), an act that is often a prelude to actual ratification.

The rapid and widespread acceptance of the Convention on the Rights of the Child is impressive and remarkable. No other specialized United Nations human rights convention has been accepted so quickly and with such apparent enthusiasm. It took at least one and one-half years, and as much as three years, for the International Convention on the Elimination of All Forms of Racial Discrimination (hereafter cited as the Convention on the Elimination of Racial Discrimination), the Convention on the Elimination of All Forms of Discrimination Against Women (hereafter cited as the Convention on the Elimination of Discrimination Against Women), and the Convention Against Torture and Other Cruel, Inhuman or Degrading Treatment or Punishment (hereafter cited as the Convention Against Torture) to enter into force. At the end of 1992, only the Convention on the Elimination of Racial Discrimination had been ratified by more states than had the Convention on the Rights of the Child, and then by a very slim margin, 133 to 127. The subject matter of these specialized conventions has undoubtedly had something to do with the variations that have occurred in their entry into force and acceptance by states. Virtually everywhere in the world, children are perceived to be vulnerable to the most serious forms of human rights abuse. Therefore, a treaty that aims to protect them is not likely to be as controversial as one that, say, deals with discrimination against women, a subject that raises a host of cultural issues in some parts of the world. Even so, the fact remains that the Convention on the Rights of the Child has become the single most important international instrument on the rights of the child in a relatively short period of time. Its status as such has been ensured in part by its widespread ratification, which has made it the primary international legal instrument on the rights of the child, and in part by its growing political significance.

As the primary international legal instrument, the convention is the most authoritative standard-setting instrument in its field (see, e.g., Cantwell, 1992; Jupp, 1991; Lopatka, 1992; Pais, 1991). It will probably also set the guidelines for all future standard-setting activity regarding children. In fact, some indications to this effect are already apparent. The Hague Conference on Private International Law (1993) completed work on a convention on intercountry adoptions in May 1993, and Articles 20 and 21 of the Convention on the Rights of the Child, which pertain to adoptions, figured prominently in the negotiations on the 1993 convention.

The growing political significance of the convention is evident in the fact that its provisions are now taken into account in all serious discussions of the rights of the child, even among states that have not ratified it. For example, delegates from 159 countries who attended the World Summit for Children at the United Nations headquarters in September 1990 adopted a Plan of Action, which states in part that the "aspirations of the international community for the well-being of children are best reflected in the Convention on the Rights of the Child" (UN GA, 1990a:8). The delegates who attended the World Conference on Human Rights in Vienna in June 1993 included statements in the Vienna Declaration and Programme of Action (World Conference, 1993) welcoming the widespread ratification of the convention, and they urged its universal ratification by 1995 as well as its effective implementation through national and international mechanisms and programs. The United Nations Children's Fund (UNICEF) (1992:7), the premier international body concerned with the status and treatment of children, has argued that the adoption of the convention, and its endorsement by conferences such as the World Summit, are signs "of a new political priority for children and of a new promise of protection in the decade ahead."

If UNICEF is correct in its assessment, the new political priority for children could not have come at a better time. Reports about the abuse and exploitation of children throughout the world are published almost every day, and they stimulate further study and investigation by governmental and nongovernmental bodies. For example, in 1990 the United Nations Commission on Human Rights launched a "program of action" on the problems of the sale of children, child prostitution, and child pornography (UN ECOSOC, 1991a), and it appointed a "special rapporteur" to study these problems and to make recommendations on what might be done to prevent their occurrence (UN ECOSOC, 1991b). While noting some signs of improvement, UNICEF (1992:5) recently reported that a "quarter million of the world's young children are dying every week, and millions more are surviving in the half-life of malnutrition and almost permanent ill health." These problems do not exist exclusively in Third World countries. Millions of children are living in poverty in the United States. In fact, according to the Washington-based Children's Defense Fund (1991:21–35), the number of poor children in the United States increased during the 1980s even as poverty decreased for other groups, particularly the elderly.

The conditions under which children are living throughout the world raise legitimate concern about whether the entry into force and widespread ratification of the Convention on the Rights of the Child will have a beneficial impact on the status and treatment of children. In fact, as UNICEF (1993:9–10) has reminded us, a successful attack on the problems confronting children will require more than a legal commitment on the part of states; it will require also a political commitment on the part of governments everywhere to find solutions and put them into effect (see also Freeman, 1992:39–43; Melton and Limber, 1992:168–69). Nonetheless, the legal commitment remains important because it can provide the standard against which government actions can be measured and evaluated, as the delegates to the World Summit and the World Conference have already indicated. This stimulates interest in the Convention on the Rights of the Child itself. Why was a convention believed necessary? What could the convention be expected to accomplish that other human rights instruments could not? How is it to be implemented, and what are the prospects for its effective implementation? These are among the questions dealt with in this book, which is divided into three parts.

The chapters of part 1 provide an overview of the convention and the status of its ratification by states around the world. Specifically, chapter 1 examines the origins of the convention and the decision to draft it in the broader context of the United Nations human rights treaty-making process. The successful conclusion of that process depends on the resolution of a number of issues and problems that require initiative, creativity, and determination on the part of states and other international actors. As we will see in chapter 1, the Polish delegation to the United Nations took the initiative in 1978 and proposed the adoption of a convention on the rights of the child. After some deliberation, the Commission on Human Rights established an "open-ended" working group to draft the convention. In chapter 2, we will appraise the participation of the representatives of states and international governmental and nongovernmental organizations in the working group.

As we approach the issues and problems dealt with in part 1, it should be borne in mind that the proposal to draft the Convention on the Rights of the Child raised the fundamental philosophical question of whether a special convention was either necessary or desirable. Many opponents of a special treaty argued, among other things, that the rights of the child should be addressed only within the larger context of human rights, and they believed that the human rights instruments already adopted by the United Nations and other international organizations provided sufficient coverage of those rights. In contrast, proponents of a special treaty argued that only a child-specific instrument could provide the protection that children need because of their vulnerability to the most serious kinds of human rights abuses.

There was something to be said on both sides of the issue. The Convention on the Rights of the Child is not the first, nor will it be the last, international instrument to proclaim or affirm rights of—or relevant to—the child. In fact, the status and treatment of children were long ago determined to be legitimate matters of international concern. The Geneva Declaration of the Rights of the Child (see appendix A), which was endorsed by the League of Nations in 1924, was the first major international instrument to affirm that idea. The United Nations adopted the Declaration of the Rights of the Child (see appendix B) in 1959. It has also adopted, along with other global and regional international organizations, many other child-specific and general-purpose human rights instruments that affirm rights of the child (Kubota, 1989). According to a survey conducted by Interights (1986), a London-based nongovernmental organization (NGO), various international organizations adopted a total of sixty-nine such instruments between the turn of the century and the mid-1980s. Philip Veerman (1991), in a study that used different criteria from those of the Interights survey, compiled a list of forty declarations and conventions that focus exclusively on the child. In the face of all these standard-setting instruments, the question could legitimately be raised, why was another convention necessary? Since children are human beings, were they not sufficiently covered by general-purpose human rights conventions? Similar questions have been raised when other specialized human rights conventions have been discussed or proposed to deal with such matters as discrimination against women, migrant workers, or indigenous peoples.

The disagreement on this fundamental issue was especially serious during the earliest stages of negotiations on the convention, and it extended beyond the confines of the United Nations, involving scholars and activists in the fields of human and children's rights. To some extent, the disagreement persists. Some scholars and activists take an extreme, liberationist point of view, advocating that children generally should have the same rights as adults. At the opposite extreme, some see children as so in need of being nurtured and protected that they should not be thought of as bearers of rights at all. Most seem to take the middle ground, favoring some limitations on the autonomy of the child but seeing a need to recognize their rights because, as Michael Freeman (1992:31) states, "possession of them is part of what is necessary to constitute personality." Some scholars (e.g., Verhellen, 1992; Veerman, 1991) have gone further and argued that the image of the child has changed in recent decades — that the child has come to be perceived as a bearer of rights and capable of exercising them. To the extent that disagreement persists on these fundamental issues, it is not likely to have much of a negative impact on future ratification of the Convention on the Rights of the Child. Indeed, as will be discussed in chapter 2, the speed with which the convention has already been accepted suggests that a special convention has become broadly perceived as necessary, or at least as more beneficial than harmful.

The chapters of part 2 focus on the norms of the convention, or the rights of the child. According to Article 1 of the convention, a "child" is every human being below the age of eighteen years unless he or she has attained the age of majority earlier in accordance with law. The drafters realized, of course, that some "older" children function more or less as adults within their societies, and for this reason, they gave some thought to the possibility of adopting a lower age limit. In fact, as we will discuss more fully in chapter 5, they adopted a lower age limit so far as the participation of young people in armed conflicts is concerned. For general purposes, however, they were persuaded to follow the precedents that have been set in other human rights instruments, making people below eighteen years of age children. Indeed, as many scholars in this field have argued, eighteen years of age is the most widely accepted upper age limit of childhood nationally and internationally (e.g., Davis and Schwartz, 1987). Thus, unless a specific exception exists, as in the case of the participation of young people in armed conflicts, the rights affirmed in the Convention on the Rights of the Child apply to all people below eighteen years of age unless they have attained majority earlier.

Traditionally, human rights have been thought of in terms of two principal categories: civil and political rights; and economic, social, and cultural rights. For much of the post–World War II period, these categories were fixtures of international ideological disputes between East and West, with some Western states, especially the United States, emphasizing civil and political rights and with some socialist and Third World states emphasizing economic, social, and cultural rights. During the 1960s, the traditional categories came under heavy attack, and the General Assembly adopted several resolutions affirming the "indivisibility" of human rights (see, e.g., van Boven, 1991:3–10). At the same time, human rights scholars and activists (e.g., Donnelly, 1989; Forsythe, 1989; Limburg Principles, 1987; Shue, 1980; van Boven, 1991) began to question the value of the traditional categories and to argue that linkages exist between different rights. For example, many now argue that it makes no sense to speak of a right to life without at the same time speaking of those rights that sustain life, such as the rights to food and to an adequate standard of health care. The substantive articles of the Convention on the Rights of the Child reflect this "new" way of thinking because they affirm a broad range of civil, political, economic, social, and cultural rights while making no formal distinctions among them.

The tendency to perceive human rights as indivisible raised the question of how to organize an examination of the rights of the child, part 2 of this book. Thomas Hammarberg (1990:99–101) developed one classification scheme applicable exclusively to the Convention on the Rights of the Child, which he called the "three P's" of "provision" (the fulfillment of basic needs such as the rights to food, health care, and education), "protection" (the right to "be shielded from harmful acts or practices" such as commercial or sexual exploitation and involvement in warfare), and "participation" (the right "to be heard on decisions affecting one's own life"). Jack Donnelly and Rhoda Howard (1988:214–15) have developed a classification scheme more broadly applicable to human rights in general. Their scheme, which was initially developed to facilitate the assessment of national human rights performance in a comparative perspective, groups rights into four main categories: "survival" rights, including not only the right to life itself but also those rights that sustain life, such as the rights to food and health care; "membership" rights, including those that relate to a person as a part of the community, such as nondiscrimination and family rights; "protection" rights, "which guard the individual against abuses of power by the state"; and "empowerment" rights, including those that make a person effectively a member of the community in which he or she exists, such as the freedom of thought, conscience, and religion, the freedom of association and assembly, and the right to education.

These two classification schemes overlap considerably, but they also differ in some important respects. Their definitions of "protection" rights, for example, are quite different, with Hammarberg's definition being much more useful in thinking about the Convention on the Rights of the Child because it deals with the need to shield children from harmful acts and practices such as sexual and economic exploitation. At the same time, Donnelly and

Howard's definition of "survival" rights is broader and preferable to Hammarberg's definition of "provision" rights because it brings into focus the right to life. Therefore, for the chapters of part 2, I have used the main categories in the classification scheme developed by Donnelly and Howard, but I have modified them somewhat, especially in the category of "protection" rights, in order to take into account those practices that are especially important to the security and well-being of children.

But even if all rights are equally important, as the new classification schemes would have us believe, they are not all likely to be equally controversial. And some of them are, in practice, likely to be considered more important than others. In fact, this is what occurred in drafting the Convention on the Rights of the Child. For these reasons, in chapters 3, 4, 5, and 6, I focus on a selected group of rights in each of the four categories of survival, membership, protection, and empowerment rights. The rights that I chose to highlight in these chapters are the ones that were the most difficult to come to agreement on for inclusion in the convention, judging by the amount of time that was devoted to them by the drafters, or they were the rights that were considered the most controversial or important by the representatives of governments and organizations that I interviewed for this book. Thus, in chapter 3 ("Survival Rights"), I focus on the right to life, including the controversial issue of abortion, and on a group of rights that sustain life, for example, the right to an adequate standard of health care; in chapter 4 ("Membership Rights"), I address the important principle of nondiscrimination, the rights to a name and nationality, and family rights; in chapter 5 ("Protection Rights"), I focus on a group of rights that guard the child from harmful acts and practices such as sexual and economic exploitation, abduction, and participation in armed conflicts; and in chapter 6 ("Empowerment Rights"), I discuss the freedom of thought, conscience, and religion and the right to education.

My objective in the chapters of part 2 is not to reach conclusions

regarding the "true" meaning of words and phrases in the substantive articles of the convention. Nor am I concerned with determining the extent to which provisions of the convention are legally
compatible or, as the case may be, incompatible with the laws of
any particular country. Judgments regarding such legal matters
properly belong to government officials, courts, and international
bodies such as the Committee on the Rights of the Child. My objective is to identify and explore the issues and problems that arose
in drafting the articles, the proposals and formulas that were advanced to resolve the problems, and the implications of the solutions that were adopted. As we shall see, defining the rights raised
important issues of emphasis and priority. Different points of view
were expressed and positions taken, requiring the development of
compromises among the drafters of the convention. Since the
compromises were reached in a multilateral context in which people of different cultures and religions participated, they will not
satisfy everyone. But the drafters managed to reach a broad consensus among themselves on the main points at issue. At the same
time, they recognized the need to maintain the normative consistency of the convention's provisions with those of other human
rights instruments.

The chapters of part 3 deal with the implementation mechanism
of the convention, the Committee on the Rights of the Child. The
entry into force of the convention in September 1990 set in motion
the procedures for conducting the first election of the CRC in February 1991. Since then, the committee has met in formal sessions to
adopt its rules of procedure, engage in discussions of topics of special interest to it, and begin the process of examining reports that
the states parties to the convention will periodically submit to the
committee.

In some respects, the provisions of the convention that pertain
to the structure and functions of the Committee on the Rights of
the Child track familiar ground. Therefore, the CRC is not unlike
some committees established under other human rights conven-

tions. It consists of "independent experts" whose main function will be to try to persuade countries that have ratified the convention to effectively comply with its provisions. In fact, the thrust of the convention is to emphasize essentially nonconfrontational implementation procedures, as though the task of the CRC will be to assist countries in meeting their obligations under the convention rather than penalizing them for failing to do so. In other respects, the convention contains some provisions regarding the CRC that are considered innovative for a human rights treaty. For example, it contemplates a role for specialized agencies of the United Nations and "other competent bodies," a phrase that was understood to refer to NGOS, in fostering compliance with its terms.

These implementation provisions of the convention were, of course, like all other provisions, the result of a process of negotiation and compromise that took place in the open-ended working group. As in the case of all other provisions, various issues and problems were raised, discussed, and resolved during the negotiations. I have divided these issues and problems into two categories. In chapter 7, we will deal with the basic structural characteristics of the CRC. In chapter 8, we will deal with the functions that the committee will perform. Since the committee has already held several sessions, I have drawn on the records of its discussions and its decisions in order to see if any early trends have emerged in its work or experience. Moreover, since the United Nations has already had a great deal of experience with the operation of other committees under several specialized human rights conventions mentioned earlier, in chapters 7 and 8 I have put the Committee on the Rights of the Child into a broader, comparative perspective alongside those other committees, including the Committee on the Elimination of Racial Discrimination (CERD), the Committee on the Elimination of Discrimination Against Women (CEDAW), and the Committee Against Torture (CAT).

In approaching the issues and problems dealt with in this book, I have relied on a variety of primary and secondary materials.

United Nations documents were vitally important, especially those of the Commission on Human Rights, the Economic and Social Council (ECOSOC), and the Third (Economic and Social) Committee of the General Assembly. These documents provided insight into the kinds of issues and problems that arose in drafting the convention and the difficulties that the drafters experienced in reaching compromises. In addition, records of the CERD, CEDAW, and CAT were especially important for chapters 7 and 8.

Interviews with governmental representatives and with representatives of organizations that were key players in the drafting of the Convention on the Rights of the Child provided additional and very important insight into the issues and problems addressed in this book. The interviews were wide-ranging in their coverage of the drafting process. To stimulate as much as possible the free flow of information, I assured all those interviewed that I would hold their comments in confidence. My objective was not to lay blame on anyone for any flaws either in the drafting process or in the final product; instead, I wanted to let the written records speak for themselves and to use the interviews to clarify the records and, in some instances, to supplement them when the written records seemed insufficient. For these reasons, it seemed appropriate to extend assurances of confidence to those interviewed.

Finally, to give depth and meaning to the norms and implementation mechanism of the convention, I have drawn on the extensive body of literature that has been developed by scholars and activists in the fields of children's rights and human rights.

ABBREVIATIONS

CAT   Committee Against Torture
CEDAW   Committee on the Elimination of Discrimination
           Against Women
CERD   Committtee on the Elimination of Racial
           Discrimination
CRC   Committee on the Rights of the Child
DCI   Defense for Children International
ECOSOC   Economic and Social Council
FAO   Food and Agriculture Organization
ICJ   International Commission of Jurists
IGO   international governmental organization
ILO   International Labour Organization
IWRAW   International Women's Rights Action Watch
NGO   nongovernmental organization
UNESCO   United Nations Educational, Scientific and Cultural
           Organization
UNHCR   United Nations High Commissioner for Refugees
UNICEF   United Nations Children's Fund
WHO   World Health Organization

THE CONVENTION ON THE
RIGHTS OF THE CHILD

PART ONE

Establishing the Convention

1 · Origins and Background

ONE OF THE MOST important ways in which the United Nations fosters the development and strengthening of international human rights law is through the adoption of treaties and conventions such as the Convention on the Rights of the Child. We shall, therefore, begin our study of the convention by putting it in the broader context of the United Nations treaty-making process. That process, from the initiation to the implementation of treaties, has been heavily criticized in recent years. Among other things, as we will see in this chapter, critics have attacked the seemingly casual way in which decisions have been made regarding the drafting of treaties and the resulting loss of what they have called "quality control" in the treaty-making process. As a result, the critics charge, normative inconsistencies have occurred among different treaties and conventions, and implementation mechanisms that do not function properly have proliferated. Would such criticisms apply as well to the Convention on the Rights of the Child? We shall begin by looking more closely at the nature and criticisms of the treaty-making process. Then, taking these into account, we shall examine the initiation stage in the conclusion of the Convention on the Rights of the Child.

THE UNITED NATIONS
TREATY-MAKING PROCESS

In the late 1970s, the General Assembly began a review of the processes then in use to conclude multilateral treaties. The review was prompted by criticisms expressed by the Australian foreign minister in a speech he made to the General Assembly in 1976. Specifically, he attacked the "varied, chancy, frequently experimental and often inefficient" ways in which treaties were concluded by the United Nations (UN LS, 1985:7). Although criticisms of this nature had occurred sporadically through the years, on this occasion the General Assembly dealt with the issue by requesting the secretary-general to prepare a report on the multilateral treaty-making processes then in use. If the report indicated a need for improvement in the United Nations procedures, the General Assembly would consider the ways and means of doing so.

The secretary-general's report, which was not completed until 1985, was based mainly on a survey of the attitudes of member states, specialized agencies, and other global and regional international governmental organizations. It also took into account the views and opinions expressed by delegates to the Sixth (Legal) Committee of the General Assembly during their discussions of the treaty-making process on several occasions during the early 1980s. The report ranged far and wide, covering the procedures of the United Nations and other international organizations. Although the report has been largely ignored and is seldom cited, it contains valuable information concerning the attitudes of states and organizations about the multilateral treaty-making process in general and the United Nations procedures in particular.

Perceptions of the Treaty-Making Process

The secretary-general's report stated that the majority of member states appeared to be satisfied with the existing United Nations treaty-making procedures (UN LS, 1985:41). This conclusion, however, was based more on the absence of explicit criticisms of the procedures than on express approval of them. In fact, only 19 of the approximately 160 member states at the time submitted written comments and observations in response to the survey. Some of these were obviously not satisfied with the procedures. The Australian government, for example, whose foreign ministers' criticisms had stimulated the study, complained about the "excesses" of treaty-making, and it suggested that the number of treaties being drafted and adopted placed "serious strains on the resources of governments, particularly those of developing countries." Although it recognized that the "elaboration of multilateral treaties on a wide variety of topics" was an "essential part of the work of the United Nations," the Australian government was concerned that the growth in the number of such treaties since the 1960s was not "matched by any rationalization of the treaty-making process" (UN LS, 1985:42). Some Third World countries echoed these views, pointing out that they faced "financial, technical or personnel difficulties that affected their effective participation in treaty-making, and they expressed the hope that the General Assembly's review might in some way come up with solutions which might reduce their burden" (UN LS, 1985:41).

The Austrian government took a somewhat different, though nonetheless critical, stand. It expressed concern about the "heavy burden" that the treaty-making enterprise placed on legal and administrative capabilities of states, but it argued that "to attribute existing problems solely or even mainly to deficiencies in the treaty-making procedure and, hence, to expect that they would disappear with a revision of the latter" would be deceiving. According to the Austrian government, the problems originated "primarily in the international community's unrestrained appetite for new international instruments," which it then had "difficulties in digesting nationally." The Austrian government suggested that this "unsatisfactory situation" could be corrected only by setting priorities and reducing the yearly output of treaties (UN LS, 1985:43)

The secretary-general's survey found that "seemingly the only generalization possible" about the treaty-making process in the United Nations was that it was almost always a "multistage process," involving in varying degrees experts, working groups, restricted bodies such as small committees, and representative bodies (UN LS, 1985:17). In some specialized organizations, such as the International Labour Organization (ILO), the process was highly structured; in others it was highly unstructured (UN LS, 1985:76). In fact, the negotiating processes varied from one organization to another, sometimes being hierarchically arranged, perhaps starting with small groups of experts and moving up to government representatives. At other times, plenary or open-ended groups were used, sometimes breaking up into small formal or informal negotiating groups that eventually reported back to the larger organs (UN LS, 1985:28).

The report also addressed the idea of devising a uniform or structured approach to the treaty-making process. Proposals to this effect have sometimes been put forward, with the ILO usually suggested as a good role model, since it has highly structured procedures (see Leary, 1992:580–619). However, many states that replied to the secretary-general's survey indicated that they did not believe it would be possible to establish uniform rules of procedure for the conclusion of most treaties because such rules were appropriate only for treaties that deal with highly technical issues, as ILO treaties usually do (UN LS, 1985:76). As the Austrian government put it, the "often quoted wisdom that the subject determines procedure ought to be borne in mind and a uniform code for all sorts of multilateral treaties should, therefore, not be attempted." It proposed, however, the development of a manual of treaty-making procedures, "annotated with practical considerations derived from experience," which would encourage choosing the most appropriate approach in the development of particular treaties (UN LS, 1985:43).

Despite these reservations about uniform procedures, the question of how to deal with the "excesses" of treaty-making remained. Some states argued that the General Assembly itself might assume a more prominent role, functioning more or less as a gatekeeper, scrutinizing proposals for the drafting of treaties and disallowing those that lacked merit (UN LS, 1985:61–62). Others argued that preliminary or preparatory studies should be carried out to assess the feasibility and desirability of all new treaties, or that priorities should be set, or that states should exercise self-restraint in proposing new treaties. But none of these proposals seemed to enjoy widespread support, and there was considerable doubt as to their efficacy. In fact, as noted earlier, many states seemed uninterested in the study itself. Those that were interested were especially pessimistic about the General Assembly assuming the role of coordinating treaty-making for various reasons: its agenda was already too crowded; other United Nations organs that had traditionally played a role in treaty-making might think the General Assembly was encroaching on their responsibilities; the member states themselves should decide if they wanted to conclude treaties in any field; and the General Assembly simply was not competent to make decisions of that sort (UN LS, 1985:68). Many states also had reservations about the ability of the International Law Commission of the United Nations to deal with the excesses of treaty-making; they believed that the commission was not well suited to handling issues of "an exclusively political character" (UN LS, 1985:92).

The secretary-general's report was thorough in its breadth of coverage, and it shed light on the problems that have plagued the multilateral treaty-making process broadly conceived. But, as we have seen, relatively few states were concerned about these problems, and fewer still were prepared to commit the time and energy that would be required to reform the system. In brief, the report's assertion that states were satisfied with existing multilateral treaty-making processes seems accurate; their satisfaction might be inferred from their silence. In any case, the problem is certainly not a lack of knowledge about the processes. The problem is essentially political. States have developed and utilized the existing processes, and they can change them if they want to do so, but they have been unwilling to invest the time and energy that would be required to develop different and perhaps better processes.

The Human Rights Treaty-Making Process

Simultaneously with the emergence of concern about the United Nations treaty-making process in general, questions were beginning to be raised specifically about treaty-making in the human rights field. In fact, that particular process has been the subject of intensive study in recent years. Theo van Boven (1979, 119 – 35; 1989:2 – 10), who served as director of the United Nations Division (now Centre) of Human Rights from 1977 to 1982, Theodor Meron (1986), B. G. Ramcharan (1989), and Philip Alston (1984) have all studied the process. So have the chairs of several human rights bodies (the Human Rights Committee, the Committee on Economic, Social and Cultural Rights, the Group of Three on Apartheid, the CERD, CEDAW, and CAT) that were established under different conventions. These chairs met jointly on three occasions, in 1984, 1988, and 1990, and were joined by the chair of the Committee on the Rights of the Child, which had only recently come into existence, at their fourth meeting in 1992. The studies have differed in approach and points of emphasis, but they have all come to the same conclusion: the need for "quality control" in the human rights treaty-making process.

The problems identified in these studies range over the entire human rights treaty-making process from proposal to implementation. A glimpse of these problems had been provided by the report that the secretary-general submitted to the General Assembly in 1985. That report claimed that human rights treaties had been initiated in principal organs of the United Nations, in subsidiary organs, and at diplomatic conferences that were convened inside and outside of the United Nations. The initial drafts had been prepared by the secretariat, ad hoc groups of experts or "working groups," specific governments, standing organs, and by the Commission on Human Rights. The General Assembly had scrutinized the final drafts in its Third (Economic and Social) Committee or Sixth (Legal) Committee, depending on the specific nature of the treaties. And the entire process of treaty-making from proposal to conclusion had run from about one year to more than one decade (UN LS, 1985:19). Overall, the secretary-general's report painted a picture of a process over which relatively little control existed. As a later study would suggest, draft human rights treaties had come to acquire a life of their own, with no express decision ever being taken on the fundamental question of their necessity or desirability (UN GA, 1989b:63).

Other studies have focused on more specific problems. In the first place, some critics have argued that insufficient attention has been given to the issue of the appropriateness of the type of instrument that should be adopted in any given instance. They have pointed out that negotiations on human rights instruments seem always to move toward the conclusion of new treaties, which establish legally binding obligations among the states that ratify them, rather than toward nonbinding agreements such as declarations. Yet, as the critics maintain, it is not clear that binding agreements are always preferable. As van Boven (1989:8) has observed, "Declarations address themselves immediately (without long ratification delays) to the whole of the UN membership and, as the case may be, to other actors and organs of society at national and international levels, thus expressing the notion of collective and universal responsibility." Hence, they may be preferable on some occasions. In cases where binding agreements may in fact be preferable, van Boven argues that protocols to existing instruments, rather than free-standing treaties, may be appropriate.

A second problem that many critics have pointed to is the normative inconsistency that sometimes occurs from one human rights instrument to another. This problem arises when different instruments that could be ratified by the same states provide different definitions of specific rights. The right to life, for example, may be defined in one instrument (e.g, the American Convention on Human Rights) in such a way as to have an impact on matters like abortion, whereas in another instrument (e.g., the International Covenant on Civil and Political Rights) it may be defined in such a way as to have no impact, or a different impact, on the same matters. The problem is potentially quite great when one considers the broad range of civil, political, economic, social, and cultural rights that may be dealt with in human rights instruments. The problem, as well as how to avoid it, has become more serious and complicated by the seemingly unending proliferation of human rights instruments. The secretary-general's report on the multilateral treaty-making process pointed out that as "the body of international law created by multilateral treaties increases, greater and greater problems arise about possible conflict between treaties already in force, whether on a world-wide or regional or otherwise restricted basis, and new proposed instruments" (UN LS, 1985:32).

The chairs of the human rights treaty bodies have also expressed concern that "inconsistencies in the provisions of international instruments and, in particular, between provisions of global instruments and those of regional instruments might raise difficulties with regard to their implementation" (UN GA, 1990b:8). Even the General Assembly has discussed the matter, and it adopted a resolution (Resolution 41/120) in 1986 in which it urged the member states and the United Nations organs to "accord priority to the implementation of existing international standards in the field of human rights." Delegates to the World Conference on Human Rights in June 1993 included a statement in the Vienna Declaration and Programme of Action (World Conference, 1993:3,1.5) reiterating the importance of the normative consistency of human rights instruments as follows:

> The World Conference, recognizing the need to maintain consistency with the high quality of existing international standards and to avoid proliferation of human rights instruments, reaffirms the guidelines relating to the elaboration of new international instruments contained in General Assembly resolution 41/120 and calls on the United Nations human rights bodies, when considering the elaboration of new international standards, to keep those guidelines in mind, to consult with human rights treaty bodies on the necessity for drafting new standards and to request the Secretariat to carry out technical reviews of proposed new instruments.

Clearly, there is broad concern that the proliferation of human rights instruments could jeopardize consistent interpretation of human rights standards and thus undermine the coherence and credibility of the treaty system itself (UN GA C.3, 1990:11; UN ECOSOC, 1988:1 – 2).

Finally, the critics have identified several practical problems that they have seen as growing out of the proliferation of human rights instruments, especially treaties and conventions. For states, of course, and especially for less developed countries, it is expensive to participate in treaty-drafting activities. Moreover, competent personnel need to be available. As we will see in chapter 2, many of the less developed states claim that they lack the financial and personnel resources to participate in treaty-drafting activities to the extent that they would like. Once treaties or conventions are adopted, different problems arise if states ratify them. Ratification can strain the domestic court systems and the administrative agencies that must fulfill reporting requirements. The financial and administrative costs are also high for the United Nations, especially for the Centre for Human Rights, which must service a growing standard-setting and implementation system while trying to ensure the consistency of the standards that are adopted (van Boven, 1989:7 – 8; UN GA, 1989b:57 – 58).

Various proposals have been put forth to address these problems, but like the general treaty-making process, they seem to have little chance of being acted on. One suggestion that is often made is that priority be given to implementing existing human rights agreements rather than to drafting new ones (UN GA, 1989b: 59 – 60); some go further to suggest that a moratorium be declared on the drafting of new instruments (UN ECOSOC, 1988a). As we have just seen, the General Assembly adopted a special resolution in 1986 in which it called on the member states to give priority to the implementation of existing human rights instruments. The idea seems sound, although there is no evidence that it has taken firm hold. States continue to propose new standards, or the revision of existing standards, and they are likely to continue to do so because the need for new standards arises in the face of changing times. These considerations make proposals to declare a moratorium on the drafting of new instruments untenable. As van Boven (1989:3–4) has rightly pointed out, concern for quality control in the development of human rights instruments, although very important, should not obscure the need to close existing gaps in human rights law that affect the rights and interests of especially vulnerable people and groups, such as those suffering from AIDS. In fact, in July 1989, the United Nations Centre for Human Rights, with the technical and financial support of the World Health Organization, organized an international "consultation" on AIDS and human rights. Among other things, the consultation recommended that human rights bodies around the world consider what actions they could take to protect the human rights of people "at risk or affected by HIV/AIDS" (United Nations, 1991:21–22).

A second—though not necessarily more realistic—suggestion has been to set priorities in standard-setting. This is an approach widely endorsed by states and organizations alike. Most frequently, the Commission on Human Rights is suggested as an appropriate body to engage in a thorough review of standard-setting activities and even to authorize only a limited amount of such activities. Those who make this suggestion are aware that it may be difficult to adhere to, since many states want to maintain flexibility in deciding which areas need further standard-setting (UN GA, 1989b). However, a certain amount of self-policing may be possible if all states are reminded of the standards laid down in General Assembly Resolution 41/120, as the 1993 World Conference on Human Rights has done. Moreover, there is no reason that proposals for new standard-setting instruments should not be accompanied by thorough studies as to their need and that a requirement could not be established that, as Alston has put it, a "specific decision be taken before the drafting of an instrument is begun" (UN GA, 1989b:63–64).

A third suggestion is that adequate steps be taken to ensure the normative consistency of human rights instruments. As noted earlier, this has come to be perceived as especially important in view of the proliferation of human rights instruments. But how is normative consistency to be achieved? Some propose making expert advice and consultation available to drafting bodies as they do their work (UN GA, 1989b:66, 1990b:8). Others suggest that careful research be done to survey existing instruments that bear on the subject matter, including instruments adopted by organizations other than the one contemplating drafting a new instrument. The International Labour Organization is usually cited as an example of an organization that has an especially well-developed practice of identifying all treaties that bear on the subject of international labor (UN LS, 1985:32). Still others suggest that draft human rights instruments be reviewed for their normative consistency with previously adopted instruments before they are finally adopted (UN GA, 1990b:9; World Conference, 1993:3,1.5). In the case of the Convention on the Rights of the Child, the United Nations secretariat conducted what was called a "technical review" of its provisions before it was adopted. The review (UN CHR, 1989a) drew on the expertise of various people and bodies, including intergovernmental and nongovernmental organizations. The drafters of the convention were quite pleased with the results of the review, although it may not have resolved all normative inconsistencies between the convention and other human rights instruments.

Since the technical review of the Convention on the Rights of the Child produced generally good results, some analysts had hoped that the procedure would become a more or less permanent feature of the human rights treaty-making process. However, the most recent experience, a technical review of the Convention on the Protection of the Rights of All Migrant Workers and Members of the Their Families, was not very satisfactory, and several states expressed displeasure with the results. The secretariat of the Centre for Human Rights was unable to prepare as thorough a review of the migrant workers convention as it might have owing to its limited personnel and financial resources (UN GA, 1990c:2 – 21). To make effective use of this procedure, therefore, will require a greater allocation of resources to the centre, and this, as we will discuss more fully in chapter 7, will be difficult in light of the financial difficulties that have affected United Nations operations since the early 1980s.

Fourth, it has been suggested that careful consideration be given to the types of human rights instruments that should be adopted. Binding instruments may not always be necessary, and if they are, perhaps consideration should be given to the adoption of protocols to existing instruments rather than new, separate treaties or conventions. This practice would help to control the potential problem of normative inconsistencies *and* the administrative and service problems that have arisen because of the proliferation of implementation systems (van Boven, 1989:8–10). The chairs of the treaty bodies have expressed somewhat different viewpoints on the relative advantages and disadvantages of protocols as opposed to separate instruments, but they have endorsed the need to contain the proliferation of implementing bodies as much as possible. Accordingly, they have suggested that "whenever possible the supervisory or monitoring functions established under new human rights treaties should be assigned to appropriate existing treaty bodies that were felt to possess the necessary competence." The chairs were aware, of course, that the uniqueness of some instruments would demand the creation of uniquely suited implementation mechanisms (UN GA, 1990b:9; see also UN GA, 1992b:18–19).

Fifth, and finally, it has been suggested that human rights lawmaking be centralized in a specialized body created for that purpose. Meron (1986:279–84) made such a suggestion after concluding a wide-ranging analysis of the problems that have arisen in the human rights lawmaking process. To develop his model, he surveyed alternative lawmaking models that have been utilized in trade, labor, and outer space negotiations, the general lawmaking model of the United Nations International Law Commission, and the lawmaking models of some regional organizations such as the Council of Europe. As Meron sees it, the United Nations should emulate the practice of the Council of Europe and "regard the task of human rights law-making not as an operation designed to produce a particular instrument, but as a continuing process, which includes extension, elaboration, consolidation, and revision." To do this, the United Nations needs an organ, which Meron calls the United Nations Human Rights Law Commission (UNHRLC), that would "devote its entire time to, and specialize exclusively in, human rights law-making." He suggests that the UNHRLC be relatively small and composed of experts. It would not matter much whether the members were governmental representatives or independent experts so long as they were, according to Meron, genuine experts. Moreover, the UNHRLC would not necessarily have a monopoly on human rights lawmaking, though it should be charged with drafting at least the most important human rights instruments of general interest (Meron, 1986:289–90).

As conceived by Meron, the effective operation of the UNHRLC would help to overcome all of the major problems that exist in the present system of human rights lawmaking. But as he anticipated, critics of his proposal have greeted it with skepticism. Alston (UN GA, 1989b:60–61), for example, has argued that the United Nations is not likely to create any new organs in light of its chronic financial problems. Moreover, he believes that the creation of a specialized body for human rights treaty-making is probably not appropriate because human rights issues are broader, more diverse, and inherently more politically controversial than are the kinds of issues normally dealt with by specialized lawmaking bodies such as the International Law Commission. But Meron's proposal is based on a presumed need for reform that has arisen because of the obvious inadequacies in the present system and that may not be as insensitive to political realities as Alston makes it out to be. In any event, as Meron (1986:269) points out, the deficiencies in the present system are "not always rooted in political factors, but often in incompetence, hasty consideration and approval, lack of adequate research and editing, and so on and therefore must not be viewed as inevitable and beyond reasonable prospects for reform."

THE ORIGINS OF THE CONVENTION

To what extent are the criticisms of the human rights treaty-making process applicable to the Convention on the Rights of the Child? At this point, we are concerned only with issues of a preliminary nature, that is, those that arose in connection with the decision to draft the convention. In subsequent chapters, we will deal with issues related to the procedure used to draft the convention, its norms, and its implementation mechanism.

The Proposal to Draft a Convention on the Rights of the Child

The Convention on the Rights of the Child originated in a proposal submitted by the Polish government to the thirty-fourth session of the United Nations Commission on Human Rights in 1978 (UN CHR, 1978a:1–5). Earlier, in 1976, the General Assembly had adopted a resolution proclaiming 1979 as the International Year of the Child. Various programs were planned in celebration of that year, and the Polish government looked to the adoption of a convention on the rights of the child as one of its most concrete achievements.

Although the proclamation of the International Year of the Child provided an opportunity for the Polish government to take this initiative, its interest in protecting children dated back to World War II (Cantwell, 1992:20–21). During the war, over two million Polish children were killed. Many had been subjected to Nazi persecution and medical experimentation. The Polish delegation to the United Nations during its formative years pressed the Commission on Human Rights to deal with the numerous child-related problems that had arisen out of the war. Preliminary work was begun on a draft declaration on the rights of the child, but it was not until 1959 that the General Assembly adopted the Declaration of the Rights of the Child. In the meantime, the Polish delegations to the United Nations continued to advocate the adoption of a legally binding instrument such as a convention (Tolley, 1987:44, 139–40).

Polish organizations also became involved in this endeavor. In January 1979, the Polish Association of Jurists hosted a conference on Legal Protection of the Rights of the Child in Warsaw. Two high-profile NGOs, the International Commission of Jurists and the International Association of Democratic Lawyers, were also listed as conference organizers, which ensured that the proceedings would get some international publicity. Numerous jurists from Poland and other East and West European countries, as well as representatives from several United Nations bodies, participated in the conference. The conference was chaired by Professor Adam Lopatka, who was then president of the Polish Association of Jurists and a delegate to the United Nations Commission on Human Rights. He subsequently chaired all sessions of the open-ended working group, discussed more fully in chapter 2, that was established by the Commission on Human Rights to draft the Convention on the Rights of the Child, and he became known as the "father" of the convention. At the close of its proceedings, the Warsaw conference issued a "Statement of Principles on the Legal Protection of the Rights of the Child," in which it elaborated the responsibilities of the state, the parents, and the child in a variety of issue areas such as education, health, and recreation. It also "demanded" an end to child labor everywhere (ICJ *Review*, 1979:63 – 66). In the main, the statement of principles took a traditional approach to the rights of the child, emphasizing their protection and the need for positive action by the state on their behalf.

Other than suggesting that the adoption of a convention on the rights of the child would be an appropriate way to celebrate the International Year of the Child, the proposal that the Polish delegation submitted to the United Nations Commission on Human Rights in 1978 provided no extensive rationale for the adoption of a convention. It claimed that there was a "need to further strengthen the comprehensive care and well-being of children all over the world" (UN CHR, 1978a:1, 1978b:10), but it cited no deficiencies in existing human rights laws, nor did it indicate any specific weaknesses in the existing human rights mechanisms that operate on behalf of children (see, e.g., Cantwell, 1992:21). To the Polish delegation, the need for a convention was presumably self-evident. But as far as the members of the Commission on Human Rights were concerned, the proposal raised two fundamental questions. First, was a convention really necessary? Second, was the time appropriate to adopt a convention?

The Commission on Human Rights discussed the Polish proposal at meetings in early March 1978, and representatives of several states and nongovernmental organizations addressed both questions explicitly and implicitly. The governmental representatives divided along traditional East/West lines not unusual for that time. Lopatka naturally defended both the need for a convention and the timing of his government's proposal (UN CHR, 1978c:2, 1978d:9–10), and he was supported by delegates from the German Democratic Republic, Bulgaria, and the Soviet Union. For the most part, their comments were heavily laced with ideological overtones. For example, Rudolf Frambach, a delegate from the German Democratic Republic, argued that a convention was necessary because children "continued to be the innocent victims of acts of aggression, colonialism, fascism and racism and were still exposed to discrimination" on various grounds (UN CHR, 1978d:11–12). V. A. Zorin, the Soviet delegate, could not imagine how anyone "who was concerned about human rights and the rights of future generations could object" to drafting a convention on the rights of the child (UN CHR, 1978d:13–14).

Representatives of some Third World countries also supported the Polish initiative. Didimo Rios of Panama, for example, stated that his government planned to commemorate the International Year of the Child in various ways. He also claimed that work on a convention could create a climate that would encourage states to enact measures to protect children (UN CHR, 1978c:2).

In contrast, representatives of Western states questioned both the need for a convention and the timing of the project. Edward

Mezvinsky of the United States argued that it would be premature to negotiate a convention that could be adopted as early as 1979 because so much work remained to be done at the national level to implement the principles affirmed in the United Nations Declaration of the Rights of the Child, which the General Assembly had adopted in 1959 (UN CHR, 1978c:2). Alan Rowe of Canada wondered if the project "should be given priority in the work" of the Commission on Human Rights and also whether it was "appropriate" to talk about drafting a convention when governments, specialized agencies, and other governmental as well as nongovernmental organizations had not yet been able to express their views on the need for one (UN CHR, 1978d:10). Hans Danelius of Sweden voiced similar concerns (UN CHR, 1978d:12). Sir Keith Unwin of the United Kingdom questioned the need for a convention, suggesting that the sponsors of the project had not "sufficiently demonstrated the advantages" of a convention and that it seemed "premature to push on at the present stage of discussions" with the project (UN CHR, 1978d:12).

But it was not only governmental representatives that took a position on the questions of the need for a convention and the timing of the Polish proposal. In February 1978, twenty NGOs accredited to the ECOSOC issued a statement on the subject. Although they generally favored the eventual conclusion of a convention, seeing it as important from the standpoint of the protection of the rights of the child, they questioned the timing of the proposal to draft a convention. As they stated at the time, several studies, surveys, and programs concerning the rights of the child, and the ways and means of implementing various international instruments in the field of children's rights, were already planned or in progress by governments, international governmental organizations (IGOs), and NGOs in connection with the International Year of the Child. In their view, the "value of a Convention on the rights of the child would be that much greater and richer if it could take into account the results of this work." For this reason, they suggested that debate on the draft convention "commence only when the results of these studies" were known, that is, not earlier than 1980 (UN CHR, 1978e:1).

The representatives of Eastern European states generally dismissed the reservations of the NGOs. Lopatka argued that NGOs should not need "several years to make their opinions known on questions which they had long had under consideration" (UN CHR, 1978d:11). Ivan Garvalov of Bulgaria took a more explicitly state-centric position, claiming that it was the views of the member states, not the NGOs, that were "particularly important, since it was they which would become parties to the Convention" (UN CHR, 1978d:13). In contrast, the representatives of several Western states supported the NGO position.

The compromise that resulted from the Commission on Human Rights deliberations was to modify the terms of the Polish draft resolution so that it would call for the conclusion of a convention on the rights of the child "if possible" at the thirty-fifth session of the Commission on Human Rights in 1979. In the meantime, the secretary-general was to invite the member states of the United Nations and IGOs and NGOs that maintained consultative status with the ECOSOC to submit their observations and suggestions regarding the draft convention to the commission (UN CHR, 1978c:2–3).

Results of the Secretary-General's Survey

Approximately 40 member states replied to the secretary-general's survey regarding a convention on the rights of the child, a relatively modest number given the total membership of the United Nations at that time (approximately 160 states), although surveys of this sort often attract little attention. In addition, the ILO, the United Nations Educational, Scientific and Cultural Organization (UNESCO), the World Health Organization (WHO), and 14 NGOs replied (UN CHR, 1978f, 1979a-e, 1980a).

The states divided into two main groups. Most of them stated that they approved the drafting of a convention, although many of their statements were highly qualified, implying perhaps serious reservations but also an unwillingness, for political reasons, to take a strong stand against the project. It is difficult enough for governments to be officially indifferent to violations of human rights; it is even more difficult to be indifferent when children are involved because they are perceived as being so vulnerable to the most serious forms of human rights abuses. Thus, even if some governments may have had legitimate objections to proceeding with the drafting of a convention on the rights of the child, they found it very difficult to oppose the idea for fear of being perceived as indifferent to the status and treatment of children. In addition, some governments may simply have concluded that it would be imprudent to oppose another government's proposal that might do some good, or at least probably do more good than harm.

Many of the other respondents made extensive comments about the Polish draft, criticizing its form and content. Several West European states—including Belgium, the Federal Republic of Germany, the Netherlands, Norway, and Sweden—expressed special concern about the fact that the draft merely repeated the principles proclaimed in the 1959 Declaration of the Rights of the Child, and they considered this inappropriate for a convention. The Belgian government, for example, flatly asserted that the "sole effect of the Polish draft" was to "give an existing declaration the form of a binding convention" but that the Declaration of the Rights of the Child "was not, and was not intended to be, drafted in such a way as to be directly usable as a convention" (UN CHR, 1978f:8). The Netherlands government argued that for a convention to be useful, it "must consist of timely, up-to-date and concrete principles, accompanied by practical guidelines for application, and supplementary to already existing instruments and activities," none of which characterized the Polish draft (UN CHR, 1978f:14). The government of the Federal Republic of Germany suggested that the Polish draft should be considered only as a "starting point for deliberations" and that it "should be subjected to a thorough, careful and unhurried review." In this connection, it proposed that "consideration should be given to the possibility of convening a group of experts to carry out a comprehensive and specialist review of all the questions which ought to be raised during the preparation of a convention, in particular, legal issues or questions relating to social policy" (UN CHR, 1978f:10–13). The Swedish government called attention to one of the most serious issues, namely, the need to be especially careful about the proposed convention's normative consistency with existing international agreements on human rights, particularly the International Covenants on Civil and Political Rights and on Economic, Social and Cultural Rights, which the General Assembly had adopted in 1966 (UN CHR, 1978f:16–17).

Some governments that had expressed serious reservations about drafting a convention when the issue was discussed in the Commission on Human Rights in 1978 reiterated their concerns, though none of them voiced strong opposition, implying, once again, that they were dissuaded from doing so by essentially political considerations. The Australian government, for example, aligned itself with a number of NGOs and suggested that the question of whether or not a convention was desirable should be deferred until after the activities that had been planned in connection with the celebration of the International Year of the Child in 1979 were over (UN CHR, 1978f:6). The United Kingdom repeated its reservations about the need for a convention and indicated that it remained convinced that the proposal needed further study, though it stated its willingness to support the elaboration of a convention if the majority of member states believed there should be one (UN CHR, 1978f:18).

The IGOs and specialized agencies of the United Nations that replied to the secretary-general's request for comments generally agreed that the project should be pursued and offered some suggestions for making technical improvements in the Polish draft (UN CHR, 1978f:20–21). The bulk of the NGOs, however, expressed grave concern about proceeding with a convention at that time. As noted earlier, twenty NGOs had issued a joint statement setting forth their reasons for opposing the project in 1978 (UN CHR, 1978e). They were concerned mainly about the timing of the preparation of a convention, but this is not to say that they wholeheartedly endorsed the need for one. In response to the secretary-general's survey, they reiterated their position that work on a convention should be delayed until after the studies and projects that had been planned for the International Year of the Child had been completed (UN CHR, 1978f:21–24).

The Convention and the Human Rights Treaty-Making Process

When we look back over the initial stages in the development of the Convention on the Rights of the Child, the weaknesses in the human rights treaty-making process discussed earlier are apparent. At no time was there serious discussion about the need for a convention. Nor was any thorough or comprehensive study undertaken to establish whether such a need existed. Yet, as we discussed in the introduction, before the adoption of the convention there had been no shortage in standard-setting activity relating to children, as the surveys by Interights (1986) and Philip Veerman (1991) have shown. Some opponents of the adoption of a convention, referring to all of this previous standard-setting activity in the field of human rights, believed that the large number of existing instruments provided sufficient coverage of the rights of the child. Proponents of a convention usually replied that although children were implicitly covered by general-purpose human rights treaties by virtue of their status as human beings, they deserved special protection because of their special needs, protection that only a child-specific instrument could provide. But the debate on this fundamental philosophical issue never really moved toward a conclusion on the merits of either viewpoint. In fact, there seems never to have been an express decision by any United Nations body on the need for a convention on the rights of the child before the drafting work actually began. Instead, the proposal developed a life of its own.

In retrospect, in the earliest stages, the drafting of the Convention on the Rights of the Child did not enjoy very broad-based support, but perhaps more important, it did not face strong and sustained opposition. Rather than opposing the project in principle, states as well as organizations concentrated their attack on the form and content of the Polish draft. This had the effect of slowing down the drafting process, but it did not block the process. Indeed, in marked contrast to the speed with which the convention entered into force, the process of drafting it proceeded very slowly, beginning in 1979 and finally ending in 1989. In the interim, the initial Polish draft was so transformed that the final text of the convention scarcely resembles the draft either in form or in content.

The draft convention began with ten very brief articles that closely tracked the norms proclaimed in the 1959 Declaration of the Rights of the Child (Cantwell, 1992:21) and with only one article regarding implementation, which would have required the states parties to report periodically to the United Nations Economic and Social Council (UN CHR, 1978a:2 – 5). In final form, the convention consists of forty-one detailed substantive articles and extensive provisions regarding its implementation through the Committee on the Rights of the Child assisted by IGOS and NGOS. Along the way, important compromises were reached regarding both the norms and the implementation mechanism, which will be the subjects of our attention in parts 2 and 3.

2 · Drafting and Ratifying the Convention

BESIDES THE QUESTION of whether there is a need for a particular human rights treaty or convention, other significant issues of public policy arise in the treaty-making process. A forum must be chosen to conduct the negotiations. The states and other actors in the international system that will be permitted to participate in the negotiations must decide whether to participate and, if so, to what extent. Governments must then decide whether to ratify, and thus to formally accept, the obligations spelled out in the treaty or convention. These issues identify our main concerns in this chapter. First, we will appraise the roles of the various actors that participated in drafting the Convention on the Rights of the Child. Second, we will analyze the practice of countries in various regions of the world in ratifying the convention.

DRAFTING THE CONVENTION

The Convention on the Rights of the Child was drafted by an "open-ended" working group established for that purpose by the United Nations Commission on Human Rights in 1979. To say that the group was open-ended means that participation in it was open to states and to nonstate actors such as IGOS and NGOS. The commission has established such groups on other occasions, most recently in connection with the drafting of the Convention on the Protection of the Rights of All Migrant Workers and Members of Their Families. In fact, open-ended working groups seem to have become the forum of choice for United Nations human rights treaty-drafting activities.

The working group usually met for a week before the regular sessions of the Commission on Human Rights until its work was completed in 1989 (UN CHR, 1979f, 1980b, 1981–1988, 1989b). Con-

sistent with the practice that has become commonplace in the deliberations of some United Nations bodies, the working group
reached its decisions by what is called "consensus," that is, no formal votes were taken. Instead, agreement was reached through debate and compromise. Precisely when a consensus can be said to
have been reached in such a group is, of course, not always clear.
The absence of any strong dissent is usually taken as an indication
of a consensus, but for all practical purposes, the chairs of meetings determine when a consensus does or does not exist on a given
point under negotiation (see Kaufmann, 1988:24–30). Obviously,
the process of reaching a consensus can tax the diplomatic skills of
the most talented chairs, and in some instances, a consensus simply cannot be said to have been reached. On such occasions, decisions must be passed on to higher bodies including the General Assembly. As we will discuss more fully in chapter 7, because of the
strong dissent of the United States, the drafters of the Convention
on the Rights of the Child could not reach a consensus on how to
finance the work of the Committee on the Rights of the Child.
Therefore, the decision on this issue was passed on to the Commission on Human Rights, which, in turn, passed it on to the General Assembly, where the outcome was determined by a roll call
vote in the Third Committee. This was the only issue on which a
formal vote was taken during the entire drafting process. The convention as a whole was adopted by consensus.

The Role of States

A great deal has been said in recent years about the emergence
of various international and transnational nonstate actors in international politics, but it is generally agreed that states remain the
primary actors in the international system (e.g., Keohane and Nye,
1989). This is certainly the case for human rights treaties.
States—and only states—can ratify such treaties, so they can be
expected to play the most important role in drafting them. For this
reason, it seems appropriate that we should begin with states in

our analysis of the roles of the various actors that participated in drafting the Convention on the Rights of the Child.

States that were members of the United Nations Commission on Human Rights were automatically entitled to participate in the open-ended working group. If they were not members of the commission, they could participate as nonvoting observers if they were member states of the United Nations or non–member states that maintained observer status (e.g., the Holy See and Switzerland) in the United Nations (Cantwell, 1992:21–22). In principle, therefore, since virtually all states in the world are members of the United Nations, participation in the working group was open to almost all states on a purely voluntary basis.

One way to gauge the interest of states in the convention is to look at the frequency with which they participated in the sessions of the working group. Beginning in 1981, the reports of the working group listed the states that were represented at the sessions. The fact that a state was listed does not, of course, mean that its representatives actively participated during the session. Nor does it tell us anything about the type of representation, for example, specialist-expert or general diplomatic, or, in the case of diplomatic representation, the level at which it took place. In fact, there were significant variations among states in these respects; developed states were generally represented by experts and higher-ranking diplomatic agents, whereas less developed states were usually represented by lower-ranking members of their permanent delegations to the United Nations (see, e.g., Cantwell, 1992:23; Johnson, 1992:96–97).

Despite these variations, the frequency with which states participated in the working group is important for two reasons. First, the simple fact that a state was represented at all at a session tells us something about the interest of that state's government in the convention and, more broadly, about its interest in the further development of international law on the rights of the child. Second, according to the information contained in the reports of the working group, it seems that the delegations that participated most frequently were also the ones that made the most significant substantive contributions—in other words, a high level of participation in quantitative terms generally translated into high-quality participation as well. Therefore, let us look more closely at the quantitative aspects of state participation in the working group.

In table 2.1, the states that participated in the sessions are grouped into the seven major geographical regions used by the United Nations for various purposes, including surveying trends in the composition of the secretariat (UN GA, 1992a:70–72). The eighth group, labeled "others," is also used by the United Nations and was included in table 2.1 to take into account states (e.g., the Holy See, Monaco, and Switzerland) that have enjoyed observer status in the United Nations. It was necessary to include these states because some of them were active participants in drafting the convention and/or have since ratified it.

The classification scheme utilized in table 2.1 is, of course, geographical and not—which some analysts might prefer—geopolitical. Thus, in this scheme, South Africa is included among African states; Australia and New Zealand are included among Asian and Pacific states; Albania is included among East European states; Israel, Cyprus, and Turkey are included among Middle Eastern states; and Canada and the United States are included among North American and Caribbean states. The member states of the United Nations themselves have developed an informal grouping that is geopolitical in nature and has been used for such things as determining equitable geographical representation in elections to various United Nations bodies (UN GA, 1990d:9, 73). In that scheme, Albania, Israel, and South Africa are not members of any regional group; countries such as Australia, Canada, New Zealand, Turkey, and the United States are considered part of a group called "West Europe and Other" for election purposes.

However, recent events in international politics, notably the breakup of the Soviet empire and the disintegration of the Soviet

Union itself, will probably have a significant impact on the informal grouping of states. Since the regions are geopolitical, how states identify themselves is important. Some states that were part of the Soviet Union itself, such as some of the Baltic states, may not want to be considered among the East European group. Some East European states, such as Poland, have joined West European states in the Council of Europe, and perhaps in the future all of these states will simply think of themselves as "European." And how will all the other new states that were formerly part of the Soviet Union — such as Azerbaijan, Kazakhstan, Kyrgyzstan, Tajikistan, Turkmenistan, and Uzbekistan — think of themselves? Even the recent United Nations practice, classifying all of these states as being part of the East European geographical region, may have to change in the future.

Since all of these issues are unresolved, it seemed best to follow the most recent United Nations classification and to group the member states into geographical regions as reflected in table 2.1 and in other tables in this book. For analytical purposes, it was important to have some way of classifying the member states into regions. Such classification will help us to explore any differences that may have occurred among the various regions in terms of their participation in the drafting of the Convention on the Rights of the Child. The convention, like other United Nations human rights treaties, is, in principle, an instrument of global applicability. Yet, we know from studies of the drafting of other United Nations human rights instruments (e.g., Burgers and Danelius, 1988; Barsh, 1989; Lerner, 1980) that West European and other highly developed states have tended to dominate the negotiations. Did this occur also in the case of the Convention on the Rights of the Child? Grouping the states into regions will also help us better understand any regional patterns that may have developed in terms of the ratification of the convention. What might explain the variations, if any? And what might be their significance?

Table 2.1

<small>STATES AS PARTICIPANTS IN THE DRAFTING PROCESS, I</small>

Region   Years Participating in the Working Group, 1981 – 1989

	At least 9 of 9 (%)	At least 8 of 9 (%)	At least 7 of 9 (%)	At least 6 of 9 (%)	At least 5 of 9 (%)
Africa (51 states)	0	0	2 (3.92)	3 (5.88)	3 (5.88)
Asia and Pacific (27 states)	2 (7.41)	4 (14.81)	4 (14.81)	6 (22.22)	7 (25.93)
Europe — East (11 states)	2 (18.18)	3 (27.27)	4 (36.36)	5 (45.45)	5 (45.45)
Europe — West (18 states)	4 (22.22)	8 (44.44)	9 (50.00)	10 (55.55)	11 (61.11)
Latin America (21 states)	2 (9.52)	3 (14.29)	4 (19.05)	5 (23.81)	6 (28.57)
Middle East (17 states)	0	0	0	0	2 (11.76)
North America and Caribbean (14 states)	2 (14.29)	2 (14.29)	2 (14.29)	2 (14.29)	2 (14.29)
Others (3 observers)	1 (33.33)	2 (66.67)	2 (66.67)	2 (66.67)	2 (66.67)
Total (162)	13 (8.02)	22 (13.58)	27 (16.67)	33 (20.37)	38 (23.46)

SOURCE: Compiled from reports prepared by the working group on the Convention on the Rights of the Child of the United Nations Commission on Human Rights for the years 1981–89.

NOTE: To simplify the compilation of data for this table, no effort was made to take into account any variations in membership in the United Nations over the years from 1981 to 1989. These variations were small and would not have had a significant impact on the results presented in this table.

AFRICA (51): Algeria; Angola; Benin; Botswana; Burkina Faso; Burundi; Cameroon; Cape Verde; Central African Republic; Chad; Comoros; Congo; Côte d'Ivoire; Djibouti; Egypt; Equatorial Guinea; Ethiopia; Gabon; Gambia; Ghana; Guinea; Guinea-Bissau; Kenya; Lesotho; Liberia; Libyan Arab Jamahiriya; Madagascar; Malawi; Mali; Mauritania; Mauri-

In constructing table 2.1, only those states that participated in a majority (at least five) of the nine working group sessions that were held between 1981 and 1989 were included. This standard is a reasonable test of the long-term commitment of states to the development of the convention. Since participation in the working group was voluntary, no distinction was made between those states that were members of the Commission on Human Rights or that participated as observers. As table 2.1 shows, the different regions varied in terms of the intensity of their participation. Excluding for the moment the group of "other" states, we see that the states in the West Europe region — the states that, as we discussed in chapter 1, were the most skeptical of the need for a convention — were the main participants. The records show that the four major participants in this region were France, the Netherlands, Norway, and the United Kingdom, all of which participated in every session between 1981 and 1989. Other important participants in this region were Sweden, Denmark, the Federal Republic of Germany, and

---

tius; Morocco; Mozambique; Niger; Nigeria; Rwanda; Sao Tome and Principe; Senegal; Seychelles; Sierra Leone; Somalia; South Africa; Sudan; Swaziland; Togo; Tunisia; Uganda; United Republic Tanzania; Zaire; Zambia; Zimbabwe.

ASIA AND PACIFIC (27): Australia; Bangladesh; Bhutan; Brunei Darussalam; Cambodia; China; Fiji; India; Indonesia; Japan; Lao People's Democratic Republic; Malaysia; Maldives; Mongolia; Myanmar; Nepal; New Zealand; Pakistan; Papua New Guinea; Philippines; Samoa; Singapore; Solomon Islands; Sri Lanka; Thailand; Vanuatu; Vietnam.

EUROPE (EAST) (11): Albania; Byelorussian SSR; Bulgaria; Czechoslovakia; German Democratic Republic; Hungary; Poland; Romania; USSR; Ukrainian SSR; Yugoslavia.

EUROPE (WEST) (18): Austria; Belgium; Denmark; Federal Republic of Germany; Finland; France; Greece; Iceland; Ireland; Italy; Luxembourg; Malta; Netherlands; Norway; Portugal; Spain; Sweden; United Kingdom.

LATIN AMERICA (21): Argentina; Bolivia; Brazil; Chile; Colombia; Costa Rica; Cuba; Dominican Republic; Ecuador; El Salvador; Guatemala; Haiti; Honduras; Mexico; Nicaragua; Panama; Paraguay; Peru; Suriname; Uruguay; Venezuela.

MIDDLE EAST (17): Afghanistan; Bahrain; Cyprus; Democratic Yemen; Islamic Republic of Iran; Iraq; Israel; Jordan; Kuwait; Lebanon; Oman; Qatar; Saudi Arabia; Syrian Arab Republic; Turkey; United Arab Emirates; Yemen.

NORTH AMERICA AND CARIBBEAN (14): Antigua and Barbuda; Bahamas; Barbados; Belize; Canada; Dominica; Grenada; Guyana; Jamaica; Saint Kitts and Nevis; Saint Lucia; Saint Vincent and the Grenadines; Trinidad and Tobago; USA.

OTHERS (3 Non–Member States): Holy See; Monaco; Switzerland.

Italy, which participated in at least eight of the nine sessions. Only two of the eighteen members of the region, Iceland and Luxembourg, did not participate in any of the sessions of the working group.

The East Europe region scored second highest. Even though it is the smallest of the regions, with eleven states, the participation rates for most of those states were high. The USSR, as one might have expected in view of its political importance in the region, was the major participant, attending every session of the working group. Poland too, whose delegation to the United Nations introduced the proposal to draft a convention on the rights of the child and whose minister, Adam Lopatka, chaired all the sessions of the working group, participated every year, sending observers to the sessions after its membership on the Commission on Human Rights ended in 1984. Other major participants in this region were the German Democratic Republic and Bulgaria; Hungary was the only state in this region not to participate in any sessions of the working group.

As table 2.1 also shows, when compared with the West and the East European regions, the Asia and Pacific and the Latin American regions had considerably lower participation rates. Only two Latin American countries (Argentina and Brazil) and two from Asia and Pacific (Australia and India) participated in all nine sessions of the working group that were held between 1981 and 1989. More of the states in both regions participated in at least five of the nine sessions, but even then, their participation rates were low when compared with those of the countries in the West Europe and the East Europe regions (seven, or 25.93 percent, for Asia and the Pacific, and six, or 28.57, percent for Latin America). The figures for the North America and Caribbean region were affected by the fact that not one of the twelve Caribbean states was represented at any of the sessions of the working group; Canada and the United States, however, attended all nine of the sessions.

Perhaps the most striking feature of the data in table 2.1 is the extremely low level of participation by states in the African and the Middle East regions. Only three of the fifty-one states in the African region (Algeria, Morocco, and Senegal) attended the sessions of the working group with any regularity. Senegal was the only African member of the Commission on Human Rights that participated extensively, attending seven of the nine sessions of the working group between 1981 and 1989. The Moroccan delegation participated as an observer for seven consecutive years from 1983 to 1989, and the Algerian delegation attended on six occasions during that same period, twice as an observer and four times as a member of the Commission on Human Rights. States in the Middle East region also participated infrequently. Only two of the seventeen countries in that region (Cyprus and Iraq) participated in a majority of the sessions of the working group.

Among the states that are classified as "Others," the Holy See and Switzerland showed great interest in the convention. Representatives of the Holy See attended all nine sessions of the working group between 1981 and 1989. Swiss representatives attended eight of the sessions.

In strictly quantitative terms, the data in table 2.1 tell us that the Western states and, to a somewhat lesser extent, the East European states were the principal drafters of the Convention on the Rights of the Child. This conclusion is consistent with the findings of other studies that have pointed out the importance — even the dominance — of Western states in drafting United Nations human rights conventions. Herman Burgers and Hans Danelius's study (1988) of the drafting of the Convention Against Torture provides a case in point (see also Barsh, 1989). Natan Lerner's study (1980) of the Convention on the Elimination of Racial Discrimination provides another example.

What accounts for the relatively low levels of participation by most other states — the great majority of which would be considered Third World countries — in this important endeavor? Needless to say, their lack of participation did not go unnoticed. In 1985, a group of NGOS, including Defense for Children International (DCI), Radda Barnen International, and the International Commission of Jurists (ICJ) submitted a statement to the Commission on Human Rights noting the importance of and need for participation by Third World countries in the working group. As these NGOS pointed out, a majority of the world's children live in the Third World, and although many of the issues that affect children are of global concern, the specific needs of children in the Third World required highlighting. As the NGOS saw it, this could be done most effectively by representatives of the Third World themselves (UN CHR, 1985b:1–2).

Despite this express appeal, the participation of Third World countries in the working group did not increase. The conventional explanation for this is that Third World countries do not have the trained personnel and financial resources to commit the time and energy that are necessary to participate effectively in standard-setting activities and certainly not on the order of the advanced Western states (see, e.g., Johnson, 1992:96–97). As noted in chapter 1 in our discussion of problems related to the human rights treaty-making process, some Third World countries have complained about scarce personnel and resources. In the case of the Convention on the Rights of the Child, this explanation is undoubtedly valid in some circumstances; it provides at least a partial explanation for the lack of participation by the poorest countries in the African region. But is it a valid explanation for the very low levels of participation by Middle Eastern states or by some states in Asia and Latin America, or even some in Africa? It seems reasonable to assume that other factors, including indifference and, in some cases, opposition to norm creation in the field of children's rights, affected the participation levels of many Third World countries.

Would a different approach produce a result different from that found in table 2.1, a result that would put Third World countries in a more favorable light? Table 2.2 is designed to test this possibility. The table carries over the last column of table 2.1 and also shows the participation rates of states in the different regions during only the last two years — 1988 and 1989 — of negotiations on the convention. Although the negotiations took place over ten years, the last two years were the most important. It was during those years that most of the negotiations concerning the structure and functions of the implementation mechanism of the convention, the Committee on the Rights of the Child, took place. It was also during those years that the "second reading" of the convention and the technical review of its draft provisions took place. For these reasons, it could be argued that the extent to which states participated in the 1988 and 1989 sessions provides a better measure of their interest in the further development of the norms and implementation mechanism of the convention than does the extent of their participation in all the sessions.

As the data in table 2.2 show, the participation rates for most of the principal regions were higher in the 1988 and 1989 sessions of the working group, and Third World countries appear in a somewhat more favorable light. The African states participated in greater numbers. So did states in the Asia and Pacific and the Latin American regions. The most impressive increase came, however, in the Middle East region, where nine of the seventeen states (52.94 percent) participated in the 1989 session of the working group. The main objective of these states was to push through last-minute substantive changes in the norms of the convention, to make them more compatible with Islamic thought and practice. We will discuss this matter more fully in various chapters of part 2. For the moment, suffice it to say that the Islamic states were especially concerned about the convention articles that pertain to freedom of religion (Article 14) and adoption (Articles 20 and 21), and significant concessions were made to them. The right of the child to choose his or her religion was dropped from Article 14; and Article 21 now applies only to states that "recognize and/or permit the system of adoption," which Islamic states neither recognize nor permit. The alterations reflect the importance of cultural factors in drafting international human rights instruments and show that the increased participation by Islamic states toward the end of the negotiations on the Convention on the Rights of the Child worked to their advantage.

Table 2.2

STATES AS PARTICIPANTS IN THE DRAFTING PROCESS, II

Region	Years Participating in the Working Group		
	At least 5 of 9 (%)	*1988 only (%)*	*1989 only (%)*
Africa (51 states)	3 (5.88)	7 (13.73)	9 (17.65)
Asia and Pacific (27 states)	7 (25.93)	8 (29.63)	10 (37.04)
Europe — East (11 states)	5 (45.45)	6 (54.55)	8 (72.73)
Europe — West (18 states)	11 (61.11)	12 (66.67)	15 (83.33)
Latin America (21 states)	6 (28.57)	7 (33.33)	10 (47.62)
Middle East (17 states)	2 (11.76)	4 (23.53)	9 (52.94)
North America and Caribbean (14 states)	2 (14.29)	2 (14.29)	2 (14.29)
Others (3 observers)	2 (66.67)	2 (66.67)	2 (66.67)
Total (162)	38 (23.46)	48 (29.63)	65 (40.12)

SOURCE: Compiled from reports prepared by the working group on the Convention on the Rights of the Child of the United Nations Commission on Human Rights for the years 1981–89.

Still, as the data in table 2.2 show, the West Europe and the East Europe regions also experienced significant increases in participation during the 1988 and 1989 sessions of the working group. At the 1989 session, fifteen of the eighteen states—over 80 percent—in the West Europe region and eight of the eleven states—over 70 percent—in the East Europe region participated. Thus, even with the increased participation of Third World countries toward the end of the negotiations on the convention, the data in table 2.2 confirm the conclusions drawn from the data in table 2.1.

The Role of IGOS, Specialized Agencies, and Other United Nations Bodies

Many nonstate actors such as IGOS, specialized agencies, and other United Nations bodies have competence in matters involving children or highly specialized competence in certain matters that would be addressed in a convention on the rights of the child. Examples include UNICEF, the ILO, the United Nations High Commissioner for Refugees (UNHCR), UNESCO, the Food and Agriculture Organization (FAO), and the WHO. Because of their interests or expertise, these organizations and agencies might have been expected to make important substantive contributions when the Convention on the Rights of the Child was drafted. The working group that drafted the convention was open to their participation. They would have participated as nonvoting observers, but this should not have been a major disincentive to them, since the working group was to reach its decisions by consensus. By contributing to the debates and discussions, they could have had an impact on the consensus reached on a variety of issues.

The records of the working group listed the IGOS, specialized agencies, and other United Nations bodies that were represented at the sessions held between 1981 and 1989. Their numbers were always small. In fact, only seven (UNICEF, the UNHCR, the ILO, UNESCO, the WHO, the League of Arab States, and the Inter-American Children's Institute of the Organization of American States) were listed as having participated in the final session of 1989. Although this figure is small when compared with the number of states—and, as we will see in a moment, the number of NGOs—that were usually involved in the negotiations every year, it is actually large when compared with what had happened in previous years. In most other years, only two or three IGOs, specialized agencies, or other United Nations bodies (usually UNICEF, the ILO, and the UNHCR) were listed as having sent representatives. Quantitatively, therefore, it would seem that agencies or organizations of this type showed relatively little interest in participating in drafting the Convention on the Rights of the Child.

But what about the quality of their participation, even if it was not extensive? As we will see in the chapters of part 2, some agencies or organizations took positions on matters of special interest to them during the negotiations. A few examples may be cited here: the ILO and the convention articles that deal with child labor and the exploitation of children; the WHO and the article on health care; and the International Committee of the Red Cross and the article pertaining to the involvement of children in situations of armed conflict. UNICEF showed considerable interest in the implementation provisions of the convention and made significant financial contributions that facilitated meetings of the NGO group discussed below. These agencies or organizations made substantive suggestions that were taken into account by the working group and often influenced the consensus that emerged. Overall, however, it would be fair to say that they tended to have narrow rather than general interests in the evolving convention.

Was this experience unusual? Could more have realistically been expected? The NGOs and some governmental representatives certainly expected more (see Cantwell, 1992:23–24). In fact, representatives of NGOs interviewed for this book were uniformly critical of the IGOs, specialized agencies, and other United Nations bodies for not taking a more active and constructive role in drafting the convention. UNICEF, of course, was credited for its financial contributions mentioned above, but it was widely criticized for not having taken a broader interest in the convention, particularly in the normative provisions. Overall, the NGOs were dissatisfied with what they considered low levels of attendance by the IGOs and specialized agencies at the sessions of the working group and claimed that the IGOs and agencies had been timid in bringing their expertise to bear on substantive issues.

The NGOs may have had unrealistic expectations. It is true, of course, that some IGOs have played important roles in the standard-setting or norm-creation process at the international level. The ILO, for example, has a long history of involvement in human rights standard-setting dating back to the immediate post–World War I period (Galenson, 1981; Leary, 1979, 1992; Lubin and Winslow, 1990). In fact, Leary (1992:586–87) argues that standard-setting has been more important in the totality of the ILO's work than it has been in the work of the United Nations and that its methods are more unified, standardized, and effective than are those of the United Nations. In other areas, even small and relatively obscure, United Nations bodies have been known to play important roles in the standard-setting or norm-creation process. Richard Benedick (1991), for example, in his work entitled *Ozone Diplomacy*, has shown how the United Nations Environment Programme (UNEP) was instrumental in the difficult and complex process of reaching an international consensus on the need to protect the ozone layer.

Nonetheless, IGOs such as the ILO tend to have relatively narrow interests. Even if, as Leary (1992:586–88) shows, the ILO has taken a more holistic approach to human rights issues, emphasizing both civil and political as well as economic and social rights, its long and commendable experience is precisely in those areas that relate to labor. Thus, it could not really have been expected to become seriously interested in all the many articles of the Convention on the Rights of the Child that dealt with issues not related to labor and economic exploitation. The same would have been true for other organizations and United Nations bodies such as the WHO and the UNHCR, which tend to have relatively narrow interests.

It is also not clear how much more could have been expected of specialized agencies like UNICEF. Although it may rightly be considered the premier international agency concerned with the status and welfare of children, UNICEF is primarily an operating agency and is only secondarily, if at all, a standard-setting agency. In fact, although it may possess substantial expertise that, in an ideal setting, should be shared with states and other actors involved in the elaboration of international norms, it faces realities that limit its potential value and effectiveness in such a process. It was created by governments and, for the most part, remains a creature of governments. Governments prescribe its mandate, establish much of its agenda, and provide most of its budget—all of which can serve to limit its independence or autonomy. Like other agencies or organizations of this type, it may be susceptible to political pressures and therefore may find an advantage to being prudent in its relations with states, allowing them to be primarily responsible for standard-setting and focusing its own energies on operational concerns (Rodley, 1979:157–78). In fact, as we will see at other points in this book, UNICEF has emphasized the importance of the Convention on the Rights of the child in its literature and has taken its provisions into account in developing its work programs in various countries.

The Role of NGOS

The work of NGOs in the field of human rights has long been the subject of observation and study. In fact, a large body of literature has been built up in this field (e.g., Chiang Pei-heng, 1981; Livezey, 1988; Steiner, 1991; Rodley, 1979; Wiseberg and Scoble, 1979; Weissbrodt, 1984; Armstrong, 1986; Tolley, 1989). Much of the research has focused on the work that NGOs do on behalf of the victims of human rights violations, and many scholars believe that they are very effective in this field, or at least more effective than governments could ever be expected to be. After all, governments are usually the violators of human rights, whereas NGOs have established their reputations as champions of the victims of human rights violations.

But NGOs have also been involved in human rights in other ways. They have lobbied governments and participated in educational or publicity campaigns, and they have been actively involved in the elaboration of international human rights norms. We know that NGOs were energetic in lobbying governments in favor of the inclusion of many of the provisions relating to human rights in the United Nations Charter (Humphrey, 1989). Since then, they have been involved in the elaboration of other human rights norms. Peter Baehr (1989:36–53) has shown how Amnesty International and the International Commission of Jurists played crucial roles in the development of the Convention Against Torture, which was adopted by the General Assembly in December 1984. According to Baehr, they "were of crucial importance in putting the issue on the international political agenda in the first place." By convening an international conference on the abolition of torture in 1973, Amnesty International helped to "mobilize interest in the subject among government officials and politicians alike." When work on drafting the Convention Against Torture began, NGOs such as the International Commission of Jurists took an active part in the debates.

In general, research has shown that NGOs can participate in the human rights norm-creation process in a variety of ways, including attending conferences, suggesting draft articles for inclusion in norm-creating instruments, criticizing articles in draft stage, doing research, providing advice and assistance, lobbying governments and other organizations, conducting publicity campaigns, and offering legal expertise and advice. The extent to which any particular NGO is able to engage in any of these activities depends on a number of factors, including the size and expertise of its staff and the availability of resources, and many of them face serious problems in these regards. Nonetheless, what is important is that NGOS could become involved in a very broad range of activities in the norm-creation process.

In the case of the Convention on the Rights of the Child, NGOS were involved in a variety of ways in the drafting process. The reports issued by the open-ended working group indicate that many NGOS attended its sessions. From 1983 to 1989, an average of twenty NGOS participated, and their numbers increased in the last two years of negotiations. Some participated individually and only sporadically through the years, and some were narrowly focused on specific issues. But what was most significant from the standpoint of NGO involvement was that, beginning in 1983, a group of organizations came together to form the Informal NGO Ad Hoc Group on the Drafting of the Convention on the Rights of the Child. The Geneva-based DCI served as the secretariat, and Nigel Cantwell of its staff served as the chief spokesman. The DCI was created in 1979, the year proclaimed by the General Assembly as the International Year of the Child, for the purpose of fostering international action toward promoting and protecting the rights of the child. By virtue of its location, interests, and very capable staff, the DCI was well suited to serving the NGO Ad Hoc Group.

The Ad Hoc Group provided a convenient vehicle through which a large number — thirty-five NGOS endorsed a joint statement on the convention at the close of the negotiations — of NGOS could consult and attempt to reach a consensus on the substantive articles as well as implementation provisions of the convention (DCI, 1983 – 1988). Since the group was large and very diverse, consisting of some human rights NGOS that were not necessarily focused on children, it could have been expected that a core group would have emerged and played a leading role. In fact, this occurred, with the DCI, the International Catholic Child Bureau (ICCB), Radda Barnen, Human Rights Internet, and the ICJ becoming the core group.

The Ad Hoc Group reached consensus on many important issues, and its members then lobbied the governmental delegations in the working group. However, since the group was composed of diverse NGOs, which had their own particular agendas, its reports always indicated that all of its members did not necessarily subscribe to every proposal or recommendation. In fact, according to Cynthia Price Cohen (1990:137–47), who represented Human Rights Internet and became widely respected among NGO and governmental representatives for her work on the convention, the Ad Hoc Group refused to be drawn into every area of concern in the field of children's rights, as in the case of the rights of the unborn child that will be discussed in chapter 3. Therefore, NGOs that wished to pursue their own agendas on such specific issues were free to do so. At the same time, the group assisted NGOs that were otherwise operating independently when it was asked for help and could reach a consensus (Cohen, 1990:141–42).

In addition to engaging in the traditional lobbying activities of trying to secure the inclusion of specific provisions in the convention, the Ad Hoc Group did a great deal to stimulate awareness of the work that was being done on the draft convention. Various NGOs sponsored or supported conferences, symposia, and exhibitions throughout the world on the convention or on specific topics in the field of children's rights that are covered by the convention. Regional seminars and workshops were also held. These activities helped to make the convention become perhaps better known than many other specialized human rights instruments, and they probably also had an impact so far as its rapid ratification is concerned. In fact, the NGOs continued their educational campaigns after the convention was adopted by the General Assembly. In August 1990, for example, a group of three Dutch NGOs sponsored an international child labor seminar in Amsterdam (Schaule Jullens, 1991), which was attended by eighty persons from all over the world. The recommendations of the seminar were then disseminated at two much larger meetings held in September 1990: the Eighth International Congress on Child Abuse, held in Hamburg, Germany, and the World Summit for Children, held at the United Nations.

At the close of the negotiations on the convention, the NGOS were generally satisfied with their accomplishments, although they had some misgivings. Speaking on behalf of thirty-five NGOS, Cantwell, spokesman for the Ad Hoc Group, stated that the NGOS would support the adoption of the convention if the governments of the world believed that its text reflected what was just and good. However, he went on to say that his group had some misgivings about the content of specific provisions of the convention.

We will deal more fully with some of the accomplishments as well as misgivings of the NGOS in the chapters of part 2. For the moment, suffice it to say that the NGOS successfully lobbied for such things as gender-free language throughout the convention and various specific rights or aspects of rights, as in the area of the exploitation of children; but they remained especially concerned about the failure of the convention to make an explicit statement protecting children from medical experimentation and about what they considered the "amazingly low level of protection" that the convention gives to children in situations of armed conflict (UN CHR, 1989c:18). Other NGO representatives criticized the content of specific articles that their organizations were especially concerned about (UN CHR, 1989d:3). Despite these reservations, most NGOS were satisfied with the outcome of the negotiations, believing that they had exercised substantial influence in improving the text of the convention and that any remaining weaknesses could be dealt with later through the adoption of protocols to the convention or additional specialized conventions.

The NGOS could also take comfort from the fact that many of the governmental representatives who were involved in drafting the convention were pleased with their contributions and made comments to this effect in the Commission on Human Rights and the General Assembly (UN GA C.3, 1989a:7). Some, such as Per Miljeteig-Olssen (1990:151−52), who represented Norway in the working group, have written about the experience. As she puts it, there were times when some NGOS "might have acted too much as single issue agencies, not able to take a general point of view" on the convention as a whole. And sometimes they took a more idealistic rather than realistic position on some issues, such as medical experimentation, traditional practices, and the involvement of young people in armed conflicts, a position that irritated some governmental delegations. But overall, she believed that the NGOs had engaged in a "constructive dialogue" with governmental delegates rather than being antagonistic. Furthermore, by emphasizing the welfare of children, the NGOs acted as a "balancing factor" against the tendency of the governmental delegates to become absorbed in legalistic disputes.

The question for the future is whether the NGOs will be able to maintain the high degree of cooperation they achieved during the drafting stage. This will be especially important in view of the fact that, as we will discuss in chapter 8, the NGOs will have a role to play in the implementation of the convention. Among other things, they will be in a position to provide "expert advice." Effective collaboration among the NGOs would maximize their impact in this endeavor, but it remains to be seen if they will be able to continue their cooperative efforts from the norm-creation stage to the implementation stage or if they will return to focusing on their own, more narrowly defined interests and concerns.

RATIFICATION OF THE CONVENTION

To the great satisfaction of many children's rights activists, the Convention on the Rights of the Child has been ratified at record-breaking rates; no other specialized United Nations human rights treaty has entered into force so quickly and been ratified by so many states in such a short period of time. But what states have been inclined to ratify? Have any patterns emerged among states in the various regions of the world? And under what, if any, conditions have these states ratified the convention?

Patterns of Ratification

We begin our analysis by looking at the extent to which countries in the various regions have ratified the Convention on the
Rights of the Child. The data in tables 2.3 and 2.4 provide insight
into this matter. Table 2.3 is based on data provided by the United
Nations secretary-general to the states parties to the convention as
they were preparing to conduct the first election of the Committee
on the Rights of the Child in February 1991. Among other things,
the secretary-general supplied the parties with a list of states that
had ratified the convention as of January 31, 1991 — the only states
that, in accordance with Article 43 of the convention, were eligible
to nominate candidates for election to the committee and to vote
in the first election (UN CHR, 1991). Table 2.4 is based on more recent data on the number of states that had ratified the convention
as of December 31, 1992 (UN LS, 1993:187 – 95).

Table 2.3

STATES PARTIES TO THE CONVENTION, I

Region	Number of States in Region	Number of States Parties as of January 31, 1991	%
Africa[a]	52	26	50.00
Asia and Pacific	27	9	33.33
Europe — East[b]	10	5	50.00
Europe — West[c]	19	6	31.58
Latin America	21	17	80.95
Middle East[d]	16	0	0
North America and Caribbean	14	5	35.71
Others[e]	4	2	50.00
Total	163	70	42.94

SOURCE: UN CRC, 1991a.

[a] Namibia became a member of the United Nations in April 1990 and has been added to this
group.

The data in table 2.3 are revealing. In the main, the states that were the most involved in drafting the convention were not as quick to ratify it. As the table shows, only six (France, Malta, Norway, Portugal, Spain, and Sweden) of the nineteen states (31.58 percent) in the West Europe region had ratified the convention by January 31, 1991. Yet, as shown earlier in tables 2.1 and 2.2, this region ranked the highest in terms of states participating in the sessions of the working group. However, it must be borne in mind that the West European states differ from each other in their approach to the ratification of conventions. Some (e.g., Sweden) ratify first and then adjust their domestic legislation if need be; others (e.g., the Netherlands) prefer to adjust their legislation first and then ratify. As we have seen, Sweden ratified the convention before the first election of the members of the crc was conducted; the Nether-

---

b The German Democratic Republic has been deleted from this group. Although it ratified the convention on October 2, 1990, it ceased to exist on October 3, 1990, when it united with the Federal Republic of Germany to form one sovereign state. "Germany" now represents this united state in the United Nations.

c Liechtenstein became a member of the United Nations in September 1990 and has been added to this group.

d The People's Democratic Republic of Yemen has been deleted from this group because in May 1990 it merged with the Yemen Arab Republic to form the "Republic of Yemen."

e The Democratic People's Republic of Korea has been added to this group. Although it was not a member state of the United Nations before January 31, 1991, it had ratified the convention in September 1990.

NOTE: Except for the additions or deletions indicated above, the states included in the various regions are the same as those listed in table 2.1.

AFRICA (26): Angola; Benin; Burkina Faso; Burundi; Chad; Djibouti; Egypt; Gambia; Ghana; Guinea; Guinea-Bissau; Kenya; Malawi; Mali; Mauritius; Namibia; Niger; Rwanda; Senegal; Seychelles; Sierra Leone; Sudan; Togo; Uganda; Zaire; Zimbabwe.

ASIA AND PACIFIC (9): Australia; Bangladesh; Bhutan; Indonesia; Mongolia; Nepal; Pakistan; Philippines; Vietnam.

EUROPE (EAST) (5): Byelorussian SSR; Czechoslovakia; Romania; USSR; Yugoslavia.

EUROPE (WEST) (6): France; Malta; Norway; Portugal; Spain; Sweden.

LATIN AMERICA (17): Argentina; Bolivia; Brazil; Chile; Colombia; Costa Rica; Ecuador; El Salvador; Guatemala; Honduras; Mexico; Nicaragua; Panama; Paraguay; Peru; Uruguay; Venezuela.

NORTH AMERICA AND CARIBBEAN (5): Barbados; Belize; Grenada; Guyana; Saint Kitts and Nevis.

OTHERS (2): Democratic People's Republic of Korea; Holy See.

lands had still not ratified by the end of 1992, though it was sure to do so. As we can see in table 2.4, by the end of December 1992, a huge increase in the number of West European states ratifying the convention had occurred. By that time, sixteen of the twenty states (80.00 percent) in the region had ratified.

Table 2.4

STATES PARTIES TO THE CONVENTION, II

Region	Number of States in Region	Number of States Parties as of December 31, 1992	%
Africa	52	39	75.00
Asia and Pacific[a]	31	19	61.29
Europe — East[b]	25	16	64.00
Europe — West[c]	20	16	80.00
Latin America	21	19	90.48
Middle East	16	7	43.75
North America and Caribbean	14	10	71.43
Others[d]	3	1	33.33
Total[e]	182	127	69.78

SOURCE: UN LS, 1993:187–95.

[a] The Democratic People's Republic of Korea, Marshall Islands, Micronesia, and the Republic of Korea became members of the United Nations during 1991 and have been added to this group.

[b] Between January 31, 1991, and December 31, 1992, the composition of this group underwent profound changes because of the breakup of the Soviet Union. The twenty-five members of the this group are as follows: Albania; Armenia; Azerbaijan; Belarus; Bosnia and Herzegovina; Bulgaria; Croatia; Czechoslovakia; Estonia; Georgia; Hungary; Kazakhstan; Kyrgyzstan; Latvia; Lithuania; Poland; Republic of Moldova; Romania; Russian Federation; Slovenia; Tajikistan; Turkmenistan; Ukraine; Uzbekistan; Yugoslavia.

[c] San Marino became a member of the United Nations in 1992 and has been added to this group.

[d] The Democratic People's Republic of Korea has been deleted from this group and added to "Asia and Pacific." See note (a) above.

[e] The total includes 179 member states and 3 non–member state observers (Holy See, Monaco, and Switzerland).

In the earliest stages, states in the East Europe region ratified the convention at about the same rate at which they participated in the open-ended working group. As table 2.3 shows, five (Byelorussian SSR, Czechoslovakia, Romania, the USSR, and Yugoslavia) of the ten states in the region had ratified the convention by January 31, 1991. As shown in table 2.4, by the end of 1992 this region had more than doubled in size, to twenty-five states, owing to the disintegration of the Soviet Union; most of these states (sixteen, or 64.00 percent) had ratified the convention.

What is most noteworthy about the data in table 2.3 is that the states in the African and Latin American regions, which scarcely participated in the drafting process, ranked very high in ratifying the convention. At the time of the first election of the Committee on the Rights of the Child, one-half of the states in the African region and more than two-thirds of those in the Latin American region had ratified the convention. As shown in table 2.4, these

---

NOTE: Except for the additions or deletions indicated above, the states included in the various regions are the same as those listed in tables 2.1 and 2.3.

AFRICA (39): Angola; Benin; Burkina Faso; Burundi; Cape Verde; Central African Republic; Chad; Côte d'Ivoire; Djibouti; Egypt; Equatorial Guinea; Ethiopia; Gambia; Ghana; Guinea; Guinea-Bissau; Kenya; Lesotho; Madagascar; Malawi; Mali; Mauritania; Mauritius; Namibia; Niger; Nigeria; Rwanda; Sao Tome and Principe; Senegal; Seychelles; Sierra Leone; Sudan; Togo; Tunisia; Uganda; United Republic Tanzania; Zaire; Zambia; Zimbabwe.

ASIA AND PACIFIC (19): Australia; Bangladesh; Bhutan; Cambodia; China; Democratic People's Republic of Korea; India; Indonesia; Lao People's Democratic Republic; Maldives; Mongolia; Myanmar; Nepal; Pakistan; Philippines; Republic of Korea; Sri Lanka; Thailand; Vietnam.

EUROPE (EAST) (16): Albania; Azerbaijan; Belarus; Bulgaria; Croatia; Czechoslovakia; Estonia; Hungary; Latvia; Lithuania; Poland; Romania; Russian Federation; Slovenia; Ukraine; Yugoslavia.

EUROPE (WEST) (16): Austria; Belgium; Denmark; Finland; France; Germany; Iceland; Ireland; Italy; Malta; Norway; Portugal; San Marino; Spain; Sweden; United Kingdom.

LATIN AMERICA (19): Argentina; Bolivia; Brazil; Chile; Colombia; Costa Rica; Cuba; Dominican Republic; Ecuador; El Salvador; Guatemala; Honduras; Mexico; Nicaragua; Panama; Paraguay; Peru; Uruguay; Venezuela.

MIDDLE EAST (7): Bahrain; Cyprus; Israel; Jordan; Kuwait; Lebanon; Yemen.

NORTH AMERICA AND CARIBBEAN (10): Bahamas; Barbados; Belize; Canada; Dominica; Grenada; Guyana; Jamaica; Saint Kitts and Nevis; Trinidad and Tobago.

OTHERS (1): Holy See.

figures continued to increase. By the end of December 1992, thirty-nine of the fifty-two African states (75.00 percent) had ratified the convention and nineteen of the twenty-one Latin American states (90.48 percent) had ratified it. Similarly, by the end of 1992, almost three-quarters of the states in the North American and Caribbean region had ratified the convention, whereas only two of them, Canada and the United States, had participated in drafting it. Canada was among the ten states in this region to have ratified the convention, but the United States was not.

Taken together, the data in tables 2.3 and 2.4 show that the states in the Asia and Pacific and the Middle East regions have lagged behind the states in other regions in terms of ratifying the convention, but their figures in this regard are consistent with their lower participation rates in the sessions of the working group that drafted the convention. Even so, their ratification percentages are impressive, especially those of the Middle East region. Only two of the states in that region had participated in a majority of the sessions of the working group, but as the data in table 2.4 show, seven of thcm (43.75 percent) had ratified the convention by the end of 1992.

Reservations and Other Conditions of Ratification

It is noteworthy that some of the states in all of the regions ratified the convention conditionally, that is, subject to what they have called "reservations" or "declarations." As table 2.5 shows, 35 of the 127 parties (almost 30 percent) to the convention at the end of 1992 had ratified it with at least one reservation; 19 of the parties (some of these had also made reservations) had ratified it with at least one declaration. Overall, these figures are consistent with what we know about other specialized human rights conventions. Some research (e.g., Clark, 1991; Coccia, 1985) and data gathered by the United Nations (un ls, 1993:99–106, 162–83) indicate that between 30 and 40 percent of the parties to the Convention on the Elimination of Racial Discrimination, the Convention on the

Elimination of Discrimination Against Women, and the Convention Against Torture ratified these conventions with reservations. But it is not just the number of states that have ratified the convention with reservations that is of concern to us. In this chapter, and in the chapters of part 2, we are also concerned about the impact of the reservations on the convention — or the extent to which they might undermine its effective application.

Theoretically, there is an important difference between reservations and declarations. A reservation is a statement that modifies or excludes the application of a provision of a treaty to the reserving state and, therefore, has legal implications. Declarations, or other statements such as "interpretive understandings," are not as serious. Their purpose is merely to indicate how a party to a treaty understands or interprets its provisions. Since these interpretations are presumably consistent with the actual provisions of the treaty, declarations or interpretive understandings do not change the nature of the treaty obligations. But, according to Article 2 of the Vienna Convention on the Law of Treaties of 1969, which elaborates the rules of treaty law that most states recognize as authoritative (see, e.g., Bourguignon, 1989; Clark, 1991; Coccia, 1985; Piper, 1985), the substance of a statement, not the label that a state attaches to it, is crucial in determining what it is. In other words, if a statement purports to modify or exclude the application of a provision of a treaty, it is a reservation regardless how the reserving state labels it.

Moreover, according to Articles 19 – 21 of the Vienna Convention, states are limited in making reservations to treaties. In some cases, a treaty may itself stipulate that no reservations are permissible; in others, specific types of reservations may be prohibited by the treaty. According to the Vienna Convention, states would be obliged to follow such specific rules. In all other cases, states may make only those reservations that are compatible with the object and purpose of a treaty. Should a state propose to ratify a treaty with a reservation that a state party judges to be incompatible with the object and purpose of that treaty, the state party could object to the reservation. The effects of the objection would depend on the intentions of the objecting state. We shall return to this point below.

The so-called substance test of the Vienna Convention is potentially problematic. To begin with, the question arises as to whether a reservation can be incompatible with the object and purpose of a treaty even if other parties to the treaty do not object to it on that ground. If so, what would be the status of the state party making the reservation? Moreover, one need only look at the long lists of reservations, declarations, and interpretive declarations that states have made when ratifying human rights conventions to appreciate the problems that could arise in reaching judgments as to their substance. Disputes could easily arise over the subjective judgments that unavoidably enter into such an evaluation process. Despite these difficulties, the mere existence of the substance test has the effect of putting all states on notice that they cannot use labels in such a way as to mislead — or attempt to mislead — other states about their intentions in making reservations. In addition, it at least allows states to use their own judgment in evaluating the acceptability of the reservations that are proposed by others. In this way, objecting states may be able to prevent other states from ratifying treaties or conventions with reservations that undermine the integrity of their provisions.

In the compilation of the data for table 2.5, the substance of the conditions of ratification of the states parties to the Convention on the Rights of the Child was taken into account. Few of the parties were deemed to have mislabeled their conditions. For example, Djibouti ratified the convention with a "declaration" stating that it "shall not consider itself bound by any provisions or articles that are incompatible with its religion and its traditional values" (UN LS, 1993:190). Substantively, this statement obviously has far-reaching implications for the application of the convention and is truly a reservation. Support for this judgment can be found in the practice of other Islamic states (e.g., Kuwait, Mauritania, and Pakistan) that ratified the convention with statements that were similar to Djibouti's but that they labeled as "reservations." In addition, states (e.g., Ireland, Norway, and Portugal) that objected to Djibouti's statement considered it a "reservation" (UN LS, 1993:195). For these reasons, Djibouti's "declaration" was tabulated as a reservation in table 2.5.

Table 2.5

CONDITIONS OF RATIFICATION AS OF DECEMBER 31, 1992

Region	*In Region*	*States Parties With Reservations (%)*	*States Parties With Declarations (%)*
Africa	39	6 (15.38)	1 (2.56)
Asia and Pacific	19	9 (47.37)	1 (5.26)
Europe — East	16	5 (31.25)	1 (6.25)
Europe — West	16	8 (50.00)	8 (50.00)
Latin America	19	2 (10.53)	6 (31.58)
Middle East	7	2 (28.57)	0
North America and Caribbean	10	2 (20.00)	1 (10.00)
Others	1	1 (100.00)	1 (100.00)
Total	127	35 (27.56)	19 (14.96)

SOURCE: UN LS, 1993:187–95.

Another example, this one of a declaration that was labeled as a reservation, is the "reservation" of Uruguay, in which it expressed its regret that the convention did not prohibit using young people below eighteen years of age in armed hostilities (UN LS, 1993:194). Other Latin American states (e.g., Argentina, Ecuador, and Guatemala) made similar statements and in every case labeled them as "declarations" (UN LS, 1993:188–91). Since none of these statements modify or exclude the legal effect of any provisions of the convention (to the contrary, they imply that the states will interpret certain provisions of the convention more liberally than they would otherwise be required to), Argentina, Ecuador, Guatemala, and Uruguay were counted among the Latin American states in table 2.5 as having made declarations concerning the involvement of young people in armed conflicts regardless of how they labeled their statements.

As table 2.5 shows, there are some variations in the number of states in the different regions that have ratified the convention with reservations and/or declarations. States in the West Europe region have been more inclined than those in any other region to ratify the convention with reservations and declarations. In the main, their conditions have been very carefully and precisely framed and directed to specific words or phrases in the convention. For the most part, they show a concern for upholding specific domestic laws or practices that they feel provide better protection to children, or affirm their rights in a better way, than does the convention. In contrast, the reservations or declarations of some Third World states in Africa, Asia, and the Middle East reflect more concern for defending religious precepts (especially Islam) and national sovereignty (the supremacy of national constitutions over the convention). Examples of these different types of reservations will be discussed in the chapters of part 2.

The question of whether the states parties to the convention should be limited in specific ways in making reservations was discussed during several sessions of the working group that drafted the convention. In the earliest stages, Sweden proposed some restrictions, namely, prohibiting altogether reservations to some specific articles and requiring that all other reservations be compatible with the object and purpose of the convention. The rationale behind these limitations was that "it was of the utmost importance that the draft convention should not be undermined by States parties making reservations but should lead to the improvement of national laws to comply with international standards" (UN CHR, 1988:43–44). But Sweden was in the minority on this issue. Most states wanted to maintain their laws rather than have to modify them to comply with the provisions of the convention. Therefore, they wanted to maximize their discretion in making reservations when ratifying the convention (UN CHR, 1988:44). Since there was no consensus on the Swedish proposal, it was withdrawn in favor of adopting Article 51.

The only limitation that Article 51 imposes on the parties to the convention is that they cannot make reservations that are incompatible with the object and purpose of the convention. As we have seen, this is a restriction that is widely accepted under general international treaty law as elaborated in the Vienna Convention on the Law of Treaties. In principle, the limitation is entirely reasonable. But what if states should ratify the convention with reservations that others believe are incompatible with its object and purpose? Under those circumstances, the concerned states could formally object. The effect of their objections could range from the mild and inconsequential (they could simply object, leaving the matter there) to the severe (they could indicate that they do not consider themselves in treaty relations with the reserving state).

Table 2.6 presents data on objections that have been filed to the reservations made to the Convention on the Rights of the Child. The data clearly show that the states parties have been very much disinclined to object to the reservations made by other states. As of the end of 1992, only 7 of the 127 parties to the convention had objected to the reservations made by other parties. Of these states, 6 were West European (Finland, Germany, Ireland, Norway, Portugal, and Sweden) and 1 East European (Czechoslovakia). And although 35 of the 127 parties had made at least one reservation (table 2.5), the seven objecting states objected to the reservations of only 10 parties, mostly in the Asia and Pacific region. The fact that so many objecting states were West European and expressed almost identical objections indicates that they had coordinated their policies on the reservations they found especially offensive. The main concerns of the objecting states were reservations that invoked domestic law (including religious precepts) as a reason for not fulfilling treaty obligations, because, in their view, such reservations created doubts as to the reserving state's commitment to the object

Table 2.6

OBJECTIONS TO RESERVATIONS AS OF DECEMBER 31, 1992

Region	In Region	States Parties That Object to Reservations	States Parties Whose Reservations Are Objected to
Africa	39	0	2
Asia and Pacific	19	0	5
Europe — East	16	1	0
Europe — West	16	6	0
Latin America	19	0	0
Middle East	7	0	3[a]
North America and Caribbean	10	0	0
Others	1	0	0
Total	127	7	10

SOURCE: UN LS, 1993:187–95.

[a] This figure includes Turkey, who at the time of signature reserved the right to "interpret and apply" provisions of Articles 17, 29, and 30 of the convention in accordance with the "letter and spirit" of its constitution and the Treaty of Lausanne of 1923. This reservation was objected to by Ireland and Portugal on the ground that it raised doubts about the commitment of Turkey to the convention and could undermine the basis of international treaty law. Turkey still had not ratified the convention as of December 31, 1992.

and purpose of the convention. But however offensive the objecting states may have believed these reservations to be, none of these states indicated that they did not consider themselves to be in treaty relations with the reserving states. To the contrary, many of them indicated that they did not consider their objection to be an obstacle to the entry into force of the convention between them and the reserving states (UN LS, 1993:194–95).

Several factors seem to explain the conclusions that emerge from an analysis of the data in table 2.6. The great majority of states are apparently unwilling and/or unable to invest the amount of time and energy that would be required to do an effective job of monitoring the reservations made by other parties to the convention. States may be unable to do so because of the weakness of their bureaucratic infrastructure, an especially serious problem for many Third World countries. In fact, as we have seen, most of the states that have objected to reservations are Western states. Similar patterns have been observed in other studies of objections to different treaties (Clark, 1991:312–13; Coccia, 1985:1–51).

States may be unwilling to object to the reservations of other states for various political reasons. To begin with, they might want to avoid engaging in actions that other states might perceive as hostile. Moreover, if they object, they might be accused of "cultural imperialism," especially if the objection comes from a Western state and is lodged against the reservation of a Third World state. States might also be unwilling to object to the reservations of their close allies, geographical neighbors, or states that they are otherwise dependent on for trade or natural resources. As table 2.6 shows, the West European states objected to the reservations of states from regions other than their own. Finally, states might see no practical benefits to be derived from objecting to the reservations of other states. In other words, they have nothing to gain, as they might in the case of a reciprocal rights treaty; nor do they have any reason to expect that their objections will lead other states to withdraw their reservations. None of the reservations to the Convention on the Rights of the Child have been withdrawn. In fact, very few reservations to other human rights conventions have ever been withdrawn, and of those that have, most were withdrawn more because of fundamental changes in policy or political systems than because of an objection raised by another state.

Experience with the reservations that have been made to other human rights treaties suggests that the reservations made to the Convention on the Rights of the Child will add to the difficulties of implementing the convention. The CEDAW, the committee that is charged with implementing the Convention on the Elimination of Discrimination Against Women, has devoted a considerable amount of its time to discussing the impact of reservations that many analysts have considered incompatible with the object and purpose of the convention (Cook, 1990:643–716; Galey, 1984:463–90; Grannes, 1990:9–10). In 1983, it requested an opinion of the United Nations Office of Legal Affairs on what it might do about the reservations (UN GA, 1984:47, 56). It was told, in effect, that the most the CEDAW could do was to comment on the reservations in its reports to the General Assembly (UN GA, 1984: 56; 1986a:7; 1986b:1–2). Although a few of the committee members have been aggressive on the issue (UN CEDAW, 1986a:5–7; Jacobson, 1992:469), no effective way of dealing with the reservations has been found.

Like the CEDAW, the Committee on the Rights of the Child, whose structure and functions will be discussed in chapters 7 and 8, will have to deal with reservations. In fact, the committee has already discussed the potential problems that could arise. Recognizing that it is limited in what it can do about the reservations (UN CRC, 1991b:4–6), it agreed that it would have to deal with them in the course of the dialogue it plans to have with the states parties when it examines the periodic reports they will be obliged to submit (UN CRC, 1992a:6). The committee realizes, as we discussed earlier, that some reservations or declarations tend to reinforce rather than undermine the standards of the convention and are, therefore, no cause for concern. It expects, however, that it will have to raise the issue of the problematic reservations when it examines reports and that it will encourage states that have made such reservations to withdraw them (UN CRC, 1992a:18).

Human rights committees other than the CEDAW and CRC have experienced problems with reservations, and they have been discussed by the chairs of United Nations treaty bodies that receive and examine reports from states (UN GA, 1992b:12 – 18). The chairs made several very strong and potentially controversial recommendations: (1) that treaty bodies should themselves ask the ECOSOC or the General Assembly to request an advisory opinion of the International Court of Justice when they believe that reservations are incompatible with the object and purpose of the conventions they are charged with implementing; (2) that the General Assembly should commission a comprehensive study, perhaps by the Commission on Human Rights, of reservations to human rights treaties; (3) that states should be encouraged to keep to a minimum the number and scope of reservations they make and that they should keep them always under review with an eye toward withdrawing them; (4) that the states parties to treaties should seriously consider objecting to reservations when they consider it appropriate to do so; and (5) that when new human rights treaties are being drafted, careful consideration should be given to identifying certain provisions as being not subject to reservations, and that any body charged with implementing that treaty should be authorized to request an advisory opinion of the ICJ when it believes a reservation to be incompatible with the treaty. The World Conference on Human Rights (1993:3.1.4) took a much milder stand, merely urging states to exercise care in formulating reservations and to keep the reservations constantly under review with a view to withdrawing them when they are no longer necessary.

In view of the problems that have arisen with reservations, the recommendations of the chairs of the treaty bodies have great merit. However, taking effective action on each of them would require the exercise of considerable political will on the part of states and the United Nations as an organization. This may not be forthcoming because of the many pressing problems that need urgent attention and because several of the recommendations would require many states to fundamentally rethink their traditional policies regarding reservations. Still, the recommendations have merit. Perhaps the chairs of the treaty bodies and individual committee members will be sufficiently motivated to continue to call attention to the issues.

Why the Different Patterns of Ratification?

Overall, the data in tables 2.3 to 2.6 tell us that many states in the Third World were quick to ratify the convention even though they were not at all active in drafting it. Western and Eastern European states, the main drafters of the convention, were slower to ratify, although they have since come on board. Substantial numbers of states have ratified the convention with reservations that may be problematic, though few states parties have objected to the reservations. What explains these different trends? Several explanations are possible.

First, it may be that Third World countries have been quick to ratify the convention in such large numbers because they truly endorse the provisions of the convention and intend to implement them to the best of their ability. This is the most generous and optimistic of all explanations of their actions. The problem with this explanation is precisely that it may be too generous and optimistic. Very large numbers of Third World states have ratified other specialized United Nations human rights conventions, and the records of many of those states in living up to their obligations have left much to be desired.

A second possible explanation is that Third World states have been quick to ratify the convention because they have believed that ratification is the politically correct thing to do. As suggested earlier, it is difficult to argue against doing something to promote and protect the human rights of children because they seem so vulnerable to abuse. Given the laudable objectives, it would seem almost shameful to not ratify the Convention on the Rights of the Child. Only the "bad" states of the world are not likely to ratify; the "good" states are sure to do so. This view would create a powerful incentive for Third World countries to want to ratify. As David Johnson (1990:3), editor of the *International Children's Rights Monitor*, put it, "Some who have observed the Convention's rapid entry into force have remarked that it is an 'easy' Convention to ratify, that it is essentially a question of 'motherhood issues.'"

The third possible explanation concerns the discretion that states can exercise in ratifying the convention with reservations. The limitation that Article 51 imposes on states, namely, that they cannot make reservations that are incompatible with the object and purpose of the convention, is mainly of theoretical interest. In practice, it appears that the states parties are virtually unrestrained in making reservations. Most of the parties have shown that they are not likely to object to reservations. To make matters worse, experience with other human rights bodies suggests that the Committee on the Rights of the Child will be unable to take states to task for their reservations, even if the reservations appear to the committee to be incompatible with the object and purpose of the convention. Moreover, the convention prescribes no procedures for resolving any disputes that might arise concerning any reservations or their impact on the interpretation or application of the convention. Although the United Nations Legal Counsel (UN CHR, 1989a:7), when it participated in the technical review of the convention in 1988, suggested that the convention contain an article on the settlement of disputes, the drafters failed to act on its recommendation.

The fourth possible explanation for the different trends relates to state perceptions of international law and its effectiveness. At one extreme, skeptics and cynics might say that Third World states have been quick to ratify the Convention on the Rights of the Child because international law means nothing to them. The implementation mechanism of the convention is likely to be as weak and ineffective as others have been. It is at best difficult to hold states accountable even for serious failure to live up to their international human rights obligations, so the ratification of human rights instruments carries little, if any, risk of censure. It is therefore possible to ratify international instruments and violate them with impunity if and when the need arises.

Less cynical and skeptical analysts might argue that the Third World states' perception of international law simply differs from that of Western states—that they hold to different views about the meaning and importance of the law. In general, for Western states, laws are rules that must be respected, and although they may be violated, institutions exist for the purpose of providing redress of grievances. One of the main arguments that is sometimes made against ratification of human rights treaties by the United States, for example, is that they would have to be taken seriously here and now. In other words, a treaty is worth more than simply the paper it is written on—it has more than just symbolic value. This demands that serious attention be given to precisely what norms and rules are being endorsed through ratification. As we will see in the chapters of part 2, the Convention on the Rights of the Child is sweeping in its terms and breadth of coverage. It seems unlikely that many countries in the world—particularly Third World countries—would be able to live up to the convention's expectations now or in the near future. Why, then, would so many ratify? Perhaps because they perceive international law differently, as something not necessarily to be respected here and now but as something that one strives to live up to. If this explanation is correct, the future may hold more promise for the effective implementation of the convention.

PART TWO

Defining Children's Rights

~

3 · Survival Rights

WE SHALL BEGIN our survey of the rights of the child with survival rights. "Survival," as Jack Donnelly and Rhoda Howard (1988:217) have argued, is the "prerequisite to all other human rights." It includes not only the right to life but also those rights that sustain life, such as the rights to an adequate standard of living and health care. Defined in this way, the category of survival rights emphasizes the indivisibility of both civil and political and economic, social, and cultural human rights, a conception that the drafters of the Convention on the Rights of the Child clearly shared.

As Article 6 of the convention states:

> 1. States Parties recognize that every child has the inherent right to life.
> 2. States Parties shall ensure to the maximum extent possible the survival and development of the child.

The principles affirmed in this basic article are further clarified and reinforced by several other provisions of the convention. Some of these provisions (e.g., whether or not the death penalty can be imposed) pertain to the right to life as it is more traditionally conceived; others (e.g., the need to provide an adequate standard of living and health care) concern the newer conception of the right to life by emphasizing the notion of the survival and development of the child (see, e.g., Cook, 1986). In this chapter, we shall use these two conceptions to organize our discussion of how the drafters resolved the various issues and problems that arose in framing articles that affirm survival rights.

THE RIGHT TO LIFE

Issues directly related to the right to life as it has been traditionally conceived are dealt with in several places in the convention. As noted above, Article 6(1) states, "Every child has the inherent right to life." Understood in its simplest meaning, this statement would surely be universally endorsed. But it leaves two main issues unresolved. In the first place, it says nothing about when life begins. One might argue, of course, and many do, that this question need not have been addressed at all. As we will see below, however, the drafters found discussion of the issue unavoidable, and extremely contentious, in connection with other provisions that are closely related to Article 6, namely, Article 1 and a paragraph of the preamble. Second, Article 6 says nothing about any conditions under which the "right" to life might be denied, for example, through the application of the death penalty. This issue too is dealt with in a separate article, Article 37.

Abortion and the Rights of the Unborn Child

If the definition of the child in the initial Polish draft of Article 1 of the convention had been accepted, there would have been no controversy over the issue of abortion. The draft defined the child as "every human being from the moment of his birth to the age of 18 years unless, under the law of his state, he has attained his age of majority earlier" (UN CHR, 1980c:2). This approach to the question of when life begins was consistent with the terms of most other human rights treaties, including the International Covenants on Human Rights and the European Convention on Human Rights, which do not deal with the question of when life begins, thus leaving it up to individual states to reach decisions on the matter. The exception to this general rule is the American Convention on Human Rights, which is open to ratification by states in the Western Hemisphere. Article 4(1) of that convention establishes the obligation of the states parties to protect the right to life "in general, from the moment of conception."

It became obvious early in the debates over the Convention on the Rights of the Child that the position taken on the question of when life begins in the Polish draft of Article 1 would encounter serious opposition in the working group. In fact, the issue of abortion was raised at the earliest stages in the negotiations (UN CHR, 1979f:60–65). The issue was brought to the fore when, in 1980, the Holy See's delegation submitted a proposal that would have inserted language from the 1959 Declaration of the Rights of the Child—to the effect that children should have particular care and assistance "before as well as after birth"—in one of the preambular paragraphs of the convention. The proposal divided the participants in the working group into those who opposed abortion and those who supported abortion rights. The division persisted throughout the negotiations and, as we will see later, has continued in the aftermath of the adoption of the convention itself.

The antiabortion group supported the Holy See's position on various grounds. Some supported it on the ground that their national legislation contained provisions that protected the rights of what they called "unborn children" from the moment of conception. Others supported it on the ground that it was actually flexible inasmuch as it did not preclude the possibility of abortion, which was recognized in many countries, particularly when the health of the mother was threatened. Still others supported it on the ground that it was "sufficiently neutral" on the issue of abortion because it did not "specify the length of the period before birth that was covered" (UN CHR, 1980b:2–3).

On the other side, some delegates opposed the Holy See's proposal because they wanted the preamble of the convention to be "indisputably neutral" on issues such as abortion. These delegates generally believed that the effort to establish a "beginning point" for life should be abandoned and that only language compatible with the variety of existing domestic legislation on the subject of abortion should be adopted. As they saw it, if the convention took sides on this issue, and did not yield to state practices, it might not be widely ratified. They made similar demands for the "indisputable neutrality" of Article 1 of the convention and in that case achieved it early in the debate by securing the deletion of the words "from the moment of his birth," which appeared in the Polish draft of the article (UN CHR, 1980b:2–5). Henceforth, Article 1 would simply define a child as any human being under eighteen years of age unless the age of majority had been attained earlier.

The issues continued to be raised sporadically through the years that the convention was under negotiation. In 1989, the delegations of Malta and Senegal, supported by the Holy See, attempted to reopen the issue by proposing an amendment of Article 1 that would define the life of the child as beginning at the moment of conception (UN CHR, 1989b:15–16). They had to abandon this effort, however, because of strenuous opposition from many delegations, and instead they worked toward a compromise that would allow for the inclusion of a provision they would find acceptable in the preamble of the convention (Cantwell, 1992:26). The final compromise was reflected in the text of the ninth preambular paragraph: "*Bearing in mind* that, as indicated in the Declaration of the Rights of the Child adopted by the General Assembly on 20 November 1959, 'the child, by reason of his physical and mental immaturity, needs special safeguards and care, including appropriate legal protection, before as well as after birth.'"

The Federal Republic of Germany and delegations from several predominantly Catholic and Moslem countries (e.g., Argentina, Colombia, Egypt, Italy, Kuwait, the Philippines, Senegal, and Venezuela) joined together to support the compromise. In addition, the International Right to Life Federation, an NGO that attended only the last two sessions of the working group in 1988 and 1989 and that limited its activity to the single issue of abortion, also supported the compromise. Among this group, the Federal Republic of Germany's representative was the most outspoken on the issue of abortion and threatened to force a vote on the preambular paragraph if consensus could not be achieved (UN CHR, 1989b:10).

The delegations that were the most strongly opposed to the compromise text were those of Australia, Canada, China, Denmark, the German Democratic Republic, India, the Netherlands,

Norway, Sweden, and the USSR. These delegations argued that the "unborn child" was not literally a person whose rights could be protected and that the main thrust of the convention was to affirm "the rights and freedoms of every human being after his birth and to the age of 18 years." They also argued that it was not necessary to adhere firmly to all the provisions of the 1959 Declaration of the Rights of the Child, since it was about thirty years old and would, in any case, be superseded by the new convention (UN CHR, 1989b:10).

The differences of opinion on the matter were so strong that it was necessary to set up an informal drafting group consisting of the Federal Republic of Germany, Ireland, Italy, the Netherlands, Poland, Sweden, and the United States in the hope of finding a compromise. The drafting group recommended the adoption of the ninth preambular paragraph, but it also recommended that a statement be included in the *travaux preparatoires* to the effect that, in adopting the paragraph, the working group did "not intend to prejudice the interpretation of article 1 or any other provision of the Convention by States Parties" (UN CHR, 1989b:11). The interpretive statement indicated that those in favor of defending abortion rights carried greater weight in the working group.

The compromise was greeted by the working group as a whole with mixed skepticism and concern, although it was adopted. The delegate of Senegal, for example, doubted that the inclusion of a statement in the *travaux* would be of much value. In contrast, the United Kingdom's delegate, obviously concerned about the impact of the preambular paragraph on the abortion policies and practices of states, requested confirmation from the United Nations Legal Counsel that the working group's "statement would be taken into account if, in the future, doubts were raised as to the method of interpreting" Article 1 of the convention (UN CHR, 1989b:11).

In his opinion on this matter, the legal counsel, Carl Fleischauer, indicated that preambles of conventions usually set out the motivations that lie behind their adoption. For this reason, it seemed "strange" to him that a statement was to be included in the *travaux* "for the purpose of depriving a particular preambular paragraph of its usual purpose, i.e., to form part of the basis for the interpretation of the treaty." He warned, however, that the statement might not "fulfil the intended purpose" because, under "article 32 of the Vienna Convention on the Law of Treaties, *travaux preparatoires* constitute a 'supplementary means of interpretation' and hence recourse to *travaux preparatoires* may only be had if the relevant treaty provisions are in fact found by those interpreting the treaty to be unclear." Although Fleischauer found no "prohibition in law or practice" against including statements in *travaux*, he thought it might be more appropriate to adopt a separate resolution on the subject (UN CHR, 1989b:144). However, the working group went ahead and simply included its interpretive statement in its report. For his part, the United Kingdom's delegate made a statement at the close of the negotiations indicating that his delegation understood the clarifying statement made with regard to Article 1 as also applying to Article 6, which, as we have seen, states that every child has the "inherent right to life" (UN CHR, 1989b:143).

Commentators such as Philip Alston (1990:157) have seen the adoption of the ninth preambular paragraph of the convention as a "typical compromise" solution that failed to resolve the controversy over abortion definitely one way or the other. In fact, Alston argues that the compromise was "assumed by most observers to have carefully left the way clear to individual states which might ratify the Convention to adopt whatever position they prefer with respect to the rights of the unborn child, provided they act in conformity with other applicable provisions of international human rights law." But Alston acknowledges that such compromises "tend subsequently to be subject to a range of different interpretations" and that "partisans" of one view or another are likely to read into the convention what they want to see there. Consequently, he has tried to give a more objective view by analyzing the provisions of the convention in the broad perspective of the relevant provisions of international law.

After conducting a survey of provisions of several international instruments, including the 1924 and 1959 Declarations on the Rights of the Child, the Polish drafts of the Convention on the Rights of the Child, the Universal Declaration of Human Rights, and the American Convention on Human Rights, Alston concluded that "while there is no basis for asserting" that the "unborn child" has been "authoritatively rejected by international human rights law" as a subject of the law, "there has been a consistent pattern of avoiding any explicit recognition of such rights, thereby leaving the matter to be dealt with outside the international legal framework" (Alston, 1990:161). Regarding specifically the Convention on the Rights of the Child, Alston found the "most striking feature of the initial responses" of governments to the Polish proposal to draft a convention to be the "paucity of concern with the issue of [the rights of the unborn child], which would seem to demonstrate a generally shared, but certainly unstated, consensus that the matter would be best left unaddressed or at least unresolved." Nevertheless, he conceded that "the matter would in fact be raised from time to time over the next decade" in connection with several provisions of the convention. Like other analysts, however, Alston doubted the effectiveness of the "interpretive statement" that was included in the records of the working group so far as Article 1 or any other article of the convention is concerned (Alston, 1990:170–72). He concluded, "It is clear that neither the text of the Convention itself, nor any of the relevant circumstances surrounding its adoption, lend support, either of a legal or other nature, to the suggestion that the Convention requires legislation to recognize and protect the right to life of the fetus" (Alston, 1990:177–78).

As Alston suspected, "partisans" of different points of view have read into the compromise what they have wanted to see. During the final stages of preparing the convention for adoption by the General Assembly, the Holy See's representative on the Third Committee, Archbishop Renato R. Martino, said that "defending the rights of the child was a central obligation" of the Catholic

Church. He believed that it was "very significant" that the convention "recognized clearly the right to life of the unborn child." Although the "Holy See would have preferred to see further elaboration of that right in the articles of the draft convention, it was confident that the ninth preambular paragraph would serve as a guide for interpreting the rest of the convention" (UN GA C.3, 1989h:8 – 9). Later, on ratification, the Holy See made a declaration stating that it perceived the convention as "a proper and laudable instrument aimed at protecting the rights and interests of children" and that it believed the convention would "safeguard the rights of the child before as well as after birth." In this connection, the Holy See remained "confident" that the ninth preambular paragraph would "serve as the perspective through which the rest of the convention" would be interpreted (UN LS, 1993:191).

Several other states parties to the convention have followed the Holy See in making statements about how they interpret the convention provisions that relate to the practice of abortion. Argentina, for example, made declarations, on signature and later on ratification, that Article 1 "must be interpreted to the effect that a child means every human being from the moment of conception up to the age of 18" (UN LS, 1993:188). Similarly, on signing the convention, Guatemala made a declaration that it would interpret Article 1 of the convention in light of Article 3 of its constitution, which provides, "The State guarantees and protects human life from the time of its conception, as well as the integrity and security of the individual" (UN LS, 1993:191).

In contrast, France made a declaration on signing the convention and confirmed it on ratification that Article 6 "cannot be interpreted as constituting any obstacle to the implementation of the provisions of French legislation relating to the voluntary interruption of pregnancy" (UN LS, 1993:190). Similarly, Tunisia made a declaration that stated, "The Preamble to and the provisions of the Convention, in particular article 6, shall not be interpreted in such a way as to impede the application of Tunisian legislation concerning voluntary termination of pregnancy" (UN LS, 1993:193). China made a reservation stating that it would "fulfil its obligations provided by article 6 of the Convention under the prerequisite that the Convention accords with the provisions of article 25 concerning family planning of the Constitution of the People's Republic of China and in conformity with the provisions of article 2 of the Law of Minor Children of the People's Republic of China" (UN LS, 1993:189), though it did not say specifically what these laws provide. Indonesia made a declaration on ratification that it would "apply" Article 1 of the convention "in conformity with its Constitution," though it did not elaborate on what its constitution has to say about the issues dealt with in the article (UN LS, 1993:192). The United Kingdom ratified the convention with a declaration stating as follows: "The United Kingdom interprets the Convention as applicable only following a live birth" (UN LS, 1993:194).

Other than these few states, however, the vast majority of the parties to the convention have ignored the issue, indicating that, for all practical purposes, they reached the same conclusion as Alston did in interpreting the preamble and Articles 1 and 6 of the convention. Thus, if they favored abortion rights, no declaration or reservation was necessary. If they opposed abortion rights, no declaration or reservation was necessary. Still, it is noteworthy that, in view of all the controversy that surrounded the adoption of the preambular paragraph and Article 1 of the Convention, so few states made declarations regarding how they interpreted the right to life.

The Death Penalty

Like the issue of abortion, the application of the death penalty to "minors" has attracted a great deal of attention in recent years. NGOs such as Amnesty International and the International Commission of Jurists as well as a number of scholars have done research in this field and lobbied governments to ban the application of the death penalty to minors, usually defined as people below the age of eighteen when they commit their crimes. This issue too has been highly emotion-charged.

The issue arose in connection with the drafting of Article 37 of the Convention on the Rights of the Child, which deals broadly with protecting children from torture and other cruel, inhuman, or degrading treatment or punishment and unlawful and arbitrary deprivations of liberty. Article 37(a) flatly states, "Neither capital punishment nor life imprisonment without possibility of release shall be imposed for offenses committed by persons below eighteen years of age." The crucial issue, then, is when the offense is committed. Capital punishment cannot be imposed on, say, a twenty-five-year-old person who committed his or her offense when under eighteen years of age.

The principle affirmed in Article 37(a), along with others, was originally proposed by the Canadian government (UN CHR, 1986a:22). The United States' representative raised objections to the proposal on the ground that its phrasing was "too arbitrary" (UN CHR, 1986a:24), but the real reason is not hard to find. The imposition of the death penalty on people who committed their crimes when they were below the age of eighteen has been a matter of great concern to some groups and individuals in the United States for quite some time, and as we will see below, the Supreme Court has ruled on the issue in recent years. The Canadian proposal enjoyed such widespread support among other delegations, however, that the U.S. delegates chose not to block consensus, so long as it was "understood that the United States maintained its right to make a reservation on this point and that it was implicitly understood that a child committing an offence which, if committed by an adult, would be criminal could be treated as an adult" (UN CHR, 1986a:24).

The observers for Amnesty International and the International Commission of Jurists, among others, took exception to the U.S. objections. They argued that eighteen years of age was accepted as a limitation on the imposition of the death penalty in several international instruments, including the International Covenants on Human Rights and General Assembly resolutions (UN CHR, 1986a:24). Others have made similar arguments. Daniel O'Donnell (1989:23–26), for example, has argued that the provisions of various treaties (e.g., the International Covenant on Civil and Political Rights, the American Convention on Human Rights, and the Geneva Conventions on International Humanitarian Law and their Optional Protocols) and resolutions adopted by the United Nations General Assembly (e.g., Resolution 39/118) that prohibit the execution of people under the age of eighteen are evidence of a "growing consensus within the international community that application of the death penalty to persons under the age of 18 is a violation of minimum standards of human rights law binding on all members of that community." Nonetheless, O'Donnell cited a 1989 Amnesty International study, entitled *When the State Kills*, that showed that many states have not yet brought their legislation into conformity with the minimum international standard. According to the Amnesty study, of one hundred countries that apply the death penalty for ordinary offenses, thirty-seven did not expressly prohibit its application to people who were eighteen years of age or under when they committed their offense. Moreover, of the eighteen countries that retained the death penalty only for military offenses or offenses that are committed during wartime, thirteen of them did not expressly prohibit its application to people under eighteen years of age. It would appear, then, that the death penalty can be imposed on people who were eighteen years of age or under when they committed their offenses in some fifty countries (O'Donnell, 1989:23).

But what about the actual practices of states? Even if their laws may permit the execution of minors, have they in practice done so? The Amnesty study suggests that very few of them have. In fact, minors were executed in only six states in the 1980s — Bangladesh, Barbados, Iran, Iraq, Pakistan, and the United States. Barbados has since changed its law and abolished capital punishment for people under eighteen years of age (O'Donnell, 1989:24). In the United States, in 1988 the Supreme Court ruled, in *Thompson v. Oklahoma* (487 U.S. 815), that the execution of people who were under the age of sixteen when they committed their offenses was unconstitutional. In 1989, however, in *Stanford v. Kentucky* (492 U.S. 361), the court decided that the execution of people who were sixteen or seventeen at the time they committed their crimes does not constitute cruel and unusual punishment and is thus not a violation of the Eighth Amendment of the U.S. Constitution. In the wake of these cases, approximately thirty people remained on death row in the United States for crimes they committed when they were sixteen or seventeen years old (O'Donnell, 1989:24). Clearly, current law and practice in the United States would be in conflict with Article 37(a) of the Convention on the Rights of the Child.

The unequivocal ban on the application of the death penalty to children, as they are defined by the Convention on the Rights of the Child, reflected the strength of the forces against the death penalty among the drafters. However, reservations to Article 37 — and specifically to paragraph (a), which pertains to the death penalty — are apparently permissible, or at least they were understood to be permissible by the United States. It is significant, however, that none of the 127 parties to the convention as of the end of 1992 had ratified it with a reservation specifically to that paragraph. If the United States ratifies the convention, it will apparently do so with a reservation.

SURVIVAL AND DEVELOPMENT OF THE CHILD

The indivisibility of civil and political rights and economic, social, and cultural rights so far as the right to life is concerned is introduced in Article 6(2) of the convention. That paragraph affirms the connection between the right to life and the survival and development of the child. There was considerable debate and discussion about this issue among the drafters. In the 1988 session of the working group, the Indian delegation introduced a proposal that provided: "The States Parties to the present Convention undertake to create an environment, within their capacities and constitutional processes, which ensures, to the maximum extent possible, the survival and healthy development of the child" (UN CHR, 1988:5).

Debate on this proposal ranged over matters of principle as well as potential practical problems. The Indian delegation argued that the right to survival should be stressed in the convention because many children were dying from preventable causes, as the work of UNICEF and other international agencies showed. The Indian delegation believed that if the convention affirmed that the right to life and the right to survival were "complementary and not mutually exclusive," many problems affecting children, such as infant mortality, could be attacked (UN CHR, 1988:5–6). The Indian delegation also argued that the "right to survival carried with it a more positive connotation than the right to life," because it "meant the right to have positive steps taken to prolong the life of the child" (UN CHR, 1988:6).

Some delegates opposed the adoption of the Indian proposal on the ground that the right to survival did not have a widely accepted legal definition and would, therefore, prove difficult to implement (UN CHR, 1988:5). However, it was widely recognized that one of the advantages of the proposal was that it took a positive approach to the right to life by taking into account economic and social conditions that affect the survival of children (UN CHR, 1988:7). The working group appointed the representatives of Argentina, Bulgaria, India, Italy, Norway, the United Kingdom, and UNICEF to work out a compromise draft article. The compromise was adopted as Article 6(2) (UN CHR, 1988:7). The word *survival* in Article 6(2) was used instead of the word *growth* because it has a special meaning in the movement for children's rights. The word *survival*, according to UNICEF, has a very broad meaning and signifies "growth monitoring, oral rehydration and disease control, breast-

feeding, immunization, child spacing, food and female literacy."
The word *growth* has a narrower meaning, signifying "only a part
of the concept of 'survival.'" To have used the word *growth* in Article 6(2) would, therefore, have been a step backward from standards that had already been accepted (UN CHR, 1989b:17).

But how is the survival and development of the child to be realized? It is one thing to affirm that the right to life and the survival
and development of the child are inextricably linked, but it is another matter to map out how that linkage will be recognized and
addressed in practice. The convention affirms several rights that
are relevant to the survival and development of the child, including the right to an adequate standard of living (which recognizes
the importance of international cooperation), the right to social
security, and the right to an adequate standard of health care. As
we shall see in a moment, the articles that affirm each of these
rights make their realization conditional on the existence of favorable economic conditions. According to the terms of Article 4 of
the convention, however, which applies to all the convention provisions that deal with economic, social, and cultural rights, the
"States Parties shall undertake such measures to the maximum extent of their available resources and, where needed, within the
framework of international co-operation."

The Right to an Adequate Standard of Living

According to Article 27 of the Convention on the Rights of the
Child, the states parties "recognize the right of every child to a
standard of living adequate for the child's physical, mental, spiritual, moral and social development." The actual provision of this
standard of living is recognized as being the "primary responsibility" of the child's parents, "within their abilities and financial capacities." Article 27 goes on to say, however, that the states parties
pledge themselves, "in accordance with national conditions and
within their means," to take "appropriate measures to assist parents and others responsible for the child to implement" the right

to an adequate standard of living. Moreover, "in case of need" the states parties shall "provide material assistance and support programmes, particularly with regard to nutrition, clothing and housing." Finally, Article 27 also includes the rather interesting provision that the states parties will take all necessary measures to "secure the recovery of maintenance for the child from the parents or other persons having financial responsibility for the child, both within the State Party and from abroad."

Although the terms of Article 27 enjoyed broad support in the working group, some delegations were concerned about qualifying phrases, such as "within their abilities," which were included in the article on the insistence of the United States. The critics were concerned that the qualifying phrases weakened the principles being endorsed (UN CHR, 1985a:8 – 12, 1987:29, 1988:17, 1989b:78 – 79). But the fact that the article and the convention as a whole stressed the importance of international cooperation and assistance in improving the standards of living of children helped to make it more acceptable, especially to delegations from Third World countries. In fact, Third World countries succeeded in pushing the adoption of one preambular paragraph that is specifically devoted to the notion of the need for international cooperation. It provides for agreement to the convention by the states parties, "*recognizing* the importance of international co-operation for improving the living conditions of children in every country, in particular in the developing countries." In debate over this paragraph too, the U.S. representatives had reservations, arguing that the convention should focus on the "obligations of ratifying governments to respect the rights of, and to render assistance to, their own citizens." Thus, according to the U.S. representatives, although governments *should* cooperate in the economic realm, the drafters "should let other legal instruments and other fora deal with the subject of international assistance" (UN CHR, 1989b:14).

As we will see in our discussion of other rights that have traditionally been considered economic, social, or cultural in nature, this was not the only occasion on which the U.S. delegates expressed concern about whether and, if so, how the convention should deal with such rights. At the same time, they took very strong positions in favor of affirming in detail a broad range of traditional civil and political rights. This more conservative attitude toward the rights of the child was not surprising in view of the U.S. position on international human rights issues in general. In the past, the United States has argued that such matters as a person's standard of living and access to health care and social security are not really "rights" at all but rather "social benefits." By taking this position in international fora, the United States has promoted a policy more or less consistent with the domestic situation in the country, where health care services, social security, and the like are usually referred to as "social benefits" or "entitlements" rather than as "rights." Most other states in the world take a different position, recognizing the authenticity of economic, social, and cultural rights as human rights. They are also more likely to endorse the notion of the indivisibility of human rights.

The Right to Social Security

The role of international cooperation arose again in connection with the affirmation of the right of the child to "benefit from social security, including social insurance," as Article 26 of the convention puts it. There was some debate as to how this right could be realized. The Iranian delegation, for example, wanted the article to stress the need for international cooperation in this field. The ILO proposed that the article might not only recognize the kinds of difficulties that states might face in securing the realization of this right but also bind states to "take appropriate legal and administrative measures to guarantee the implementation" of the right (UN CHR, 1984:16–17).

Article 26, of course, recognizes that the social security benefits "should, where appropriate, be granted, taking into account the resources and the circumstances of the child and persons having responsibility for the maintenance of the child, as well as any other consideration relevant to an application for benefits made by or on behalf of the child."

The Right to Health Care

The health of children throughout the world, especially in the Third World, has been of great concern to many international governmental and nongovernmental organizations for many years. It was also an important topic of the agenda of the World Summit for Children, which was held at the United Nations in September 1990 and which adopted a World Plan of Action that included, among other things, goals regarding health standards for children to be achieved by the year 2000 (UN GA, 1990a; UNICEF, 1991:1–7). The World Conference on Human Rights in June 1993 reiterated the importance of working toward the implementation of the World Summit's goals (World Conference, 1993:3.2.D).

The statistics in this field show very clearly the need to give serious and sustained attention to the health of children throughout the world, particularly in the less developed world but also in the developed world (see, e.g., Graham, 1992:203–12). According to recent UNICEF estimates, some 35,000 children under five years old die in the less developed world every day; on an annual basis, this figure translates into approximately 12.8 million children every year. Roughly 60 percent of these deaths are "caused by just three diseases—pneumonia, diarrhoea and measles—all of which can now be prevented or treated by means which are tried and tested, available and affordable" (UNICEF, 1993:5).

As staggering as the figures are, it is encouraging to know that some progress, albeit uneven, has been made in reducing deaths among very young children. Advances in immunizations alone during the 1980s are now believed to be preventing the deaths of as many as three million children under five years old each year in the less developed world and preventing the occurrence of as many as 400,000 polio cases each year (UNICEF, 1993:16, 24). Still, a great deal needs to be done, as the leaders gathered at the World Summit realized (UNICEF, 1991:2 – 3). Formal political commitments at the highest levels are necessary if, as UNICEF has argued, "available solutions are to be put into action *on a national scale.*" But these commitments can "only be translated into action by the dedication of the professional services; by the mobilization of today's communications capacities; by the widespread support of politicians, press, and public; and by the reliable and sustained support of the international community" (UNICEF, 1993:9 – 10).

The right to health, broadly conceived to include not only health care but also the provision of health care services, was first discussed in depth in the open-ended working group that drafted the Convention on the Rights of the Child in 1985. The delegations of Poland and Canada had submitted draft articles on health, and the working group decided to use the more extensive article proposed by Canada as the basis for its discussions (UN CHR, 1985a:4 – 5). Near the end of the negotiations in 1989, the drafters adopted two articles, Articles 24 and 25, on health. In view of the importance of these articles, they are quoted here in full. Article 24 provides:

> 1. States Parties recognize the right of the child to the enjoyment of the highest attainable standard of health and to facilities for the treatment of illness and rehabilitation of health. States Parties shall strive to ensure that no child is deprived of his or her right of access to such health care services.
> 2. States Parties shall pursue full implementation of this right and, in particular, shall take appropriate measures:
>   (a) To diminish infant and child mortality;
>   (b) To ensure the provision of necessary medical assistance and health care to all children with emphasis on the development of primary health care;
>   (c) To combat disease and malnutrition, including within the framework of primary health care, through, *inter alia*, the application of readily available technology and through the provision of adequate nutritious foods and clean drinking-

water, taking into consideration the dangers and risks of environmental pollution;

(d) To ensure appropriate pre- and post-natal health care for mothers;

(e) To ensure that all segments of society, in particular parents and children, are informed, have access to education and are supported in the use of basic knowledge of child health and nutrition, the advantages of breast-feeding, hygiene and environmental sanitation and the prevention of accidents;

(f) To develop preventive health care, guidance for parents and family planning education and services.

3. States Parties shall take all effective and appropriate measures with a view to abolishing traditional practices prejudicial to the health of children.

4. States Parties undertake to promote and encourage international co-operation with a view to achieving progressively the full realization of the right recognized in the present article. In this regard, particular account shall be taken of the needs of developing countries.

Article 25 provides:

States Parties recognize the right of a child who has been placed by the competent authorities for the purposes of care, protection or treatment of his or her physical or mental health, to a periodic review of the treatment provided to the child and all other circumstances relevant to his or her placement.

The discussion of these articles in the working group revealed some serious disagreements among the drafters of the convention on numerous issues. These can be divided into three main categories: the appropriate role of the state in the provision of health care services; traditional practices that are prejudicial to the health of children; and the question of consent to medical experimentation. Let us look at how the drafters resolved their disagreements in each of these areas.

Serious ideological disagreements occurred among the delegates over the question of the role of the state in providing health care services. The delegates from the Soviet Union, with the support of some other socialist states, proposed that Article 24(1) affirm that health care services would be provided to children "free of charge" (UN CHR, 1985a:4–5). Sweden proposed that children as well as mothers should be mentioned as the beneficiaries of pre- and postnatal health care under Article 24(2)(d) (UN CHR, 1985a:6). At the other extreme, the United States, once again taking a conservative position, objected to these proposals, maintaining, among other things, that to say that the state would in all circumstances have to provide "health care free of charge might entail a misappropriation of resources" (UN CHR, 1985a:4). In fact, the United States went further and suggested that Article 24(2)(b) establish the obligation of the state to provide health care to children only "in case of need."

Other specific issues that arose in connection with the provision of health care services concerned the matter of family planning and education for family planning. Elements of Article 24(2) are relevant to these concerns. Article 24(2)(f), for example, states that the states parties shall take appropriate measures to "develop preventive health care, guidance for parents and family planning education and services." For some states, these issues raised questions of morality and concerns about state intervention in such areas as family planning.

The United States was partially successful in gaining support for its perspective on the role of the state in the provision of health care services. Article 24 does not affirm that services must be provided to children free of charge. But the conservative U.S. stance on this issue actually enjoyed little support, even among the closest allies of the United States (UN CHR, 1985a:5–8, 1989b:72), and this is reflected in other provisions of Article 24. For example, despite U.S. objections, the article recognizes the importance of pre- and postnatal care of mothers. Furthermore, in general, the terms of the article are quite far-reaching on the issue of the provision of health care services.

Only a few states, when ratifying the convention, made state-ments regarding the question of the role of the state in the provi-sion of health care services, and all of those statements had to do with the matter of family planning. Argentina (UN LS, 1993:188) made a declaration: "Questions relating to family planning are the exclusive concern of parents in accordance with ethical and moral principles." It understood Article 24 as obliging states "to adopt measures providing guidance for parents and education for re-sponsible parenthood." The Holy See made a reservation (UN LS, 1993:191) to Article 24(2), stating that it understood it to "mean only those methods of family planning which it considers morally acceptable, that is, the natural methods of family planning." Poland (UN LS, 1993:193) also made a declaration: "Family plan-ning and education services for parents should be in keeping with the principles of morality."

The second, and more controversial, issue regarding the right to health concerned the terms of Article 24(3), which requires the states parties to "take all effective and appropriate measures with a view to abolishing traditional practices prejudicial to the health of children." This was perhaps the most controversial provision of the entire article. It seems to have originated in a proposal introduced by Radda Barnen International on behalf of the Informal NGO Ad Hoc Group in 1986. That proposal, however, was more specific in its terms. It provided: "The States Parties to the present Conven-tion shall seek to eradicate traditional practices harmful to the health of children and shall take all appropriate action including necessary legislative, administrative, social and educational mea-sures to ensure that children are not subjected to such practices" (UN CHR, 1986a:11).

No decision was taken on this proposal in 1986, but it was raised again in a somewhat different form by the Australian delegation in 1987. Although the proposal did not expressly so indicate on either occasion, everyone knew that it was directed at female circumci-sion, which is a traditional practice in some areas of the world. The practice of female circumcision in different forms, which vary in degree of severity, has been around for about twenty-five hundred years, and it continues to be practiced in over forty countries, mainly in Africa and some countries of the Middle East. In one study by Alison Slack (1988:439, 443), the practice was found to be especially prevalent in Ethiopia, Somalia, and Sudan, where as many as nine out of ten females are circumcised. In fact, during the early 1980s, tens of millions of women — estimates have run as high as eighty-four million — were believed to have been circumcised. Slack argues that the practice "is primarily found in areas where there is much poverty, illiteracy, hunger, unsanitary conditions, and where there is little in the way of health care facilities. Furthermore, the economic and social status of women is characteristically low." Various reasons are cited for the persistence of the practice, including religion, cultural traditions, and a desire to control the sexuality of females (Slack, 1988:445 – 49). But the practice has tremendous adverse effects on the physical and mental health and well-being of girls and women (Slack, 1988:450 – 59). For this reason, Slack argues (1988:439) that "tradition" is hardly a valid defense of the practice because a serious human rights violation results from that tradition.

The subject of female circumcision has been discussed in numerous United Nations forums. The Committee on the Elimination of Discrimination Against Women, for example, began to give serious consideration to the adoption of a "general recommendation" on the subject at its seventh session in 1988. Not all committee members were enthusiastic about the prospects of adopting such a recommendation, however. Guan Minqian of China, for one, feared that the committee would be taken to task if it ventured into this "delicate subject," and she argued that it should defer its consideration of the subject until a later date (UN CEDAW, 1988b:2). This concern was not totally unjustified. The committee's intentions were completely misunderstood when, at its sixth session in 1987, it had called on the United Nations system as a whole to promote or undertake studies on the status of women in Islamic countries (UN GA, 1987:80). The committee had merely hoped to acquire information that would assist it in understanding the status of women in Islamic societies, but it was severely criticized by some representatives of Islamic countries in the ECOSOC and in the Third Committee of the General Assembly who had misinterpreted its request for studies as a criticism of their societies (UN GA, 1988b:17–18).

The CEDAW did defer further consideration of female circumcision until it had acquired more basic information, but it was determined not to drop the issue altogether (UN CEDAW, 1988b:3; UN GA, 1990f:73). The committee was in a better position to act at its ninth session in 1990, and it adopted a general recommendation that "appropriate and effective" measures be taken "with a view to eradicating the practice of female circumcision" (UN GA, 1990e:10). Among these measures, the committee specifically recommended the collection and dissemination of information on female circumcision by universities, medical associations, and women's organizations; the support of women's organizations at the national and subnational levels working for the elimination of the practice; the encouragement of politicians, professionals, and religious and community leaders in influencing attitudes about the practice; and the introduction of educational and training programs about the problems arising from female circumcision (UN GA, 1990e:80–81).

With this background in mind, the paragraph proposed by the Informal NGO Ad Hoc Group for inclusion in Article 24 of the Convention on the Rights of the Child could have been expected to stimulate vigorous debate among the delegates to the open-ended working group. In fact, it did. The delegate of Senegal, for example, a state in which female circumcision is practiced, "counselled prudence when dealing with issues that entailed differences in cultural values, and emphasized the dangers of forcing practices into clandestinity if they were prohibited by legislation" (UN CHR, 1987:8). But most other delegates were not prepared to be as tolerant of divergent cultural values. The Italian delegate, for example, referred to the female circumcision report that had come out of the 1985 Nairobi Conference on Women. The report noted that young girls had been subjected to female circumcision without their consent, that it had caused great suffering, and that it was often conducted in unsanitary conditions. Although the Italian delegate "recognized the importance of plurality of cultures," she "nevertheless appealed for changes in attitudes which would eliminate this problem" (UN CHR, 1987:9).

Other delegates argued that the concept of "traditional practices" as used in the NGO proposal was too broad and needed more precision to have a greater impact. Delegates from the United Kingdom and the United States argued that Article 24(3) should specifically mention the practice of female circumcision as the traditional practice that was of greatest concern. But others argued that there were additional traditional practices that were also harmful to children, for example, preferential feeding of male children. These delegates were concerned that if only female circumcision was mentioned in Article 24(3), the article might acquire an unintended narrow focus (UN CHR, 1987:9).

In an effort to reach a compromise on the different viewpoints, the drafters gave some consideration to indicating in Article 24(3) that the term "traditional practices included all those practices outlined in the 1986 report of the Working Group on Traditional Practices Affecting the Health of Women and Children" (UN CHR, 1987:9 – 10). That report had focused on female circumcision, the preference for male children, and traditional birth practices such as dietary restrictions on pregnant women and unsanitary conditions and practices during and immediately after birth (UN CHR, 1986b:1 – 41). Although this idea attracted some support, the drafters decided to accept instead a Senegalese proposal whereby the states parties to the convention would merely commit themselves to take all appropriate measures to abolish traditional practices that are prejudicial to the health of children, not specifically mentioning female circumcision (UN CHR, 1987:9–10). This compromise, reflected in Article 24(3), was a significant concession to Third World states. It is one of the most important examples of how the cultural diversity of the United Nations forced a compromise that, rather than making advances in the area of children's rights, actually resulted in the adoption of very weak norms.

Finally, it is noteworthy that neither Article 24 nor Article 25 addresses the issue of medical experimentation as an aspect of the child's right to health care. This matter was, however, discussed among the drafters in the working group. Two different proposals were introduced on this subject. One proposal was introduced by the Informal NGO Ad Hoc Group in 1985. It was in the form of a paragraph that would have been included in Article 24: "The States Parties to the present Convention shall undertake to protect children from any medical investigation or treatment detrimental to their physical or psychological health and development, and to take appropriate and necessary measures to prevent children being subjected to traditional practices harmful to their health" (UN CHR, 1985a:8).

The working group decided that it was not ready to discuss this proposal when first introduced. Although the reasons were not explicitly stated, the fact that the proposal also addressed the controversial issue of traditional practices undoubtedly had something to do with the working group's decision. The issue was raised again in 1989, however, and for a while a paragraph was included on the subject of medical experimentation in Article 24. It provided: "States Parties shall ensure that a child shall not be subject to any medical or scientific experimentation or treatment unless it is with the free and informed consent of the child or where appropriate that of the child's parents. In any case, such experimentation or treatment shall not be adverse to the child and shall be in the furtherance of child health" (UN CHR, 1989b:71).

This paragraph enjoyed broad support among the drafters of the convention when it was first discussed. Soon, however, objections to some of its specific provisions opened the way for more serious objections, which undermined the consensus that had developed at the outset. The Soviet delegation, for example, suggested that perhaps the consent of both parents and the child should be required for medical experimentation. The Portuguese delegation suggested that the last sentence of the paragraph should be clarified to make it clear that the experimentation need benefit only the health of the child who was subjected to the experimentation or treatment, not necessarily the health of all children of the world, which a literal interpretation of the sentence seemed to indicate (UN CHR, 1989b:73).

These questions led to more serious ones. The Venezuelan representative, for example, indicated that her delegation would not be able to join in any consensus on the article, since adopting it in its draft form might lead to abusive interpretations, as the concerns expressed by the Soviet and Portuguese delegates showed, and she suggested that the experts from the World Health Organization be called on to assist in the revision of the article. Despite objections from delegations such as those of Norway and the United States, the chair of the working group declared that no consensus existed on the paragraph and that it would therefore not be included in Article 24. Some believed that the issue of medical experimentation injurious to the health of the child was covered by other articles of the convention because such experimentation would not be in the "best interests of the child" (UN CHR, 1989b:73). But again, the quibbling over words and phrases created a situation in which the drafters missed an opportunity to make a contribution to the expansion of norms regarding the status and treatment of children.

Implementing Survival Rights

To many observers, the survival rights we have discussed above may seem like good ideas that will be difficult if not impossible to implement in many countries, especially in those Third World countries that are affected by massive poverty and acute shortages of resources and trained personnel. The issues addressed in the articles are essentially economic, social, and cultural in nature, and governments may be expected to invoke the numerous escape clauses that are built into them. But careful monitoring of government policies and practices by the Committee on the Rights of the Child could make a difference, and the committee has already demonstrated that it intends to do precisely that.

As we will discuss more fully in chapter 8, the Committee on the Rights of the Child is charged with examining reports that the states parties will be required to submit on the measures they have taken toward the implementation of the convention and the problems and obstacles they have encountered in doing so. The committee has decided that it will issue "concluding observations" after it has examined these reports; it will indicate, among other things, suggestions and recommendations to the governments of the states parties concerned on how they might go about more effectively implementing the convention. The committee's experience is as yet very limited, as we will see in chapter 8, but it has shown that it intends to put a lot of emphasis on rights of an economic, social, and cultural nature. The committee has recognized that some governments that have already submitted reports have experienced serious economic problems in recent years, problems that have affected their ability to fund their social programs to the extent that they would have preferred (e.g., Bolivia, Egypt, and the Russian Federation); but the committee has reminded these states that, in accordance with Article 4 of the convention, they are required to implement economic, social, and cultural rights to the *maximum* extent of their available resources (UN CRC, 1993i, 1993l, and 1993k). In general, the committee is interested in knowing about the overall state plan for children — how children are integrated into the overall development policy of states.

Moreover, the committee has repeatedly stressed, even when examining reports of highly developed states such as Sweden (UN

CRC, 1993j), that it is concerned about the policies that states pursue with regard to the most vulnerable and least privileged children. The committee is also clearly concerned about the quality of medical care that children enjoy. The report of the Russian Federation (UN CRC, 1992j:26–30), for example, provided statistics and a discussion of government projects involving such things as inoculations, family planning, and services provided to children and mothers. The report freely admitted shortcomings, some of which were due to the economic changes and difficulties going on in the country. Among other things, it reported that abortion remained "the principal method of family planning." Although the number of abortions had declined in very recent years, there were still one hundred abortions per one thousand women of childbearing age. Moreover, a relatively small proportion of women were using "modern methods" of birth control such as intrauterine devices or the pill (UN CRC, 1992j:27–28).

In issuing its concluding observations and recommendations (UN CRC, 1993k:3–4), the Committee on the Rights of the Child expressed concern about the problems the Russian government had experienced in its "immunization programme, the level of antenatal care, family planning programmes and the training of local community health workers." It also noted its "concern at the frequent recourse to abortion as what appears to be a method of family planning." The committee then went on to recommend that the "primary health care system be improved regarding the effectiveness of, *inter alia*, antenatal care, health education, including sex education, family planning and immunization programmes." It also recommended that, in the case of the immunization program in particular, the Russian Federation government "should look to international cooperation for support in the procurement and manufacturing of vaccines."

In the case of Bolivia, the committee also expressed serious concern about health issues. In particular, it noted "that only 47 per cent of births are supervised by qualified health care workers." The committee was "alarmed at the implications that this may have for increased likelihood of sickness and disability arising from preventable problems occurring during delivery." The committee believed that more "budgetary support is needed to correct this situation, as well as sufficient support to programmes benefiting the mental and physical development of children" (UN CRC, 1993i:3).

In general, the committee's practice in dealing with the reports it has thus far received suggests that although the committee will be patient with states that are experiencing severe economic difficulties that impinge on their ability to meet their conventional obligations regarding survival rights, it will nevertheless seize the opportunity to remind them that they have a serious obligation to work toward the realization of those rights.

4 · Membership Rights

INDIVIDUALS EXIST as part of a larger community, so survival rights alone will not fulfill all their needs. The importance of communities to individuals can be seen in a variety of ways, ranging from membership in national communities down to families (Donnelly and Howard, 1988:223 – 24). The safety of these communities is important to everyone, perhaps especially to children, who are so vulnerable to attack. In this chapter, we will focus on three particular "membership" rights, or groups of rights, that are affirmed in the Convention on the Rights of the Child. First, we shall look at the obligation of the states parties to respect and ensure the enjoyment of all rights of the child without discrimination. Second, we shall look at the rights to have a name and a nationality. And third, we shall look at family rights and the rights of the child within the context of the family.

NONDISCRIMINATION

The importance of nondiscrimination to human rights is recognized in virtually all international instruments. The three principal instruments in the so-called international bill of human rights—the Universal Declaration of Human Rights, the International Covenant on Civil and Political Rights, and the International Covenant on Economic, Social and Cultural Rights—affirm the principle in broad terms. So do the main regional human rights treaties, the American Convention on Human Rights and the European Convention on Human Rights. All of these instruments stress the basic equality of all human beings to enjoy the exercise of the rights proclaimed or affirmed in them. The fundamental principle is that all human beings should be able to enjoy their rights without regard to characteristics such as race, gender, language, or national origin.

Like the instruments in the international bill of rights, the Convention on the Rights of the Child also deals with nondiscrimination. In fact, it treats the issue in several articles. Article 2 establishes the general obligation of the states parties to respect and ensure the rights affirmed in the convention without discrimination. It provides:

> 1. The States Parties to the present Convention shall respect and ensure the rights set forth in the Convention to each child within their respective jurisdiction without discrimination of any kind, irrespective of the child's or his or her parent's or legal guardian's race, color, sex, language, religion, political or other opinion, national, ethnic or social origin, property, disability, birth or other status.
> 2. States Parties shall take all appropriate measures to ensure that the child is protected against all forms of discrimination or punishment on the basis of the status, activities, expressed opinions, or beliefs of the child's parents, legal guardians, or family members.

The Scope of Application of the Convention

One of the important issues addressed in Article 2(1) is that the states parties "shall respect and ensure the rights set forth in the Convention to each child within their respective jurisdiction." The drafters had some difficulty with this phrase, and several different formulas were proposed. The Polish draft of Article 2, for example, provided that countries would be obliged to respect and ensure the rights affirmed in the convention to "all children in their territories." The United States proposed that a state party be obliged to apply the convention to "all children lawfully in its territory" (UN CHR, 1981:7).

The problem with the Polish formula was that it would have made the scope of the application of the convention narrow, or at least more narrow than the formula that was eventually adopted for Article 2, because children could be subject to a state's jurisdiction but not necessarily within its territory. Nonetheless, the Polish formula would have been preferable to the one advanced by the United States, according to which the states parties to the convention would have been under an obligation to respect the rights only of those children who were "lawfully" within their territories. Critics of the U.S. proposal objected to it precisely because they believed that *all* children subject to a state's jurisdiction—which could be more than those within its territory—should enjoy the rights affirmed in the convention. Furthermore, they believed that no state should be able to limit the rights of children simply because their parents may have entered the territories or jurisdictions illegally (UN CHR, 1981:7). Although the drafters seriously considered all the various alternatives, toward the end of the negotiations they decided to adopt the broader formula as affirmed in Article 2(1) (UN CHR, 1989b:28 – 29).

The Grounds of Nondiscrimination

On what grounds should Article 2 prohibit discrimination? The main difficulty that the drafters faced in answering this question was that they ran the risk of specifying either too many conditions or not enough of them. To ensure the highest degree of normative consistency between the convention and other human rights instruments, the drafters took into account the provisions of the Universal Declaration, the two International Covenants, the Convention on the Elimination of Racial Discrimination, and the UN ESCO Convention against Discrimination in Education (UN CHR, 1981:7 – 8). The drafters were successful in maintaining the normative consistency of the convention with these other instruments so far as the *grounds* of nondiscrimination are concerned. In fact, Article 2(1) of the Convention on the Rights of the Child goes somewhat further. In addition to prohibiting discrimination on the same grounds as those specified in the Universal Declaration of Human Rights and the International Covenants (e.g., race, color, gender, language, etc.), it also prohibits discrimination on the ground of disability. And since the convention is child-specific, it indicates that the prohibition against discrimination is irrespective of the "child's or his or her parent's or legal guardian's" race, color, gender, language, etc.

Moreover, according to Article 2(2), the states parties are to take appropriate measures to ensure that children are not discriminated against *or punished* because of the "status, activities, expressed opinions, or beliefs of the child's parents, legal guardians, or family members." Children have often become victims of serious human rights violations, including arbitrary imprisonment and even torture, because of actions that their parents or family members have engaged in or have been accused of engaging in. Article 2(2) was designed to provide an additional, and very important, measure of protection to children who might find themselves in such circumstances.

Very few of the parties to the convention have interpreted Article 2 as a source of potential problems. In fact, only three states have ratified the convention with statements concerning the article. The Bahamas ratified with a reservation (UN LS, 1993:189) that is difficult to comprehend but that apparently excludes the application of the article to the "conferment of citizenship upon a child." Belgium ratified the convention with a statement that it called an "interpretive declaration" (UN LS, 1993:189) to the effect that it does not interpret the ban against discrimination on the ground of national origin in Article 2(1) as necessarily implying "the obligation for States automatically to guarantee foreigners the same rights as their nationals." It continued, "This concept should be understood as designed to rule out all arbitrary conduct but not differences in treatment based on objective and reasonable considerations, in accordance with the principles prevailing in democratic societies." Tunisia ratified the convention with a reservation (UN LS, 1993:193), claiming that Article 2 "may not impede implementation of the provisions of its national legislation concerning personal status, particularly in relation to marriage and inheritance rights." Ireland is the only state party that objected (UN LS,

1993:195) to any of these conditions, and it objected only to Tunisia's reservation on the ground that it created doubts as to Tunisia's commitment to the object and purpose of the convention. One wonders if the reservation of the Bahamas and the "interpretive understanding" of Belgium would not create similar doubts.

The Committee on the Rights of the Child has shown interest in how the states parties to the convention understand and implement their obligations under Article 2. There is also evidence that states themselves are concerned about discrimination against children on various grounds covered by the convention. The government of Sweden, for example, in the report that it submitted to the Committee on the Rights of the Child in 1992, claimed that the objectives of Article 2 of the convention are met through its constitution and laws. It conceded, however, that "disturbing signs of growing intolerance towards other nationalities and cultures" had been noticeable in Sweden in recent years. The government had undertaken a number of measures to combat intolerance, and the Swedish Youth Affairs Committee had done a report on the subject. That committee found it "impossible to generalize on the question of whether young immigrants or second-generation immigrants are at a disadvantage," reasoning that socioeconomic "identity can do more than ethnic origin to decide how young persons cope in Swedish society." Still, the Youth Affairs Committee was struggling to educate society about the problems that arise from stereotyping minority and ethnic groups (UN CRC, 1992h:15).

When issuing its concluding observations and recommendations on the Swedish report, the Committee on the Rights of the Child expressed concern that the law apparently did not provide protection from all forms of discrimination as specified in Article 2 of the convention. It also emphasized "the importance of monitoring the situation of foreign children and other vulnerable groups" in the country, and it requested that the government of Sweden provide "fuller statistical and other indicators for these groups, including the incidence of HIV infection and AIDS," in its next report (UN CRC, 1993j:2–3).

The committee was also very concerned about discrimination in Egyptian society. It noted that "although Egyptian laws and regulations guarantee equality between the sexes, there is in reality still a pattern of disparity between boys and girls, in particular as far as access to education is concerned" (UN CRC, 1993l:2−3). Thus, it made the following suggestion:

> The committee emphasizes that the principle of nondiscrimination, as provided for under article 2 of the Convention, must be vigorously applied. A more active approach should be taken to eliminating discrimination against certain groups of children, in particular girl children and children in rural areas. With regard to the gap in literacy and school enrollment mentioned in the report, obstacles facing girls should be adequately addressed so that they can enjoy their right to go to school; further measures might be taken to increase the awareness of parents in this regard. (UN CRC, 1993l:3)

In the case of Bolivia, the committee expressed broad concern about discrimination on various grounds. As it stated in its concluding observations and recommendations on a report submitted by the Bolivian government:

> In this regard, the Committee notes with concern the disparities in the status and treatment of children in Bolivia conforming to distinctions based on race, sex, language and ethnic or social origin. Vulnerable groups of children, including girl children, indigenous children and children living in poverty, are particularly disadvantaged in their access to adequate health and educational facilities and are the primary victims of such abuses as sale and trafficking, child labour and sexual and other forms of exploitation. The diminished level of protection for girl children inherent in the lower minimum age for marriage is discriminatory and, as a result, deprives this group of children of the benefit of other protections afforded by the Convention. (UN CRC, 1993i:3)
>
> The committee then went on to say that the application of Article 2 and other general principles of the convention "cannot be dependent upon budgetary resources." In fact, regarding budgetary priorities in the allocation of resources, the committee suggested that the Bolivian government be

"guided by the principle of the best interest of the child, as provided for in article 3 of the Convention, particularly as this applies to the most vulnerable groups of children, such as girl children, indigenous children, and children living in poverty, including abandoned children" (UN CRC, 1993i:4).

Children Born out of Wedlock

However broad in scope Article 2 is, it does not expressly ban discrimination against children born out of wedlock. The Polish draft of the convention had aimed to ban discrimination against children born "in lawful wedlock or out of wedlock" (UN CHR, 1980c:3), and the issue was raised by delegations from several countries as early as the first year of negotiations on the convention (UN CHR, 1979f:61; see also DCI, 1984:4). However, the issue was not seriously discussed until the Chinese delegation made a specific proposal regarding the matter in 1986. The Chinese argued that either Article 2 or some other article of the convention should state that the parties "shall take all effective measures to ensure that a child born out of wedlock shall enjoy the same legal rights as those enjoyed by a child born in wedlock, in particular the rights enumerated in the present Convention" (UN CHR, 1986a:4).

The Chinese proposal enjoyed the support of a few states, but it was criticized by delegates from a broad range of developed and Third World countries that claimed it would be contrary to their domestic laws on succession. For these representatives, it was not a question of trying to find a way of making the article more compatible with their domestic legislation. They rejected in principle the idea of granting children born out of wedlock the same legal rights as those born in wedlock, and this made it impossible for the working group to reach a consensus on the matter. Thus, although the idea was discussed at several times during the negotiations on the convention, the chair ruled that no consensus had been reached, and the issue was dropped from discussion (UN CHR, 1986a:5).

The failure of the convention explicitly to provide protection to children born out of wedlock was viewed by some delegates to the working group as one of its most serious shortcomings. At the close of the negotiations on the convention, the delegate of the Federal Republic of Germany, for example, indicated that he was especially disappointed that "nothing more could be done for the protection of an extremely weak group of children, the children born out of wedlock" (UN CHR, 1989b:139). The Swedish representative took a different viewpoint, claiming that he understood the prohibition of discrimination on the ground of any "other status" under Article 2 as covering children born out of wedlock (UN CHR, 1989b:29). Any state party to the convention could act on the basis of the most liberal interpretations of its articles, so the Swedish government would be able to extend the application of the convention to children born out of wedlock if it wished to do so. In fact, Article 41 actually encourages the most liberal interpretations of the convention's articles by stating that nothing in the convention affects any provisions of domestic law or international agreements that are "more conducive to the realization of the rights of the child." Nonetheless, the words "other status" in Article 2 would not seem to oblige states parties to prohibit discrimination against children born out of wedlock because the drafters of the convention specifically discussed, but could not reach a consensus on, protecting such children.

Children with Disabilities

In contrast to children born out of wedlock, those who are mentally or physically disabled not only are protected from discrimination under the terms of Article 2 but are the beneficiaries of positive measures prescribed by another article of the convention. Article 23 provides:

> 1. States Parties recognize that a mentally or physically disabled child should enjoy a full and decent life, in conditions which ensure dignity, promote self-reliance and facilitate the child's active participation in the community.
> 2. States Parties recognize the right of the disabled child to special care and shall encourage and ensure the extension,

subject to available resources, to the eligible child and those responsible for his or her care, of assistance for which application is made and which is appropriate to the child's condition and to the circumstances of the parents or others caring for the child.

3. Recognizing the special needs of a disabled child, assistance extended in accordance with paragraph 2 shall be provided free of charge, whenever possible, taking into account the financial resources of the parents or others caring for the child, and shall be designed to ensure that the disabled child has effective access to and receives education, training, health care services, rehabilitation services, preparation for employment and recreation opportunities in a manner conducive to the child's achieving the fullest possible social integration and individual development, including his or her cultural and spiritual development.

4. States Parties shall promote, in the spirit of international co-operation, the exchange of appropriate information in the field of preventive health care and of medical, psychological and functional treatment of disabled children, including dissemination of and access to information concerning methods of rehabilitation education and vocational services, with the aim of enabling States Parties to improve their capabilities and skills and to widen their experience in these areas. In this regard, particular account shall be taken of the needs of developing countries.

Over the history of the negotiations on the convention, the notion that positive measures should be taken to ensure that disabled children are integrated into the community, and thus made to feel as though they are full members, always enjoyed broad-based support. The earliest drafts of the convention contained proposals regarding disabled children, and many governmental delegations as well as NGOS and IGOS made constructive suggestions regarding the content of what eventually became Article 23 (UN CHR, 1982:68–70). Toward the end of the negotiations, suggestions made by UNICEF, and ideas that were generated by the technical review of the convention carried out by the secretariat, were especially useful in framing the final text of Article 23.

Along the way, the drafters expressed fundamental philosophical differences of opinion on specific provisions of the article. Some drafters believed that the care of disabled children rested primarily with governments and that care should be provided free of charge. Others believed that parents and close relatives were primarily responsible but that the state and private organizations might be called on to provide certain services. Still others believed that the state should be heavily involved but that the convention should recognize the needs of poor countries in providing assistance to disabled children and should mandate some forms of assistance for these children (UN CHR, 1983:13–18, 67). The compromise that emerged out of these different points of view is reflected in the terms of Article 23(2), (3), and (4), which establish the basic principles that are to guide assistance to disabled children within the context of available family resources augmented by national and international assistance.

The extent to which governments can take seriously their obligations under Article 23 will depend, of course, on their material resources. Some countries that have submitted reports to the Committee on the Rights of the Child already have well-established plans and programs that address the needs of disabled children. Sweden, for example, claims to have given a very high priority to a broad range of issues involving disabled persons. The government realizes that one of the greatest threats facing disabled children is that they will become isolated and cut off from their society, community, family, and other children. Hence, government policy has been to integrate these children into society at large (UN CRC, 1992h:47–50). Similarly, the Russian Federation has devoted considerable attention to problems involving disabled children and, in fact, claims that educational institutions geared toward disabled children are "more generously financed than ordinary educational institutions" (UN CRC, 1992j:28–29). However, the Committee on the Rights of the Child has expressed concern that Russian "society is not sufficiently sensitive to the needs and situation of children from particularly vulnerable and disadvantaged groups, such as the disabled," and the committee questioned if they may not be victims of discrimination contrary to the terms of Article 2 of the convention (UN CRC, 1993k:2).

The committee has found the status of disabled children in other countries to be of even greater concern. In the case of Egypt, for example, the committee expressed special concern about the status of disabled children, especially about the very low number of such children who are enrolled in school, "which might reflect an insufficient sensitiveness of the society to the specific needs and situation of those children" (UN CRC, 1993l:2). The committee therefore went on to recommend to the Egyptian government that steps "be undertaken to afford adequate protection to disabled children, including the possibility, in particular through education, to integrate them into society and to raise the awareness of their families about their specific needs. Efforts for the early detection of the incidence of handicap are important" (UN CRC, 1993l:3).

Children of Indigenous Origin

The status of indigenous peoples has been the subject of discussion in various international fora in recent years. The Sub-commission on Prevention of Discrimination and Protection of Minorities of the United Nations Commission on Human Rights established a working group on indigenous peoples in the early 1980s, and it has for some years been working on a Declaration on the Rights of Indigenous Peoples (Tolley, 1987:143–44). At the World Conference on Human Rights in Vienna in June 1993, the delegates discussed indigenous peoples and agreed to recommend that the General Assembly proclaim an International Decade of the World's Indigenous People, to begin in January 1994. The World Conference envisioned this decade as a time in which action-oriented programs would be developed in partnership with indigenous peoples themselves. It also envisioned the establishment of a Voluntary Trust Fund for indigenous peoples and the establishment of a permanent forum in the United Nations to act on their behalf (World Conference, 1993:3.2.B[bis]).

Discrimination against children of indigenous origin is not expressly prohibited under the terms of Article 2 of the Convention on the Rights of the Child, but such children may be covered under other terms used in the article, terms such as "ethnic." Whether or not they are covered in this way, it is noteworthy that, like the problems of disabled children, the problems of children of indigenous origin were extensively discussed when the convention was drafted, and these children are the beneficiaries of special protection under several provisions of the convention. Article 17(d), for example, provides that the states parties shall "encourage the mass media to have particular regard to the linguistic needs of the child who belongs to a minority group or who is indigenous." Article 29(1)(d) states that the education of children should be directed toward, among other things, tolerance for and friendship with persons of indigenous origin. And Article 30 provides: "In those States in which ethnic, religious or linguistic minorities or persons of indigenous origin exist, a child belonging to such a minority or who is indigenous shall not be denied the right, in community with other members of his or her group, to enjoy his or her own culture, to profess and practice his or her own religion, or to use his or her own language."

Article 30 originated in a proposal introduced by the nongovernmental organization Four Directions Council, which lobbied aggressively, and mainly, for the protection of indigenous children. Its draft article, however, differed from Article 30 in that it focused exclusively on indigenous children (UN CHR, 1986a:13). Although most drafters supported the Four Directions Council's initiative, they believed that the article should not apply exclusively to indigenous children but should also cover other minorities (UN CHR, 1987:13 – 15). Some drafters believed that the article was actually discriminatory, reasoning that, on the one hand, Article 2 aimed to ban discrimination but that, on the other, Article 30 implied that minority children were different from the other children of the world (UN CHR, 1989b:87 – 88). But the prevailing sentiment among the drafters was that it would do no harm to single out minority children and could even do some good by calling specific attention to their status and treatment in many countries throughout the world. In this way, the consensus on Article 30 was reached.

According to *The American Heritage Dictionary of the English Language*, the word *indigenous* refers to something occurring or living naturally in an area. The words *native* and *aboriginal* are synonyms. By this definition, American Indians might be considered indigenous or aboriginal peoples, and so might some "native" Indian tribes in Canada and other countries of the world. But practice seems to vary considerably among countries as to whether such peoples should be thought of as "indigenous" or simply as a "minority." In Canada, the words *indigenous* and *aboriginal* seem to be widely used, and in fact, indigenous people were the subject of great concern in constitutional debates in the early 1990s. It is indicative of how important this debate has been that when Canada ratified the Convention on the Rights of the Child, it made two statements (UN LS, 1993:189) relating to its treatment of indigenous peoples. One statement, which it labeled a "statement of understanding" regarding Article 30 of the convention, provides as follows:

> It is the understanding of the Government of Canada that, in matters relating to aboriginal peoples of Canada, the fulfilment of its responsibilities under article 4 of the Convention [undertaking all measures regarding economic, social, and cultural rights to the maximum extent of available resources] must take into account the provisions of article 30. In particular, assessing what measures are appropriate to implement the rights recognized in the Convention for aboriginal children, due regard must be paid to not denying their right, in community with other members of their group, to enjoy their own culture, to profess and practice their own religion and to use their own language.

The other statement is a reservation in which Canada reserved the right not to apply the provisions of Article 21 of the convention, which pertains to adoption, "to the extent that they may be inconsistent with customary forms of care among aboriginal peoples in Canada." Both of these conditions of ratification are intended to benefit indigenous children, and no other party to the convention has objected to them. It seems unlikely that the Committee on the Rights of the Child would have anything critical to say about the conditions, though it would probably want to know more about the status of indigenous children in Canada when the Canadian government submits its report.

Besides Canada, only France among all the other parties to the convention ratified the convention with a statement regarding Article 30. France declared (UN LS, 1993:190) that Article 30 is not applicable to it because of the provisions of Article 2 of its constitution. Article 2 of the French constitution provides, among other things, that the republic shall ensure the equality of all citizens before the law without distinction on the ground of origin, race, or religion. No other party to the convention has objected to the French "declaration," though the Committee on the Rights of the Child may be interested in exploring its implications.

THE RIGHTS TO A NAME AND NATIONALITY

The rights to a name and a nationality are crucial to a person's identity and are important membership rights. Of the two, the right to a name seems to be taken for granted, not even being mentioned in some human rights instruments. The Universal Declaration of Human Rights, for example, does not expressly recognize the right. However, the Declaration of the Rights of the Child (Principle 3) proclaims the right; and Article 24(2) of the International Covenant on Civil and Political Rights affirms, "Every child shall be registered after birth and shall have a name." Article 7(1) of the Convention on the Rights of the Child follows up on this point and affirms, "The child shall be registered immediately after birth and shall have the right from birth to a name." Article 8 provides that the states parties "undertake to respect the right of the child to preserve his or her identity, including [his or her] name." A consensus was easily forged on these provisions; the question of whether every child should have a right to a name was never a contentious issue in drafting the convention. The same was not true, however, regarding the right to a nationality.

In contrast to the right to a name, discussions of the right to a nationality are usually characterized by sharp differences in viewpoints, and the negotiations on the Convention on the Rights of the Child were no exception. Virtually everyone agrees with the basic principle that all persons have a right to a nationality. As Article 15 of the Universal Declaration of Human Rights puts it, "Everyone has the right to a nationality." The Universal Declaration continues, "No one shall be arbitrarily deprived of his nationality nor denied the right to change his nationality." The Declaration of the Rights of the Child (Principle 3) states that the child "shall be entitled from his birth" to a nationality. However, Article 24(3) of the International Covenant on Civil and Political Rights hedges on the issue, stating, "Every child has the right to acquire a nationality." Of course, the right to *acquire* something is not the same as a right *to* something.

The different ways in which the so-called right to a nationality is framed suggest that although there is general agreement in principle on the right, there is disagreement over specific issues regarding the acquisition of nationality. Historically, countries have applied different rules regarding the acquisition of nationality. In some cases, children are entitled to the nationality of the territory in which they are born (*jus soli*), whereas in others they acquire the nationality of their parents (*jus sanguinis*). The different rules mean that children could possess dual nationality when, for example, they are born in a country that grants nationality on the basis of *jus soli* but of parents from a country that applies the rule of *jus sanguinis*. However, under some circumstances children may have no nationality, when, for example, they are born in a country that does not grant nationality on the basis of *jus soli* and their parents have no nationality or are stateless. Serious problems involving immigration in recent years, in Western Europe and elsewhere, have added to the difficulty in trying to address the issues that arise regarding the right to a nationality.

The various issues and problems came to the fore in drafting Article 7 of the Convention on the Rights of the Child. In full, the article provides:

> 1. The child shall be registered immediately after birth and shall have the right from birth to a name, the right to acquire a nationality and, as far as possible, the right to know and be cared for by his or her parents.
>
> 2. States Parties shall ensure the implementation of these rights in accordance with their national law and their obligations under the relevant international instruments in this field, in particular where the child would otherwise be stateless.

According to Article 7(1), the child has a right "to acquire a nationality," and in this respect the convention is normatively consistent with the International Covenant on Civil and Political Rights. Article 7(2) then ventures into the area of the conditions under which the child might acquire a nationality, stating that the states parties would grant nationality in accordance with their national law and their international legal obligations, particularly "where the child would otherwise be stateless." These provisions emerged as a compromise following criticisms that some drafters, particularly from European countries and Japan, expressed about the Polish draft of Article 7. The Polish draft had provided as follows (UN CHR, 1980b:6–7):

> 1. The child shall have the right from his birth to a name and a nationality.
>
> 2. The States Parties to the present Convention undertake to introduce into their legislation the principle according to which a child shall acquire the nationality of the state in the territory of which he has been born if, at the time of the child's birth, the application of the proper national law would not grant him any nationality whatever.

The Polish draft was widely recognized to be inspired by humanitarian principles, in particular to prevent statelessness among children. According to the draft, children would have acquired the nationality of the country in which they were born if they would otherwise have been stateless (UN CHR, 1981:2–3). Some drafters believed that the draft article would have brought the Convention on the Rights of the Child more or less in line with the provisions of the Convention on the Reduction of Statelessness, which was adopted in 1961 and which affirms the basic principle that states should grant nationality to people born in their territory if those people would otherwise be stateless. But the Convention on the Reduction of Statelessness was slow in gaining acceptance, not entering into force until 1975. In fact, by the end of December 1992, it had been ratified by only sixteen countries (UN LS, 1993:219–20). This fact alone indicates how exceedingly controversial the question of the acquisition of nationality is.

Obviously, the conditions under which states grant nationality affect their policies and laws on immigration. The Polish draft of Article 7 was unacceptable to some countries precisely because they perceived it as having undesirable implications for their immigration policies and laws. Two countries in particular, the Federal Republic of Germany and the Netherlands, were especially concerned and argued for more flexible rules so that the convention would be more compatible with their domestic laws on the subject of immigration. The delegate of the Federal Republic of Germany, for example, argued that a child should be able to acquire the nationality of the state in which he or she is born under certain conditions, for example, on application (UN CHR, 1989b:18–19). The Netherlands favored a more detailed provision that would have specified waiting periods of varying times depending on the circumstances (UN CHR, 1989b:19). The compromise that emerged from the different positions on the matter is evident in the terms of Article 7(2), namely, that the nationality of children will be determined in accordance with the national law and international legal obligations of the states parties to the convention (UN CHR, 1989b:20–21).

Although the compromise significantly weakened the "right" to a nationality, some states were still anxious to express their concern about any implications it might have for their immigration laws. When the working group adopted the convention by consensus in 1969, the United Kingdom's delegate stated, "Nothing in this convention may be interpreted as affecting in any way the operation of the United Kingdom immigration or nationality legislation in so far as it relates to the entry of aliens and the terms and conditions of their stay in the United Kingdom, and to the acquisition and possession of citizenship" (UN CHR, 1989b:7). The delegate of the Federal Republic of Germany claimed, "Nothing in the Convention on the Rights of the Child shall be interpreted as legitimizing the illegal entry and presence on the territory of the Federal Republic of Germany of any alien, nor shall any provision be interpreted as restricting the right of the Federal Republic of Germany to promulgate laws and regulations concerning the entry of aliens and the conditions of their stay or to establish differences between nationals and aliens" (UN CHR, 1989b:139). The Japanese delegate indicated that his government would have to consider the implications of Article 7 as well as other articles of the convention for Japan's immigration laws (UN CHR, 1989b:7); after the convention was adopted by the Third Committee of the General Assembly on November 15, 1989, the Japanese delegate stated that his government did not interpret Article 7(2) as requiring states "to give their nationality to any persons who were born or had become stateless in their territory" (UN GA C.3, 1989f:17).

Since the terms of Article 7(2) make it clear that the states parties to the convention are only obligated to apply their national laws and relevant international obligations to the granting of nationality to children, it would seem that none of them would have had to make reservations to the paragraph, or declarations indicating how they interpreted it, when they ratified the convention.

In fact, very few did so. Kuwait made a declaration, and Thailand and Tunisia made reservations, indicating that they would apply their domestic laws and regulations to matters such as the acquisition and loss of nationality (un ls, 1993:192–93).

The Federal Republic of Germany and the United Kingdom, however, evidently wanting to leave no room for doubt about the matter, made more extensive statements. The Federal Republic of Germany's declaration (un ls, 1993:191) stated: "Nothing in the Convention may be interpreted as implying that unlawful entry by an alien into the territory of the Federal Republic of Germany or his unlawful stay there is permitted; nor may any provision be interpreted to mean that it restricts the right of the Federal Republic of Germany to pass laws and regulations concerning the entry of aliens and the conditions of their stay or to make a distinction between nationals and aliens." The United Kingdom made a reservation (un ls, 1993:194) as follows: "The United Kingdom reserves the right to apply such legislation, in so far as it relates to the entry into, stay in and departure from the United Kingdom of those who do not have the right under the law of the United Kingdom to enter and remain in the United Kingdom, and to the acquisition and possession of citizenship, as it may deem necessary from time to time."

FAMILY RIGHTS

The family is often said to be the basic unit of society. Its importance to the rights of the child is evident in the large number of articles included in the Convention on the Rights of the Child that in some way pertain to the child within the family structure. Article 5 of the convention sets the basic framework. It provides:

> States Parties shall respect the responsibilities, rights and duties of parents or, where applicable, the members of the extended family or community as provided for by local custom, legal guardians or other persons legally responsible for the child, to provide, in a manner consistent with the evolving

capacities of the child, appropriate direction and guidance in the exercise by the child of the rights recognized in the present Convention.

This article originated in a proposal submitted to the working group by the United States and Australia in 1987 (UN CHR, 1987:24). The proposal stimulated considerable controversy. On the one hand, the United States and Australia argued that the convention should emphasize the importance of the family and of the responsibility of the family for the care, upbringing, and development of the child. They perceived the family as the "natural and fundamental group unit of society." Furthermore, they maintained that a convention article that recognized the importance of the family would be normatively consistent with provisions of the International Covenants on Civil and Political Rights and on Economic, Social and Cultural Rights.

On the other hand, critics of the proposal argued that the International Covenant on Civil and Political Rights protected "the family from the state" and that it was important that the Convention on the Rights of the Child not set out to protect the family at the "expense of the child." As the Canadian delegation to the working group put it, the rights of the child should not "be left solely to the wishes of the family, without any protection whatsoever from the State; in other words, in protecting the family from the State, the family must not be given arbitrary control over the child. Any protection from the State given to the family must be equally balanced with the protection of the child within the family" (UN CHR, 1987:25).

The need for "balance" was supported by most delegations, some of which expressed misgivings about the draft of Article 5 (UN CHR, 1988:8–9). The compromise that was reached was believed to take a balanced stand. It is noteworthy that Article 5 provides a somewhat broader definition of the family than the traditional definition. It refers not only to parents but also to members of the extended family, community, legal guardians, or other persons legally responsible for the child. The earliest drafts of the article did not include the reference to "members of the extended family or community as provided for by local custom," and some drafters were concerned that its adoption would change the essentially "traditional triangular responsibility" of the child, parents, and state for the well-being of the child (UN CHR, 1989b:31–32). But the drafters wanted to adopt a broader definition.

Parental Rights and Duties Regarding the Child

Other articles of the convention reflect the continuing need to balance the rights and duties of parents and guardians and those of the child. According to Article 18, for example, parents and legal guardians have "the primary responsibility for the upbringing and development of the child," but "the best interests of the child will be their basic concern." According to the same article, the state has a responsibility — albeit secondary — to provide "appropriate assistance" to parents and legal guardians in meeting their responsibilities (UN CHR, 1981:16–18, 1989b:50–52).

Articles 9 and 10 deal essentially with matters of child custody. According to Article 9, the states parties "shall ensure that the child shall not be separated from his or her parents against their will, except when competent authorities subject to judicial review determine . . . that such separation is necessary for the best interests of the child." The qualification was intended to make allowances for the involuntary separation of children from their parents in cases of abuse and neglect, when it may be determined that a child should be removed from parental control. Article 9(2) adds that "all interested parties shall be given an opportunity to participate in the proceedings" that are conducted to reach decisions regarding separations of children from parents and shall be able to "make their views known."

Some states parties to the convention have had reservations about specific provisions of Article 9. Iceland, for example, ratified the convention with a declaration (UN LS, 1993:191) that "under

Icelandic law the administrative authorities can take final decisions" in some matters referred to in Article 9. Those decisions are,
however, "subject to judicial review in the sense that it is a principle of Icelandic law that courts can nullify administrative decisions
if they conclude that they are based on unlawful premises." Croatia ratified with a reservation (UN LS, 1993:189) to Article 9(1)
"since the internal legislation of the Republic of Croatia provides
for the right of competent authorities (Centres for Social Work) to
determine on separation of a child from his/her parents without a
previous judicial review." Yugoslavia made a similar reservation
(UN LS, 1993:194). The Republic of Korea, one of the principal
"sending" countries in intercountry adoptions, made a reservation
(UN LS, 1993:193) stipulating that Korea "considers itself not
bound" specifically to Article 9(3), which provides that the states
parties "shall respect the right of the child who is separated from
one or both parents to maintain personal relations and direct contact with both parents on a regular basis, except if it is contrary to
the child's best interests."

Whereas Article 9 deals with parental control mainly in domestic situations, Article 10 deals with problems that can arise internationally. Article 10(2) provides as follows:

> A child whose parents reside in different States shall have the
> right to maintain on a regular basis save in exceptional cir-
> cumstances personal relations and direct contacts with both
> parents. Towards that end and in accordance with the obli-
> gation of States Parties under article 9, paragraph 2, States
> Parties shall respect the right of the child and his or her par-
> ents to leave any country, including their own, and to enter
> their own country. The right to leave any country shall be
> subject only to such restrictions as are prescribed by law and
> which are necessary to protect the national security, public
> order (*ordre public*), public health or morals or the rights and
> freedoms of others and are consistent with the other rights
> recognized in the present Convention.

This paragraph originated in proposals submitted to the working group by the delegations of France and the United States in 1982 (UN CHR, 1983:5). The United States was especially concerned about the right of the child and his or her parents to leave their country and to return to it. There was a clear political purpose behind the U.S. initiative in this regard. In fact, the proposal reflected the tense state of U.S.-Soviet bilateral relations before the thaw in the cold war (UN CHR, 1986a:6). The right to leave and to return to one's country had become an issue between the United States and the Soviet Union soon after the end of World War II. It became an even more serious problem during the 1970s and the increasing controversy over restrictions on the emigration of Soviet Jews. It was not surprising, therefore, that in the earlier stages of the negotiations on the Convention on the Rights of the Child, the Soviet delegates opposed the U.S. proposal regarding Article 10(2). Toward the end of the 1980s, however, as the U.S. and Soviet delegates began to work on much better terms, they were able to share in the consensus on the article as a whole (UN CHR, 1987:4 – 6).

The part of Article 10(2) that affirms the right of the child to maintain contact with his or her parents when they are living in different countries was introduced by the French delegation to the working group. The proposal was intended to draw attention to the situation of children of parents who are separated by divorce or for other reasons and who are of different nationalities or who may reside in different countries. The French delegation noted the "need of the child in such a situation to retain his links with both his parents," and it believed that its provision could serve as a "bench-mark" for cooperative agreements among states on the issue of child-parent reunifications under such circumstances (UN CHR, 1982:51).

Like the U.S. proposal regarding the right to leave and to return to one's own country, the French proposal regarding the right of children to maintain contact with both parents when they reside in different countries had a clear political purpose. The proposal addressed a serious problem that has arisen in recent years involving the abduction of children, and for this reason we shall return to it in chapter 5 in connection with the protection rights of the child. For the moment, it should be noted that the French government has been very interested in this matter because, according to the French Ministry of Justice, approximately one thousand children are abducted across international boundaries every year (UN CHR, 1982:51). In part, the problem is to secure recognition and enforcement of judicial and administrative decisions regarding child custody disputes. Some multilateral conventions have already been concluded on the subject (UN CHR, 1982:51), but more remains to be done, and the French proposal regarding Article 10(2) was designed to emphasize the point in the Convention on the Rights of the Child.

Overall, Article 10 enjoyed broad support among the drafters, but some were concerned, as they were in the case of Article 9, about its implications for their immigration laws. Richard Jaeger, representative of the Federal Republic of Germany, stated that although his government "generally welcomed the provisions regarding family reunification" in Article 10, application "should not undermine legislation concerning aliens." As he put it, the "Federal Republic of Germany was not an immigration country and reserved the right to take its own decisions concerning the reunification of families of aliens living in its territory" (UN CHR, 1989g:18). The delegate from Japan, Shozo Fujita, also stated that representatives of his government did not understand Article 10 as establishing or regulating their "immigration laws in accordance with their international obligations" (UN CHR, 1989d:7). However, none of the parties ratified the convention with reservations or declarations regarding the article.

Alternative Means of Child Care

Although the convention emphasizes the primary responsibility of the family for the care of the child, it recognizes that under some circumstances children might become, or have to be, separated from their family environment either temporarily or permanently. For the drafters, this possibility raised the question of whether the convention should deal with alternative means of child care. The Polish draft convention had contained a brief article that enunciated a few principles—for example, that a child deprived of parental care should be entitled to assistance provided by the state and that the state would take measures to facilitate the adoption of children and create conditions favorable to the establishment of foster homes (UN CHR, 1980c:4). The drafters took these basic principles into account in their discussions of how to address the issue of alternative means of child care. In addition, they took into account the provisions of other international instruments on the subject, especially the Declaration on Social and Legal Principles Relating to the Protection and Welfare of Children, with Special Reference to Foster Placement and Adoption Nationally and Internationally, which was adopted (Resolution 41/85) by the General Assembly in December 1986. The convention contains two articles on alternative means of child care. Article 20 provides:

> 1. A child temporarily or permanently deprived of his or her family environment, or in whose own best interests cannot be allowed to remain in that environment, shall be entitled to special protection and assistance provided by the State.
> 2. States Parties shall in accordance with their national laws ensure alternative care for such a child.
> 3. Such care could include, *inter alia*, foster placement, *kafalah* of Islamic law, adoption, or if necessary placement in suitable institutions for the care of children. When considering solutions, due regard shall be paid to the desirability of continuity in a child's upbringing and to the child's ethnic, religious, cultural and linguistic background.

Article 21 provides:

> States Parties that recognize and/or permit the system of adoption shall ensure that the best interests of the child shall be the paramount consideration and they shall:
> (a) Ensure that the adoption of a child is authorized only

by competent authorities who determine, in accordance with applicable law and procedures and on the basis of all pertinent and reliable information, that the adoption is permissible in view of the child's status concerning parents, relatives and legal guardians and that, if required, the persons concerned have given their informed consent to the adoption on the basis of such counselling as may be necessary;

(b) Recognize that inter-country adoption may be considered as an alternative means of child's care, if the child cannot be placed in a foster or an adoptive family or cannot in any suitable manner be cared for in the child's country of origin;

(c) Ensure that the child concerned by inter-country adoption enjoys safeguards and standards equivalent to those existing in the case of national adoption;

(d) Take all appropriate measures to ensure that, in inter-country adoption, the placement does not result in improper financial gain for those involved in it;

(e) Promote, where appropriate, the objectives of the present article by concluding bilateral or multilateral arrangements or agreements, and endeavour, within this framework, to ensure that the placement of the child in another country is carried out by competent authorities or organs.

The drafters began to consider the content of these two articles as early as the 1982 session of the working group (UN CHR, 1982:56–64). Article 20 concerns basic principles regarding alternative means of child care. Again we find the familiar theme that runs throughout the convention, namely, the "best interests" of the child. In addition, the article stresses the need for "special protection and assistance provided by the State" for children who are deprived of their family environment.

Initially, Article 20 dealt only with foster placement and adoption as alternative means of child care. The concept of *kafalah,* or bond, from Islamic law was introduced into Article 20(3) near the end of the negotiations on the convention, a concession to a group of Islamic states that wanted the convention to incorporate the principal features of all legal systems (UN CHR, 1989b:56–58). The drafters of the convention very strongly supported the principle that "due regard shall be paid to the desirability of continuity in a child's upbringing and to the child's ethnic, religious, cultural and linguistic background" in making arrangements for alternative care.

Article 21 concerns the adoption of children within countries and intercountry adoptions. At the earliest stages of the negotiations on the convention, most of the participants seemed interested in establishing an obligation on the part of the states parties to "undertake measures so as to facilitate adoption of children" and alternative methods of caring for children such as foster families (UN CHR, 1982:59–64). Second, they were interested in establishing the basic guidelines for regulating the system of adoptions, by making them subject to authorization by "competent authorities" and by emphasizing the concept of the "best interests of the child" (UN CHR, 1982:60–61). During the negotiations, however, the drafters abandoned some of these objectives. Article 21 is applicable only to states "that recognize and/or permit the system of adoption." If they do, they must ensure that the "best interests of the child" are the "paramount consideration" in cases of adoption. The article does not, therefore, mandate that the states parties take measures to facilitate the adoption of children.

The optional application of Article 21 was another concession that the drafters of the convention made to a group of Islamic states toward the end of the negotiations (UN CHR, 1989b:58–59). Still, when the convention was adopted by the Third Committee of the General Assembly (UN GA C.3, 1989f:16) and later by the General Assembly itself (UN GA, 1989c:6–7), the delegates from some Islamic states made statements regarding the terms of both Articles 20 and 21. Basically, they claimed that the articles are not binding on them because, consistent with Islamic law, they do not recognize or approve of the system of adoption.

Islamic states have followed up on their concerns by including, in their instruments of ratification, statements noting that they do not consider themselves bound by the provisions of Articles 20 and 21. Jordan, for example, ratified the convention with a reservation (UN LS, 1993:192) stating that it did not consider itself bound by Articles 20 and 21 "since they are at variance with the precepts of the tolerant Islamic Shariah." Kuwait indicated that "as it adheres to the provisions of the Islamic shariah as the main source of legislation," it does not approve of adoption (UN LS, 1993:192). The Egyptian government, whose representatives in the working group were the chief spokesmen for the Islamic group and negotiated the compromises that were so advantageous to them, also ratified the convention with a "reservation with respect to all the clauses and provisions relating to adoption" and "in particular with respect to the provisions governing adoption in articles 20 and 21 of the Convention" (UN LS, 1993:190). Other Islamic states (e.g., Djibouti, Maldives, and Mauritania) made general reservations that were based on their religious precepts and that would apparently apply to Articles 20 and 21. Some states parties (e.g., Finland, Norway, and Sweden) have objected to the reservations of some—but not all—Islamic states, claiming that states cannot invoke general principles of domestic law as reasons for failing to abide by their international legal obligations, but all of the objecting states parties indicated that they did not consider their objections as constituting obstacles to the entry into force of the convention between themselves and the states whose reservations they objected to (UN LS, 1993:194–95).

The issue of intercountry adoptions, which Article 21 also addresses, was controversial during the negotiations on the convention. The drafters set out to establish some basic guidelines, and they adopted only a few rudimentary ones (UN CHR, 1982:61–64). In fact, they left the most important work in this field to future negotiations. According to Article 21(e), the states parties agree to promote the conclusion of bilateral and multilateral agreements on intercountry adoptions. In recent years, many critics of intercountry adoptions have charged that the practice oftentimes involves the sale of and trafficking in children. In fact, the practice has stimulated highly emotional debate among NGOs and governmental representatives. Most of the concern in this field is to protect the children involved. For this reason, we shall return to the issue of intercountry adoptions in chapter 5, where we will focus on protection rights.

5 · Protection Rights

THE CONVENTION ON the Rights of the Child covers a broad range of issues and problems that are important from the standpoint of shielding children from harmful acts and practices. In fact, the convention is strongly oriented toward protection rights (see, e.g., Hammarberg, 1990:100 – 101). The reason for this is not hard to find. Children, especially younger children, are vulnerable to the most serious forms of abusive treatment, so they need to be protected. But some who have long advocated the further development and strengthening of human rights law specifically regarding children might find that the convention puts too much emphasis on protection rights, thus reinforcing, even if unintended, the traditional notion of children as objects of protection rather than bearers of rights.

Whatever the case, the fact remains that many of the articles of the convention (e.g., Articles 11, 19, 21, 32 – 38, and 40) deal with the need to protect children from various forms of abuse and mistreatment. In addition, one article, Article 39, establishes the obligation of the states parties to take measures to promote the physical and psychological recovery and social reintegration of a child that becomes a victim of abusive treatment. Although these articles cover a broad range of issues, they can be grouped into three main areas, which will provide the organizational scheme for this chapter: exploitation and abuse of children; abduction of, sale of, and trafficking in children; and the use of children in armed conflicts.

EXPLOITATION AND ABUSE

The exploitation and abuse of children occurs in so many ways that the drafters of the Convention on the Rights of the Child realized that they would not be able to address all of them in detail. Consequently, they focused on two especially serious exploitative practices, the sexual and the economic exploitation of children, and addressed other forms of exploitation in a general article (Article 36), which provides that the states parties "shall protect the child against all other forms of exploitation prejudicial to any aspects of the child's welfare."

Sexual Exploitation

The issue of the sexual exploitation of children has attracted increasing attention in recent years. Numerous governmental as well as nongovernmental organizations that are concerned about the welfare of children have done research on the subject. During the late 1980s, for example, Redd Barna, the Norwegian Save the Children Organization, sponsored a study by Ove Narvesen (1989) of the sexual exploitation of children in several developing countries. The study focused on the Philippines, Kenya, and Peru, but it also drew on previous research and data that had been collected on Thailand, Sri Lanka, India, Chile, and Brazil. According to Narvesen's report, the exploitation of children through prostitution and pornography is "probably the very worst form of exploitation of children" that occurs in the developing countries. Likening the problem to "a modern form of slavery that has grown to be a considerable problem in a number of countries," the report argued that it is "primarily the most defenceless individuals in the community, those with the greatest need for support and care, who are exploited by the sex market" (Narvesen, 1989:9).

Given the nature of the problem, it has been impossible to establish precise figures regarding the number of children who are victims of sexual exploitation. Some have suggested that on a worldwide basis, millions of children are involved. But the figures range far and wide even for individual countries. In Thailand alone, where the problem is believed to be extremely serious, estimates of the number of children involved have varied tremendously. The Center for the Protection of Children's Rights in Bangkok (DCI, 1989a:7–10), after a random sampling of prostitution houses in Bangkok and in major towns throughout the country, concluded that some 800,000 minors sixteen years of age or under were involved in the "flesh trade." A majority of these were fourteen or fifteen years old, but some were as young as eleven or twelve years old. As fantastic as these figures seem, the center argued that the "reality" of the flesh trade was much worse, that the demand far exceeded the supply and that the trade had now expanded to procuring children from hill tribes for export to neighboring countries. In stark contrast, the Thai National Youth Bureau has claimed that there are no more than 2,500 children involved in the flesh trade, whereas some other organizations, including the Women's Information Center and the Ministry of Public Welfare, claim that the correct figure is probably somewhere between 15,000 and 20,000 children (Narvesen, 1989:24). During the 1980s, the Ministry of Social Services and Development in the Philippines claimed that prostitution was almost as important as begging as an "occupation" among the estimated 50,000 to 75,000 street children in Manila (Kent, 1992:323).

Although children have been sexually exploited through the centuries, Narvesen's study (1989:21) found "strong indications that the form of commercial sexual exploitation best known today, and which is usually referred to as child prostitution, is a relatively recent phenomenon." The children who are most likely to become vulnerable to this form of sexual exploitation "are those with particularly problematic backgrounds," especially those who come from the lowest economic and social strata of the populations of their countries. These are the children who suffer from poverty, unemployment, lack of education, and lack of proper living conditions. Their families are usually large, and the children themselves usually do not have proper care and protection (Narvesen, 1989:27–28). As a United Nations study of the subject put it, children may become involved in prostitution because they are "runaways, walkaways or throwaways" (UN ECOSOC, 1991b:8).

The customers of the child prostitutes are predominantly men, though the exploited victims are both girls and boys. In other words, there are both heterosexual and homosexual customers. The customers are also relatively rich, whether or not they come from rich countries. Most come from the United States, Western Europe, Japan, and the Middle East (Kent, 1992:329). Many children have had their first experience of sexual abuse in the home. Some have been abused in employment, for example while working as housemaids. Obviously, the children suffer a great deal physically as well as emotionally and are exposed to various serious diseases including AIDS. They are also used in making pornographic pictures and videos (Kent, 1992:323–43; Narvesen, 1989:35).

Research on this problem suggests not a single cause but rather various factors that seem to lead to child prostitution. The Center for the Protection of Children's Rights in Bangkok suggests an essentially economic motive, though affecting two categories of children somewhat differently. One category consists of children who live in cities and who become involved in child prostitution mainly for financial reasons, that is, to satisfy their desire for consumer goods and services that are more abundant in urban centers and to which the children are exposed more extensively. The second category consists of children who live in the countryside and who become involved because they are sold into prostitution by their parents or relatives (DCI, 1989a:7–10). Narvesen's study also found a strong economic motive deriving from mass urbanization with its consequent dislocations and poverty, which force children into prostitution to make ends meet. But other factors are also at work, including colonial legacies, the "machismo" culture, tourism, the presence of foreign military bases, and commercialism (Narvesen, 1989:40–45).

Similarly, George Kent (1992:328–34) has argued that tourism and the presence of military bases have been very important in the growth of child prostitution as a problem in less developed countries. Military bases, which often employ thousands of people from the developed world, inject massive amounts of money into local economies and thus attract larger numbers of prostitutes. As for tourism, prostitution is both a cause and a consequence. As Kent put it, some "prostitution evolves to accommodate ordinary tourists on ordinary excursions. The availability of child prostitutes may be just one of the many amenities that make their vacations interesting. In some cases, however, tours are established specifically for tourists for whom sex is the primary objective." In fact, the avid promotion of tourism by the governments of countries such as the Philippines, Sri Lanka, and Thailand during the 1970s and 1980s apparently had a direct effect on increasing the number of child prostitutes. Owners of brothels and other businesses saw the burgeoning tourist trade as an opportunity to make a lot of money. In turn, awareness of the availability of child prostitutes spread among pedophiles throughout the world, further increasing the demand. While sex tourism is known to occur in some Western European countries, tourism that is focused on children is based in the poorer, less developed countries of the world.

The problem of child prostitution is widespread, and all indications are that it is growing. Yet, most countries have laws that regulate prostitution in one way or another. In some countries the practice is outlawed altogether. This is true even in Thailand, where all forms of prostitution are prohibited by law. In fact, in recent years the law has been modified to cover not only those who sell their bodies but also their customers and those who organize prostitution. But corruption among the police and civil servants makes it extremely difficult to enforce the relevant laws (DCI, 1989a:7–10). Moreover, the authorities are apparently reluctant to enforce the laws because of the importance of the tourist trade to the economy of the country, and tourists, as we have seen, are important customers of the prostitutes (Kent, 1992:328–29; Narvesen, 1989:52–53).

Corruption among authorities in other countries has also undermined the effective application of relevant laws. For this reason, in the opinion of many who have studied the phenomenon of child prostitution, attacking the problem will require more than legal intervention, though, to be sure, legal intervention at the national and international levels will continue to be required. Information campaigns that address the social and psychological implications of child sexual exploitation are necessary. In this connection, NGOS could be especially active and involved in gathering and disseminating information. Some analysts have also suggested that action against sex-tourism be taken in the developed as well as developing world (Narvesen, 1989:60 – 64; UN ECOSOC, 1991b:8).

In view of the nature and extent of the problem, the drafters of the Convention on the Rights of the Child could not avoid dealing with it, and they did so in Article 34. The details of the article were not contentious; therefore, the consensus on the article was easily reached. Article 34 provides:

> States Parties undertake to protect the child from all forms of sexual exploitation and sexual abuse. For these purposes, States Parties shall in particular take all appropriate national, bilateral and multilateral measures to prevent:
>
> (a) The inducement or coercion of a child to engage in any unlawful sexual activity;
>
> (b) The exploitative use of children in prostitution or other unlawful sexual practices;
>
> (c) The exploitative use of children in pornographic performances and materials.

Article 34 reflects a compromise that was reached from among different draft articles proposed by France, the Netherlands, and the Informal NGO Ad Hoc Group (UN CHR, 1987:16). As the drafters saw it, the purpose of the article was not to regulate the sex lives or activities of children, regulation that they perceived as impossible and, in some respects, undesirable. After all, children are allowed to marry at different ages in countries throughout the world. Moreover, children may want to voluntarily engage in sexual activities even at young ages. Therefore, the drafters wanted to frame the article in such a way that it would be aimed at combatting the sexual exploitation of children. For this reason, they used specific examples of practices, such as prostitution and pornography, that children are to be protected from but made it clear that it is the "exploitative" use of these practices that is at issue (UN CHR, 1987:21, 1989b:91).

Even if relatively small numbers of children were exploited for prostitution and pornography throughout the world, the practices deserve serious attention because of their emotional and physical effects on the children concerned. The Committee on the Rights of the Child has already indicated that it will address these matters in a serious manner. In issuing its concluding observations on the reports that were submitted by the Russian Federation and Sweden in 1992, the committee made comments and recommendations in which it took into account the provisions of Article 34. In fact, in the case of the Russian Federation, the committee went further and called attention to the terms of Article 39 of the convention, which oblige the states parties to take all appropriate measures to promote the physical and psychological recovery, and the social reintegration, of a child that is a victim of—among other things—any form of exploitation.

The Russian Federation report (UN CRC, 1992j:37–39), which was extremely candid in content, freely admitted that the increasingly serious economic dislocations in the country had had a deleterious impact on the status and well-being of children in many respects. It also noted that various programs had been initiated to help reintegrate children who had been abused and neglected; and it noted in particular that in April 1991, the Supreme Soviet had taken a decision to "halt the promotion of pornography and the glorification of violence and cruelty" as a measure to protect children from sexual abuse. Still, in this connection, the CRC made the following recommendation to the Russian Federation (UN CRC, 1993k:4): "The Committee emphasizes that more determined steps need to be taken to combat child prostitution; for example, the police forces should accord high priority to the investigation of such cases and the development of programmes to implement the provisions contained in article 39 of the Convention."

The Swedish report (UN CRC, 1992h:79–81) indicated that, in

Sweden, prostitution as such is not a criminal offense but that anyone who promotes, or makes improper economic use of, a person's
activity as a prostitute can be punished under the Penal Code. The
Swedish government was most concerned about the terms of Article 34(c), which relates to the exploitative use of children in pornographic performances and materials. In such matters Swedish law
apparently did not set a firm age limit for the definition of a
"child," the reason being a desire not to encroach too much on the
privacy of children. During parliamentary debate over ratification
of the convention, the view prevailed that the lack of a fixed age
limit should not stand in the way of ratification. Nonetheless, the
government decided to conduct a thorough review of the Penal
Code's provisions relating to child pornography.

The CRC was not completely satisfied with the Swedish government's explanations or intentions. In its concluding observations
on the Swedish report, the committee (UN CRC, 1993j:2–3) expressed "its concern over the lack of clarity and apparent discrep-
ancies contained in the law with regard to the definition of the
child"; and it also expressed concern "that the age of sexual maturity has not been fixed, which threatens the protection of children
from possible exploitation in the use of pornographic materials."
The committee therefore recommended that, regarding the definition of the child, the Swedish government "consider an approach
which is more coherent and more closely reflects the general principles and the provisions of the Convention."

Economic Exploitation

The second major form of child exploitation that the drafters of
the convention were concerned about is economic exploitation,
particularly the exploitation of child labor. The exploitation of
child labor is usually understood to mean the use of child labor under extremely difficult conditions such as low wage rates or no
wages at all, long working hours, and hazardous work in unhealthy
conditions such as exposure to dangerous machinery or chemicals.

Since children are less capable of defending themselves than are adults, they are vulnerable to being exposed to these forms of exploitation, separated from their parents, malnourished, and deprived of important social services such as medical treatment and education (UN ECOSOC, 1990c:6).

Numerous studies have been done on the phenomenon of child labor in different parts of the world (e.g., Alston, 1989; Bequele and Boyden, 1988; Dao, 1989; Hyndman, 1989; Weiner, 1991). In the industrialized countries, including the countries of Eastern Europe, enormous progress has been made, and child labor under abusive conditions, at least, has been virtually eliminated. In these countries, universal, or nearly universal, primary- and secondary-level education exists. And many of them have adopted laws that regulate the ages at which children can enter different occupations and the conditions under which they can work (see, e.g., Davis and Schwartz, 1987:31–34). As Assefa Bequele (1991:7) of the International Labour Organization has put it, although "there is concern about the appearance of traditional and new forms of child labour in" industrialized countries, "the magnitude of the problem is certainly much less and the possibilities for effective action are much greater than in other regions of the world."

In the poor countries of the world, however, the problem of child labor, and especially exploitative child labor, is, by most accounts, enormous. One report, released in 1990 by the Working Group on Contemporary Forms of Slavery of the Sub-Commission on Prevention of Discrimination and Protection of Minorities of the United Nations Commission on Human Rights, argued that the exploitation of child labor remained a serious problem especially in the poorer countries, and it called for action directed at the most vulnerable categories of children, including children of immigrants, street children, children of minority groups, indigenous children, and refugee children (UN ECOSOC, 1990d:9–10).

Problems of child labor vary from country to country (UN ECOSOC, 1990b; 1990c), and reliable statistics are very difficult to come by. It is generally believed that the continents of Asia and Africa account for well over 90 percent of the total child labor population of the world (Bequele, 1991:7). One study (Boonpala, 1991:65) cites "conservative" estimates of as many as 43 million child laborers in Asia alone. Another study (Burra, 1991:77) cites previous estimates of as many as 100 million child laborers in India alone. According to Weiner's (1991:3) calculations, "child laborers in India number from 13.6 million to 44 million, or more." These enormous statistical differences can be explained by the different criteria (e.g., the age of the laborers) that are used in different countries to compile the statistics.

Another factor that complicates the compilation of reliable statistics is the existence of large informal or unstructured economies, that is, economies outside of government control. As the ILO has noted, governments often find it very difficult if not impossible to measure the size of the informal economies, so they are unable to provide reliable statistics on the number of child laborers involved (UN CRC, 1992n:3).

Many analysts agree that poverty is the main cause of child labor. Some studies have listed two other causes: the huge debt burdens of less developed countries, debt that has led to cutbacks in social welfare programs, and rapid urbanization, which has led to a breakdown in family units. Since these problems are not likely to be alleviated in the foreseeable future, millions of children in poor countries will continue working (UN ECOSOC, 1990c:5 – 6). Weiner (1991:4 – 6), however, argues that, at least in India, the "low per capita income and economic situation is less relevant as an explanation than the belief systems of the state bureaucracy, a set of beliefs that are widely shared by educators, social activists, trade unionists, academic researchers, and, more broadly, by members of the Indian middle class." Moreover, he argues that these "beliefs are held by those outside as well as those within government, by observant Hindus and by those who regard themselves as secular, and by leftists as well as by centrists and rightists." The Indian view of the social order — of the respective roles of the different strata in society — is at the core of these beliefs. In any case, whether more traditional explanations involving poverty or more provocative ones such as Weiner's are accepted, the eradication of child labor may continue to be the ultimate goal, but it will remain elusive.

The drafters of the Convention on the Rights of the Child had to take these considerations into account in drafting Article 32 of the convention. It is noteworthy that the article does not affirm a goal of eradicating child labor; instead, it calls for the protection of children from exploitation and other harmful effects of child labor. Article 32 provides:

> 1. States Parties recognize the right of the child to be protected from economic exploitation and from performing any work that is likely to be hazardous or to interfere with the child's education, or to be harmful to the child's health or physical, mental, spiritual, moral or social development.
> 2. States Parties shall take legislative, administrative, social and educational measures to ensure the implementation of the present article. To this end, and having regard to the relevant provisions of other international instruments, States Parties shall in particular:
> (a) Provide for a minimum age or minimum ages for admissions to employment;
> (b) Provide for appropriate regulation of the hours and conditions of employment; and
> (c) Provide for appropriate penalties or other sanctions to ensure the effective enforcement of the present article.

Article 32 originated in proposals that were submitted to the working group by Poland, Canada, the United States, and the Informal NGO Ad Hoc Group during the mid-1980s (DCI, 1985:1–3; UN CHR, 1986a:13–16). The drafters generally agreed on the principle enunciated in the first paragraph of the article: that children need to be protected from exploitation and from performing work that is likely to be hazardous to their education or harmful to their health or well-being. However, some pointed out that in the present state of economic development in many Third World countries, children are often required to work even at the cost of their education (UN CHR, 1989b:90).

The drafters also easily reached a consensus on the main part of the second paragraph of Article 32: that states would adopt their own legislative and other measures to regulate child labor. The difficulty arose with the other parts of the paragraph. For example, Article 32(2)(a) states that the measures adopted by states would provide "for a minimum age or minimum ages for admissions to employment." One of the early proposals regarding this issue would have established fifteen years of age as the minimum age for work. However, the ILO questioned whether such a minimum age should be specified in the convention, pointing out that its Minimum Age Convention of 1973, though aiming at the "progressive raising of the minimum age for admission to employment or work to a level consistent with the fullest physical and mental development of young persons," distinguished between different kinds of work and recognized the need for establishing different age limits for different kinds of employment (UN ECOSOC, 1980:1, 1984:2). Thus, although the ILO realized that the Convention on the Rights of the Child could take a different stand on this issue, it wondered if specifying the minimum age for work might not prove unduly rigid, since it would not "make special allowance for the problems of less developed countries nor for work in connection with education or training, and would not contemplate a progressive raising of the minimum age" (UN ECOSOC, 1980:2).

The drafters of the convention accepted the ILO's advice on the issue of the minimum age for work, leaving it up to states to determine for themselves, in their own legislation and administrative and other measures, how they wished to deal with the matter. The drafters believed that this flexibility would be much more practical (UN CHR, 1986a:15). The same would be true for regulating the hours and conditions of employment and the sanctions that might be applied for violating the established standards.

The flexibility that Article 32 allows was obviously very important to many states in the world. It is noteworthy, however, that the Indian government still found it necessary to make a "declaration" concerning the article when it ratified the convention (UN LS, 1993:191). It stated:

> While fully subscribing to the objectives and purposes of the Convention, realising that certain of the rights of the child, namely those pertaining to the economic, social and cultural rights can only be progressively implemented in the developing countries, subject to the extent of available resources and within the framework of international co-operation; recognising that the child has to be protected from exploitation of all forms including economic exploitation; noting that for several reasons children of different ages do work in India; having prescribed minimum ages for employment in hazardous occupations and in certain other areas; having made regulatory provisions regarding hours and conditions of employment; and being aware that it is not practical immediately to prescribe minimum ages for admission to each and every area of employment in India — the Government of India undertakes to take measures to progressively implement the provisions of article 32, particularly paragraph 2 (a), in accordance with its national legislation and relevant international instruments to which it is a State Party.

The Committee on the Rights of the Child has already taken steps to indicate the importance it attaches to the subject addressed in Article 32. At its second session in October 1992, the committee met with officials of the ILO to discuss the phenomenon of child labor. The ILO has established programs and projects on the elimination of child labor, and the CRC wanted to discuss what the organization had done in this regard. In the view of the ILO officials, the eradication of child labor must be the ultimate objective of good social policy regarding children, but they realized that "initially the main consideration, in more pragmatic terms," is "to regulate and humanize it." As they saw it, in many countries it would be "impossible to eliminate child labour without first of all giving special attention to the improvement of overall economic conditions." Thus, the objective of the ILO's long-term International Programme on the Elimination of Child Labour was "to prevent children from taking part in hazardous work, to eliminate child slave labour, and to protect the youngest and most vulnerable." The program was currently being implemented in six countries: Brazil, India, Indonesia, Kenya, Thailand, and Turkey. Other countries had expressed an interest in the program, so the ILO had begun preparatory work to admit Bangladesh, Cameroon, Egypt, Pakistan, the Philippines, and Tanzania as participants (UN CRC, 1992m:2 – 3).

The discussion that the CRC had with the ILO about child labor provided the foundation for a larger, special study that the committee has planned on the subject of the economic exploitation of children. Acting under Article 45(c) of the convention, which we will discuss more fully in chapter 8, the committee has decided to undertake special studies that could "contribute to an increased awareness and better understanding of the provisions of the Convention and their implementation throughout the world" (UN CRC, 1992a:19 – 20). The special study of the economic exploitation of children will be one of those studies. It is clear that the committee has a broad conception of the issue, for it has indicated that although Article 32 of the convention is especially relevant to its concerns, other articles, including Articles 33, 34, and 35, which address drugs and narcotics, prostitution, and the sale and abduction of children, are also relevant because the exploitation of children in those ways often has economic undertones. Moreover, the committee has argued that all of these articles need to be considered in the light of general provisions of the convention, including Article 2 (nondiscrimination), Article 3 (the best interests of the child), Article 4 (the maximum extent of available resources), Article 6 (the survival and development of the child), and Article 12 (the child's right to be heard). In undertaking this special study, the committee expected to use country, thematic, or analytical reports that could throw light on factors that impede making progress toward bringing about an end to the economic exploitation of children (UN CRC, 1993a:annex 3).

Finally, it should be noted that the CRC has looked closely at the reports it has received from states parties to examine how they have addressed problems related to child labor and other forms of economic exploitation, and it has made suggestions and recommendations to some states in this regard. In the case of Egypt, the CRC expressed concern about the "very large number of children between 6 and 14 years of age who are enrolled in the labour force and therefore lack, wholly or partly, the possibility to go to school." The committee conceded that "children may to a certain extent contribute to seasonal activities," but it emphasized that "care should always be taken that primary education is available to them and that they should not be working in hazardous conditions" (UN CRC, 1993l:2−3). Therefore, the committee made the following recommendation to the Egyptian government:

> The recommendations of the studies on child labour under-taken with the assistance of the International Labour Organization on the problem of child employment should be implemented and Egyptian legislation on minimum age should be revised. In that regard, consideration should be given to the possibility of acceding to ILO Convention No. 138 and other conventions on minimum age of employment relating to the protection of children and young persons at work. (UN CRC, 1993l:3)

In the case of Sudan, the CRC was blunt. It found the report so lacking in substance that it had to postpone further consideration of the report until it received additional information. Nonetheless, it continued, UN CRC, 1993m:3): "The Committee . . . expresses its concern regarding the issues of forced labour and slavery" (UN CRC, 1993m:3).

ABDUCTION OF AND TRAFFICKING IN CHILDREN

The abduction of children and the trafficking in children, including the sale of children, have also attracted a lot of attention in recent years. The issues and problems that these practices have raised have been studied by governmental and nongovernmental organizations and private agencies. Concerted international action is clearly necessary to suppress these practices, and when the Convention on the Rights of the Child was being drafted, they were put on the agenda of the working group at the request of representatives of some states and NGOs. Unfortunately, however, although the drafters devoted some attention to these issues, they failed to take clear and unequivocal stands. Instead, they adopted several articles that affirm a few basic principles regarding the protection of children from abduction, sale, or traffic but left it mainly to future international instruments to determine the courses of action that would need to be taken to suppress such practices. We shall use two topics to illustrate this point: (1) the abduction of children; and (2) intercountry adoptions as a potential form of trafficking in children.

Abduction of Children

Two articles of the convention address the issue of the abduction of children. Article 11 provides:

> 1. States Parties shall take measures to combat the illicit transfer and non-return of children abroad.
> 2. To this end, States Parties shall promote the conclusion of bilateral or multilateral agreements or accession to existing agreements.

Article 35 provides:

> States Parties shall take all appropriate national, bilateral and multilateral measures to prevent the abduction, the sale of or traffic in children for any purpose or in any form.

Articles 11 and 35 are so closely related that the drafters gave some consideration to joining them (UN CHR, 1989b:40 – 41). The most controversial issue addressed by the articles is the international abduction of children. This issue was brought to the attention of the working group by the French delegation and by some NGOs. As it turned out, the issue was extremely sensitive politically because many children have been abducted in cases when the parents were of different nationalities. When the parents have divorced or separated, children have been "illegally removed" from one country to another (UN CHR, 1983:6). The French have had especially serious problems with such abductions when French women have divorced or become separated from Algerian husbands. In the hope of trying to deal with the problem in a cooperative fashion, the French government had concluded a treaty with Algeria, according to which they had established a commission to settle disputes involving abductions. The commission had evidently been able to settle some of the disputes, and a number of children had been reunited with their mothers (UN CHR, 1989g:13).

Other European countries and the United States have experienced similar difficulties involving different countries. When the mothers of abducted children have been awarded custody by the courts in their own countries, they have often been unable to persuade the courts and authorities in other countries to respect those custody judgments and to order their children returned. The religious upbringing of the children is apparently of paramount consideration in these cases, especially when Islamic countries are involved, with Muslim fathers wanting to ensure that their children will be raised in the Muslim faith. Since such considerations can very easily lead to highly emotion-charged debates, the best that the drafters of the Convention on the Rights of the Child could have expected to achieve was to urge states to work toward the conclusion of other agreements in which they might satisfactorily address the problem of international abductions.

Experience suggests, however, that a satisfactory solution to this problem is not likely in the foreseeable future. NGOs such as the Defense for Children International and the World Young Women's Christian Association have taken an interest in the problem of child abductions. The DCI has reported receiving many requests for assistance from mothers whose children have been abducted. Yet, the amount of assistance that they have been able to provide on a case-by-case basis has unfortunately been negligible. The refusal to cooperate by the authorities in the countries concerned is one of the most serious obstacles to a satisfactory resolution of the problem. In addition, the fact that the parents are usually unable to maintain any contact with each other makes a resolution of the problem most unlikely. International agreements that have already been concluded have not been widely ratified, and according to the DCI, many children will therefore "continue to find themselves torn between their feuding parents, without redress, for a long time to come" (DCI, 1990:10).

The World YWCA too has expressed concern about the fact that no effective measures have been found to deal with the problem of child abductions. It has argued that the abductions "are encouraged by the passivity of the concerned countries and by traditional legislation that allows the father to hinder the freedom of movement of children." Yet, the gravity of the problem has had extremely serious consequences for the children and also for the parents — especially the mothers, who, in the vast majority of cases, are the ones who are deprived of their rights to be together with their children. Effective cooperation among states will certainly be required to solve these problems, but states' apparent inability to cooperate has, in the meantime, meant "endless waiting" and "lost years that can never be replaced" (UN ECOSOC, 1987a:1 – 2).

Trafficking in Children

Child trafficking is seen as a particularly serious attack on the dignity and moral and physical security of children. As one study done by the DCI found (DCI, 1989b:iii), children who become the victims of child trafficking are used for three different purposes, which may sometimes overlap, namely, national and international adoption, forced labor, and sexual exploitation. According to the DCI, the mechanisms of the market for children are largely unknown and poorly monitored, and governments seem generally uninterested in the subject (DCI, 1989b:vi-vii).

Since we have already dealt with the sexual and economic exploitation of children, let us look more closely at intercountry adoptions as a potential form of trafficking in children. In recent years, the issue has attracted considerable public attention. It was perhaps most dramatically posed after the fall of Nicolae Ceausescu's regime in Romania in December 1989 (Cantwell, 1990:1, 19). Vivid photographs and films of children living in squalid conditions in various Romanian institutions were broadcast throughout the world. Americans, Canadians, and West Europeans flocked to Romania in search of children to adopt. In 1990, approximately three thousand children were adopted out of Romania; in the first two months of 1991, some thirteen hundred were adopted into the United States alone. Reports of corruption in the adoption process and of children and babies being sold by their parents were widespread; free-lance brokers entered the adoption "business," exploiting both the biological parents and the prospective parents. Although many of the children who were institutionalized suffered from serious diseases, including AIDS, few if any of them were adopted. It also remains unclear how many of the children were actually abandoned by their parents. In any event, it appears that once the abortion ban imposed during the Ceausescu years was lifted, the number of children being abandoned in Romanian maternity wards was greatly reduced (Hunt, 1991:27–53).

Although the Romanian "baby bazaar" brought the issue of intercountry adoption sharply into focus, the practice was quite widespread even before then. In 1987, for example, the DCI had submitted a statement (UN ECOSOC, 1987b:1–4) to the United Nations Commission on Human Rights regarding intercountry adoption of children with particular reference to Chile. The statement claimed that thousands of children were being adopted "clandestinely" through the efforts of organizations in Western Europe and North America, which pressured wed and unwed mothers who were too poor to care for their children to give them up for adoption.

A more recent study (DCI et al., 1991), conducted by a group of NGOs that drew on data available from twenty-five countries, found that a variety of illegal or questionable practices occur in the so-called sending as well as receiving countries. These practices include such things as *fait accompli* adoptions (children being brought into countries without proper home studies, prior clearance, etc.), improper pressure on biological parents to give up their children for adoption, falsification of documents, and unreasonable or unwarranted financial gain by agents and biological parents, financial gain that amounts to trafficking in and, in some cases, the sale of children (DCI et al., 1991:13–17; see also DCI, 1989b:iii).

Some who have studied the phenomenon of intercountry adoptions have suggested that in fact very few children are actually abandoned by their parents. Maria Josephina Becker (1989:24–25), for example, has argued that, at least so far as Latin American countries are concerned, the great majority of the children found on the streets and in public or private institutions are not abandoned. Rather, they, together with their families, are simply victims of economic conditions that make it impossible for them to live normal family lives. According to Becker, since the number of children actually abandoned is very small, the demand for children far exceeds the supply. Thus, to "the extent that they actively undertake the search for children to be adopted, couples and agencies involved in international adoption, their generous and humane motives notwithstanding, increase the pressures favouring a rupture between the poor child and his or her family rather than strengthening the ties between them." Becker maintains that these "pressures are exercised on the family directly, through descriptions of the paradise-like future (a perfect home in a country where poverty does not exist) that the parents will deny their child if they refuse to permit adoption." The local official or private child welfare agencies are also pressured to agree to intercountry adoptions, and in this way "conditions encouraging the 'production' of abandonment are created, apparently motivated by the assistance and protection of the child, but which in reality serve the interests of the adoptive parents." Yet, there is a "paucity of real knowledge" about the medium- and long-range consequences of intercountry adoptions, "especially with regard to children of different ethnic and racial origin." As Becker put it, the "fact that the child has been adopted by a family does not necessarily mean that he or she has been adopted by a society or by a country" (1989:25).

None of this is to say, of course, that all cases of intercountry adoption are problematic or involve child trafficking. Well-intentioned biological and adoptive parents, social workers, and legal and political authorities are involved in the process, and many children are undoubtedly placed in good homes. But as the Romanian and other experiences amply demonstrate, the practice of intercountry adoption raises issues that are especially important to three categories of people: the children, the biological parents, and the prospective parents. Each of these categories of people needs to be protected.

The Convention on the Rights of the Child addresses the phenomenon of intercountry adoption, but only in a rudimentary fashion. Article 21, which applies only to states parties that recognize or permit the system of adoption, emphasizes the principle that "the best interests of the child" shall be the "paramount consideration" in all cases of adoption. It then provides that the states parties shall recognize that intercountry adoption "may be considered as an alternative means of child's care, if the child cannot be placed in a foster or an adoptive family or cannot in any suitable manner be cared for in the child's country of origin." The article thus endorses the so-called principle of subsidiarity in intercountry adoptions, that is, that children should be put up for intercountry adoption only if they cannot be placed within their home countries (UN CHR, 1989b:59–61).

In addition, Article 21 addresses some procedural issues that arise specifically in cases of intercountry adoptions: it requires that safeguards and standards equivalent to those existing in cases of national adoptions be applied also in cases of intercountry adoptions; and it obliges the states parties to take measures to ensure that people involved in intercountry adoptions cannot benefit from "improper financial gain" in the process.

In the main, the provisions of Article 21 are consistent with the terms of the Declaration on Social and Legal Principles Relating to the Protection and Welfare of Children, with Special Reference to Foster Placement and Adoption Nationally and Internationally (Resolution 41/85), which was adopted by the General Assembly in December 1986. In fact, the drafters of the convention realized that they had merely reiterated some of the principles affirmed in that declaration and that they had therefore not gone far enough in protecting the children, biological parents, and prospective parents who are involved in intercountry adoption (Cantwell, 1992:26). Nonetheless, as we discussed in chapter 4, Article 21 has been the subject of reservations or declarations regarding its inapplicability to a number of states parties to the convention, mainly Islamic states (e.g., Bangladesh, Egypt, Jordan, Kuwait, and Maldives), which do not recognize the system of adoption. Be that as it may, as noted in Article 21(e), the states parties will seek to promote the objectives of the article by concluding bilateral or multilateral arrangements or agreements that will address more specifically the issues that arise in intercountry adoptions. An important step in this direction has already been taken by the Hague Conference on Private International Law.

In June 1990, a special commission on intercountry adoption of the Hague Conference on Private International Law met to set in

motion the process of drafting a convention on intercountry adoption. It agreed to establish an informal ad hoc advisory group that
would assist the Permanent Bureau of the Hague Conference in
preparing draft articles for a convention. The ad hoc group met at
the Permanent Bureau in The Hague in November 1990, and the
bureau then prepared a set of "illustrative draft articles" that were
to provide a focal point for discussions at the second meeting of
the special commission on intercountry adoption in April to May
1991 (Hague Conference, 1990b:3). The convention (see Hague
Conference, 1993) was adopted at the seventeenth session of the
Hague Conference in May 1993.

From the earliest stages of negotiations on the Hague Convention, representatives of governments and NGOs stressed the need
for normative consistency between the proposed convention and
the terms of Article 21 of the Convention on the Rights of the Child
(Hague Conference, 1990b:21, 1991b:1). The Hague Conference on
Private International Law is a free-standing international organization, so it was not obliged to make the provisions of its own convention normatively consistent with the terms of Article 21 of the
Convention on the Rights of the Child. But there was an important
reason why it was very much to its advantage to do so. The member states of the Hague Conference are also member states of the
United Nations and would, in many cases, probably want to ratify
both conventions. They would have found it difficult, if not impossible, to do so if the provisions of the two conventions con-
flicted with each other. Thus, the member states set out on a much
more productive course — to draft a convention that would aim to
provide adequate safeguards to the children, biological parents,
and prospective parents involved in intercountry adoptions
(Hague Conference, 1990b:21).

The negotiations on the Hague Convention involved numerous
complex administrative and legal problems that arise because of
the differences in cultures and legal systems in the receiving and
sending countries involved in intercountry adoptions (Hague

Conference, 1990a:11). During the negotiations, the principle of subsidiarity was strongly supported, especially by sending countries (Hague Conference, 1990a:13–15, 1990b:7, 1991a:2). Moreover, many negotiators supported the principle that "the family is to be found for the child, not the child for the family" (Hague Conference, 1991c:2). Both principles were seen by many negotiators as reinforcing the notion that adoptions are always concluded in the best interests of the child. There was also broad agreement that the convention should take steps to require the states parties to identify the administrative mechanisms that would be charged with cooperating with mechanisms in other countries to ensure that the rights of all parties involved in the adoption process were duly recognized and respected (Hague Conference, 1990a:17–19, 1991d:2).

The range of issues raised in the adoption of the Hague Convention reflected the inadequacies of the terms of Article 21 of the Convention on the Rights of the Child. What should be done when adoptions break down? Are the receiving states the only ones that are responsible for intervening in such cases? Or should the sending states also have some responsibilities? Should the child be repatriated? It appears that very few intercountry adoptions break down, though adoptive parents and children may be unable to adjust well, or social service agencies may find that the placement of the child is detrimental to his or her welfare. In some cases, the problems have arisen because of the differences between the "dreamed of child and the real child" (DCI et al., 1991b:9–12).

Other questions and issues arose. How should older children be treated in intercountry adoptions? What should be done about the nationality of the children adopted (Hague Conference, 1990a:21–25)? Should the convention aim to regulate "independent" intercountry adoptions, that is, adoptions that are not arranged through recognized agencies? Should there be a waiting period between the time of the child's arrival in the receiving country and the final adoption order (DCI et al., 1991a:3, 1991b:4–5)?

Although statistical data in the field of intercountry adoptions are, on the whole, unreliable, it seems that independent adoptions have been very common, perhaps amounting to as much as 80 or 90 percent of all intercountry adoptions. In fact, the NGO study cited earlier found that a "significant proportion" of adoptive parents in receiving countries choose to arrange independent adoptions rather than work through agencies. The major reason seems to be that the demand for children (especially babies) is greater than the supply that is available through agencies. But many families are also evidently motivated to bypass agencies because they are concerned about the amount of time it takes before the final adoption arrangements can be made; because they fear that they will be rejected; because they are worried about their financial situation; and because they sometimes have very specific requirements (e.g., age, race, religion, ethnic origin) that they believe will be more readily met through independent adoption agents (DCI et al., 1991a:7–9).

Generally, most officials from receiving as well as sending countries seem to favor agency over independent adoptions because they believe that in agency adoptions, the children are better protected. But even then, should the child have a say in whether or not he or she will be adopted, and by which family? If so, at what age should this right be said to exist (DCI et al., 1991a:10, 1991b:7)?

All of these questions concerning intercountry adoption are vitally important if the children, biological parents, and prospective parents are to be adequately protected. But none of these questions are addressed properly in Article 21 of the Convention on the Rights of the Child. To the contrary, as we have seen, paragraph (d) of the article urges the states parties to promote the conclusion of international agreements and arrangements that would adequately protect the relevant parties. Since the Hague Convention was intended to do this (Hague Conference, 1993; UN CRC, 1992o:8–9), it provides the most notable example to date of how the Convention on the Rights of the Child has stimulated further norm creation in the field of children's rights rather than created the norms itself.

PARTICIPATION IN ARMED CONFLICT

The question of how much, if any, protection should be accorded children in cases of armed conflict was probably the most controversial issue debated during the negotiations on the Convention on the Rights of the Child, and it was resolved in a manner that many delegations considered unsatisfactory (see Cantwell, 1992:26–27). In fact, as we will see, some states parties continued to express their dissatisfaction with how the issue was resolved even after the convention was adopted, and the Committee on the Rights of the Child has taken up the issue at its meetings.

The Polish draft of the convention was silent on the issue of the involvement of children in armed conflicts, but in the mid-1980s, various governmental delegations to the open-ended working group, the Informal NGO Ad Hoc Group, IGOS, and specialized agencies of the United Nations such as UNICEF submitted proposals that aimed to establish rules that would apply to children involved in situations of armed conflict (UN CHR, 1986a:28). Two of the governmental delegations that submitted proposals were the Islamic Republic of Iran and Iraq, both of which were then involved in a war in which young teenage boys were allegedly used in battle (UN CHR, 1986a:27). The Islamic Republic of Iran in particular is believed to have lost hundreds of thousands of "child inductees" in the war with Iraq, and its use of such young children was heavily criticized in various United Nations forums (Elahi, 1988).

In submitting their proposals to the working group, both states were probably trying to embarrass the other. The Iranian proposal (UN CHR, 1986a:27) approached the issue in broad terms, essentially reflecting on its own experience in the war with Iraq, stipulating that parties to the convention would "refrain from committing a military attack and bombardment of undefended cities and the civilian population, inflicting incalculable suffering, especially on children who are the most vulnerable members of the population." It also provided that the use of chemical and bacteriological weapons constitute a "crime against humanity." In contrast, the Iraqi proposal (UN CHR, 1986a:27) was more narrowly focused on children. Among other things, it affirmed that the protection of children must be ensured by the parties to armed conflicts; that the parties "must take every possible measure to ensure that children do not participate directly in hostilities and are not sent to combat areas"; and that in the event children were captured by adversaries they would continue to enjoy the rights affirmed in the convention and be separated from adult prisoners (UN CHR, 1986a:27).

Many other governmental delegations submitted proposals regarding the participation of children in armed conflicts, stimulating a great deal of debate and discord during several sessions of the working group. In 1986, consensus was reached on what was to become Article 38 of the convention, though efforts were made to reopen debate on some of its provisions in 1987 (UN CHR, 1987a:41–42) and 1988 (UN CHR, 1988a:19–20). Despite the serious objections of some delegations, in 1989, Adam Lopatka, the chair of the working group, ruled that the consensus had not been broken on Article 38 of the convention (UN CHR, 1989b:111–19). It provides:

> 1. States Parties undertake to respect and to ensure respect for rules of international humanitarian law applicable to them in armed conflicts which are relevant to the child.
> 2. States Parties shall take all feasible measures to ensure that persons who have not attained the age of fifteen years do not take a direct part in hostilities.
> 3. States Parties shall refrain from recruiting any person who has not attained the age of fifteen years into the armed forces. In recruiting among those persons who have attained the age of fifteen years but who have not attained the age of eighteen years, States Parties shall endeavour to give priority to those who are oldest.
> 4. In accordance with their obligations under international humanitarian law to protect the civilian population in armed conflicts, States Parties shall take all feasible measures to ensure protection and care of children who are affected by an armed conflict.

Article 39 of the convention obliges the states parties to take all appropriate measures "to promote physical and psychological recovery and social reintegration of a child victim of . . . armed conflicts."

The Age Limitation in Armed Conflicts

The most controversial issue of Article 38 is the age limitation that applies to young people involved in armed conflicts (which do not necessarily have to be international armed conflicts). According to Article 38(3), the states parties to the convention shall refrain from recruiting young people under fifteen years old into their armed forces; moreover, if they recruit young people between the ages of fifteen and eighteen, they "shall endeavour to give priority to those who are oldest." According to Article 38(2), the states parties are to "take all feasible measures" to ensure that people under the age of fifteen do not "take a direct part in hostilities."

The initial proposals regarding Article 38 had not mentioned the age limitation that should apply in recruiting and utilizing people in armed conflicts. It was evidently assumed by those who made the proposals that the states parties would be bound by the basic definition of childhood in Article 1 of the convention, that is, that a child is any person below the age of eighteen years (DCI, 1984:6). But when the working group began to discuss the proposals in 1986, a number of delegations, including those of the United Kingdom, Canada, the United States, and the Soviet Union, argued that Article 38 should qualify the definition of the child so far as participation in armed conflicts was concerned, and all of them suggested the age limit of fifteen years (UN CHR, 1986a:28 – 19). They were supported by observers of the International Committee of the Red Cross, who pointed out that the Additional Protocols of 1977 to the Geneva Conventions of 1949 had set fifteen years as the age below which children may not be recruited into the armed forces (UN CHR, 1986a:29; DCI, 1987:1 – 3). Thus, if Article 38 specified the same age limit, it would be normatively consistent with *ex-*

isting international humanitarian law. Although this was the easiest, and perhaps least controversial, way of dealing with the issue, it would not meet with the approval of those who believe that treaties and conventions can be used to *advance* the development of international law (see, e.g., Krill, 1992:347–56). In any event, in 1986, the working group agreed to set the recruitment age limit at fifteen years.

But some delegations were not pleased with the lower age limit, and they continued to work toward revising the terms of Article 38. At the 1987 session of the working group, for example, the Swedish and Swiss delegations argued that the convention should extend better protection to young people than did the Additional Protocols to the Geneva Conventions (UN CHR, 1987:41–42). The Swedish delegation reiterated its plea at the 1988 session as well (UN CHR, 1988:19–20). The issue was finally resolved in 1989 amid confusion regarding the motives that lay behind the proposals to revise the article. Some delegations, such as that of the United States, argued that Article 38 should merely be consistent with existing international standards regarding the use of young people in armed conflicts. According to the U.S. delegation, the Additional Protocols to the Geneva Conventions had been adopted after lengthy debates in diplomatic conferences convened for that purpose, and it believed that the working group was not "an appropriate forum to revise existing international law in this area" (UN CHR, 1989b:112). Other delegates disagreed with the U.S. position. They argued that the working group "should not feel constrained by existing international standards," that it should be able to adopt an innovative position that would help to expand and improve international law on the subject of the participation of young people in situations of armed conflict (UN CHR, 1989b: 112,115–16).

The different viewpoints on the issue caused substantial confusion, with some delegates complaining about the speed with which the issue was being addressed. Nonetheless, the chair ruled that consensus on Article 38 had not been broken (UN CHR, 1989b:114, 143).

Subsequent Consideration of Article 38

The disagreement that arose in the working group on Article 38 carried over into the Commission on Human Rights and later the Third Committee of the General Assembly. Since then, the Committee on the Rights of the Child has also taken up the question of how the convention deals with the participation of children in armed conflicts.

Speaking on behalf of the Nordic Group at the 1989 session of the Commission on Human Rights, Anders Ronquist of Sweden noted that "the Nordic countries attached particular importance to the question of the protection of children in cases of armed conflict" and that they did not believe that Article 38 accurately reflected the concerns expressed by a majority within the working group. Moreover, they regretted that the article did not extend to young people better protection than was afforded them under existing international humanitarian law (UN CHR, 1989g:10). Paul Rietjens of Belgium expressed similar concerns (UN CHR, 1989g:11). Wolfram Karl of Austria argued that only an age limit of eighteen years in Article 38 "would satisfy humanitarian requirements" and that allowing "anybody below the age of 18 to become involved in armed conflicts was strictly inconsistent with the overall objectives of the" Convention on the Rights of the Child (UN CHR, 1989c:7). Similarly, Quentin Bryce of Australia said her delegation was disappointed that Article 38 did not "increase the level of protection of children in armed conflicts under international humanitarian law" (UN CHR, 1989c:10). Representatives of these and other states continued to criticize the terms of Article 38 in meetings of the Third Committee of the General Assembly in November 1989 (UN GA C.3, 1989b:10, 1989c:5, 1989h:3, 9).

Some NGOs, including Radda Barnen International, also expressed their disappointment with the terms of Article 38

(UN CHR, 1989C:14). And Nigel Cantwell of Defense for Children International, speaking on behalf of the Informal NGO Ad Hoc Group, noted, "All non-governmental organizations were disturbed at the amazingly low level of protection that certain Governments seemed prepared to afford to children in armed conflicts, especially with regard to the direct participation of children in hostilities." As he put it, those "few Governments which had forced a consensus on such low standards should examine the practical implications of their stance and should revise their position before the General Assembly adopted the draft convention later in the year" (UN CHR, 1989C:18).

Despite the objections, the strongest proponents of establishing a lower age limit for the involvement of young people in armed conflicts held to their position, insisting that "the General Assembly and the Commission on Human Rights were not appropriate forums for revising existing international humanitarian law" (UN CHR, 1989d:6). Disappointed with this unyielding resistance, some delegates indicated that their governments would interpret Article 38 of the convention in the light of Article 41, that is, that they would apply provisions of their own laws or international obligations that extend a higher degree of protection to young people in cases of armed conflicts (UN CHR, 1989b:141; UN GA C.3, 1989f:15–16, 1989a:5).

Several governments have carried through with their intentions and have made declarations when ratifying the convention to the effect that they interpret Article 38 more liberally than its text would require. Argentina, for example, declared that "it would have liked the Convention categorically to prohibit the use of children in armed conflicts"; since the convention failed to do so, Argentina would apply its domestic law, which establishes such a prohibition (UN LS, 1993:188). Austria declared that it would "not make use of the possibility provided for in article 38, paragraph 2, to determine an age limit of 15 years for taking part in hostilities as this rule is incompatible with article 3, paragraph 1, which determines that the best interests of the child shall be a primary consideration" (UN LS, 1993:189). Germany made an almost identical declaration (UN LS, 1993:191). Colombia, Ecuador, Spain, and Uruguay also made statements that they would apply more liberal domestic legislation or simply that they were disappointed that the drafters of the convention had not seized the opportunity to be innovative so far as international humanitarian law was concerned (UN LS, 1993:189–93).

The Committee on the Rights of the Child has followed up on these indications of dissatisfaction with the terms of Article 38. In fact, the committee decided that the first special study it would undertake in accordance with Article 45(c) of the convention, mentioned earlier in connection with the economic exploitation of children, was the situation of children in armed conflicts. The committee decided to focus on this topic for several reasons. First, it believed that armed conflicts had important implications for the protection of children's rights in general. Second, it believed that many conflicts in the early 1990s had serious consequences for children, whether or not they were direct participants; specifically, it expressed concern about the suffering of children in Somalia and Bosnia-Herzegovina. Third, the committee believed that several articles of the convention, not just Article 38, were relevant to the topic because armed conflicts had an impact on the physical and mental well-being of children. Fourth, in the light of what had been happening in Somalia and Bosnia-Herzegovina, the committee believed that it was important to give some thought to the ways and means of protecting children exposed to situations of armed conflict (UN CRC, 1992p:2–3, 1993a:36–37).

Representatives of various IGOs, NGOs, and United Nations specialized agencies participated in the committee's special study of children in armed conflicts. By UNICEF estimates, over one and one-half million children were killed in wars in the last decade; more than four million were wounded; approximately five million were forced into refugee camps; and about twelve million had lost their homes (UN CRC, 1992p:3 – 4). According to a study done by the Quaker Peace and Service organization, tens of thousands of children under the age of eighteen were believed to be fighting alongside adult soldiers (UN CRC, 1992p:4 – 5). Most participants in the discussions generally agreed that it was necessary to consider ways and means to help children who have been affected by armed conflicts to readjust and become reintegrated into their societies (UN CRC, 1992p:7 – 10).

The discussions sponsored by the CRC ranged over four main areas involving children in situations of armed conflict: how to prevent children from being recruited and/or from participating in armed conflicts; whether existing international standards in this field are being sufficiently implemented; whether adequate measures are being taken to protect children from the effects of armed conflicts; and whether, in accordance with Article 39 of the convention, adequate measures are being taken toward the recovery and rehabilitation of children affected by armed conflicts (UN CRC, 1992q:4 – 5).

At the conclusion of its deliberations on the matter, the CRC found the international legal standards in this field deficient, and it took several steps at its third session in 1993. First, it prepared a draft resolution urging states involved in armed conflicts to take measures to protect children, a resolution that it hoped would be considered at the World Conference on Human Rights scheduled for June 1993 (UN CRC, 1993a:56 – 57). The conference did adopt, as part of the "Vienna Declaration and Programme of Action" (World Conference, 1993:paragraph 19), a paragraph that calls on all states and parties to armed conflicts to "strictly observe international humanitarian law." Second, the CRC made a recommendation to the General Assembly that a major study be undertaken of the problem of children in armed conflicts, particularly of the need to protect children from the adverse effects of armed conflicts, in order to focus even greater attention on the problem (UN CRC, 1993a:58). And third, the committee prepared a "Preliminary Draft Optional Protocol on Involvement of Children in Armed Conflicts," which would apply to Article 38 of the Convention on the Rights of the Child. The protocol would require the accepting states to refrain "from recruiting any person who has not attained the age of eighteen years into their armed forces"; and they would have to "take all feasible measures" to ensure that such people do not take part in hostilities. No reservations would be permitted to the protocol (UN CRC, 1993a:59 – 61).

The convention does not indicate any procedures that must be followed in adopting protocols per se, though it does contain an article that applies to the adoption of amendments and that would apparently apply to protocols as well. According to Article 50 of the convention, only states parties may propose amendments to the convention. If this should occur, and if within four months of such a proposal at least one-third of the states parties favor holding a conference to consider the amendment, the secretary-general would convene a conference. Then, the proposed amendment would have to be approved by the General Assembly and two-thirds of the states parties. The amendment would, of course, be binding only on the states parties that accept it. It would seem, then, that the CRC's strategy regarding the optional protocol to Article 38 would be to find a state party that would be willing to champion its proposal before the other states parties.

6 · Empowerment Rights

THE CATEGORY OF "empowerment" rights includes all those rights that relate to a person being heard on matters that affect his or her life. As Jack Donnelly and Rhoda Howard (1988:234−35) put it, people are "active, creative beings in charge of, or at least struggling to shape, their lives. People must not simply be protected against attacks by the state or other citizens, they must be empowered to act and to lead autonomous lives." Rights that fall into this category include freedom of thought, conscience, and religion, freedom of expression and information, and freedom of association and assembly. Donnelly and Howard also include the right to education in this category because, as they argue, "education provides much of the basic intellectual capacity that enables the individual to think seriously and critically about what it means to live a good life; to examine and appraise actions, institutions and ideas; and to choose a course of action on the basis of such appraisals" (1988:235).

Overall, the provisions of the Convention on the Rights of the Child seem weaker in dealing with the category of empowerment rights than they do with the other categories of rights discussed in previous chapters. Thomas Hammarberg (1990:100−101) suggests that this is because of the tension that exists between parents' and children's rights. This tension may be evident in the exercise of many rights, of course, but it is especially evident when it comes to the exercise of such rights as freedom of thought, conscience, and religion. Parents often claim, or at least try to claim, the right to make decisions regarding such things as the religious upbringing and education of their children. The question, therefore, is how to balance the rights of parents and children in regard to empowerment rights (see, e.g., Cohen, 1992:62). As we will see in a moment, the drafters adopted the principle of the "evolving capacities of the child" as the guiding principle in this regard.

We shall address the subject of empowerment rights in this chapter in four parts. First, we shall deal with a group of articles that relate to the child's right to freedom of expression and information. Second, we shall discuss the freedom of thought, conscience, and religion. Third, we shall take up the freedom of association and assembly. And fourth, we shall conclude with a discussion of the right to education.

FREEDOM OF EXPRESSION AND INFORMATION

Judging by the number of articles devoted to the freedom of expression and information, it is obvious that the drafters of the Convention on the Rights of the Child considered these rights important. In fact, they adopted three articles that concern the subject in some way. Articles 12 and 13 deal with the freedom of expression. Article 17 addresses the related right of access to information.

Freedom of Expression

Proposals to include an article on the freedom of expression date back to the earliest stages of the negotiations on the convention (UN CHR, 1981:13). Various issues in connection with the right were discussed at different times, and at the 1989 session of the working group, a consensus was reached on all the details of two articles that are relevant to this right, Articles 12 and 13. Article 12 of the convention provides:

> 1. States Parties shall assure to the child who is capable of forming his or her own views the right to express those views freely in all matters affecting the child, the views of the child being given due weight in accordance with the age and maturity of the child.
> 2. For this purpose, the child shall in particular be provided the opportunity to be heard in any judicial and administrative proceedings affecting the child, either directly, or through a representative or an appropriate body, in a manner consistent with the procedural rules of national law.

As noted earlier, the drafters of the convention affirmed the empowerment rights of the child in accordance with the overriding principle of the evolving capacities of the child. Article 12 makes this clear. Under the first paragraph, the states parties to the convention would be obliged to ensure the freedom of expression to a child "who is capable of forming his or her own views." Although the second paragraph provides more specificity, referring to the child's right to be heard in any judicial and administrative proceedings that affect himself or herself, the procedural rules of national law may vary from state to state and affect the exercise of that right.

For the drafters, the most difficult aspect of Article 12 concerned the question of whether it should specify the kinds of issues on which children would have the right to express their own views. An earlier Polish draft of the convention had specified some issues, including "matters concerning his own person, and in particular, marriage, choice of occupation, medical treatment, education and recreation" (UN CHR, 1981:13). This attempt at specification focused the discussion of the working group that drafted the convention, but it also stimulated disagreement among the delegates on precisely what issues should be covered by Article 12. The United States, for example, advocated a more expansive view than did the Polish delegation, suggesting that Article 12 be expanded to cover such matters as political and social beliefs, conscience, cultural and artistic expression, travel, and place of residence (UN CHR, 1981:13).

Other delegations also made proposals regarding the list of issues on which the child should enjoy freedom of expression. However, it soon became clear to most drafters that expanding the list might create more problems than it would resolve. In fact, some began to argue that the child's freedom of expression should not be "subject to the limits of a list" but rather should be left more or less open-ended, it being understood that the extent to which children could exercise the freedom of expression depended at least in part on their age and maturity and parental involvement and control. In this way, the lists proposed by Poland and the United States were deleted altogether, and the open-ended, but nonetheless qualified, definition of the conditions under which the child's freedom of expression can be exercised was adopted in Article 12 (UN CHR, 1981:14; Cohen, 1992:62 – 63).

Article 13 of the convention complements Article 12 and provides as follows:

> 1. The child shall have the right to freedom of expression; this right shall include freedom to seek, receive and impart information and ideas of all kinds, regardless of frontiers, either orally, in writing or in print, in the form of art, or through any other media of the child's choice.
> 2. The exercise of this right may be subject to certain restrictions, but these shall only be such as are provided by law and are necessary:
>   (a) For respect of the rights or reputations of others; or
>   (b) For the protection of national security or of public order (*ordre public*), or of public health or morals.

This article originated in a proposal that the United States submitted to the working group. It reflected the strong U.S. preference for emphasizing the civil and political rather than the economic, social, and cultural rights of the child, and it was based largely on the relevant article pertaining to this right contained in the International Covenant on Civil and Political Rights. As the United States argued in submitting the proposal:

> Children not only had the right to expect certain benefits from their Governments; they also had civil and political rights to protect them from abusive action of their Governments. These rights are largely the same as those enjoyed by adults, although it is generally recognized that children do not have the right to vote. While children might need direction and guidance from parents or legal guardians in the exercise of these rights, this does not affect the content of the rights themselves. The United States proposal was intended

to complete the process already begun by the working group of incorporating provisions from the International Covenant on Civil and Political Rights into the draft convention. (UN CHR, 1988:9–15)

The United States claimed that its proposal reflected the recognition embodied in the International Covenant on Civil and Political Rights "that the ability of all individuals to exercise civil and political rights is not absolute, but is subject to certain limited restrictions that may be imposed by States" (UN CHR, 1988:10). As we will see below, in addition to the right to freedom of expression and information, the United States was concerned about the rights to freedom of association and assembly and certain privacy rights (UN CHR, 1988:11).

The U.S. proposal gained widespread support in the working group and was adopted in its essential details at the 1988 session. Most delegates believed that the draft proposed by the United States very closely tracked Article 19 of the International Covenant on Civil and Political Rights. In fact, the only effort to amend the U.S. proposal came at the 1989 session of the working group when the German Democratic Republic's delegation proposed that a statement be included to the effect that the exercise of the right to freedom of expression could be restricted in the interest of the "spiritual and moral well-being of the child" (UN CHR, 1989b:45). The United States very strongly and successfully argued against this amendment on various grounds. In principle, the United States believed that "such extra restrictions of freedom of expression were to be avoided." In addition, the United States pointed out that the proposed restriction did not appear in the International Covenant on Civil and Political Rights and that it "would thus be unfair to impose it on children alone," that it might provide an "excuse to curtail the right" to freedom of expression, and that it had a "paternalistic flavour" that "was against the spirit of the Convention" (UN CHR, 1989b:45). Various delegates spoke for and against the amendment proposed by the German Democratic Republic, but since it enjoyed very little support, it was withdrawn from further consideration (UN CHR, 1989b:46).

Although one of the main concerns of the drafters in framing Article 13 was that it be normatively consistent with other international human rights instruments, a few states have remained concerned about the issue. Austria ratified the convention with a reservation (UN LS, 1993:188–89) stating that it would apply Article 13 provided that the provisions of the article would "not affect legal restrictions in accordance with article 10 and article 11 of the European Convention on the Protection of Human Rights and Fundamental Freedoms of 4 November 1950." Interestingly, Belgium made a virtually identical statement (UN LS, 1993:189), which it labeled as an "interpretive declaration," illustrating one of the problems raised by the substance test of the Vienna Convention on the Law of Treaties, discussed in chapter 2. It is not clear from the statements themselves if the Austrian and Belgian governments understand the European Convention as allowing greater legal restrictions on freedom of expression than does Article 13 of the Convention on the Rights of the Child, but they appear to say that. The fact that Austria labeled its statement a "reservation" lends support to this conclusion, and therefore, the label of "reservation" is probably more appropriate for both statements.

The Holy See also ratified the convention with a reservation (UN LS, 1993:191) to Article 13, but for an entirely different reason from that which motivated Austria and Belgium. The Holy See's reservation indicates that it interprets the article "in a way which safeguards the primary and inalienable rights of parents, particularly insofar as these rights concern education."

It is interesting that no objections have been filed to any of these reservations, particularly to those of Austria and Belgium. As we have seen, objections have been filed to the reservations of some states that have invoked considerations of domestic law as reasons for possibly not fulfilling their obligations under the Convention on the Rights of the Child. Austria and Belgium are the only states that have made reservations that invoke provisions of another international instrument they have ratified as a possible reason for not meeting their obligations under the convention. That they found it necessary to do so illustrates the difficulties that can arise in maintaining the normative consistency of human rights instruments under conditions of proliferation. It may be, of course, that neither Austria nor Belgium will ever have to invoke their reservations to Article 13. The fact that they have made them, however, raises the question of whether they regard the norms of a regional instrument (the European Convention on the Protection of Human Rights) to be "superior" to those of a global instrument (the Convention on the Rights of the Child). According to Article 41 of the convention, the states parties may apply provisions of their own law or international law that "are more conducive to the realization of the rights of the child"; it does not, of course, say that states parties may invoke more restrictive provisions of domestic or international law.

Freedom of Information

Another right closely related to the right to free expression is the right to access to information. Article 17 of the Convention on the Rights of the Child affirms this right as follows:

> States Parties recognize the important function performed by the mass media and shall ensure that the child has access to information and material from a diversity of national and international sources, especially those aimed at the promotion of his or her social, spiritual and moral well-being and physical and mental health. To this end, States Parties shall:
>
> (a) Encourage the mass media to disseminate information and material of social and cultural benefit to the child and in accordance with the spirit of article 29;
>
> (b) Encourage international co-operation in the production, exchange and dissemination of such information and material from a diversity of cultural, national and international sources;

(c) Encourage the production and dissemination of children's books;

(d) Encourage the mass media to have particular regard to the linguistic needs of the child who belongs to a minority group or who is indigenous;

(e) Encourage the development of appropriate guidelines for the protection of the child from information and material injurious to his or her well-being, bearing in mind the provisions of articles 13 and 18.

This article originated in a Polish proposal that was submitted to the working group during the earliest stages of the negotiations on the convention, but it scarcely resembles what the original authors had intended. In fact, the Polish proposal was perceived by some delegations as threatening freedom of expression and the operation of the mass media because it called for the protection of the child from the "harmful influence that mass media, and in particular the radio, film, television, printed materials and exhibitions, on account of their contents, may exert on his mental and moral development" (UN CHR, 1981:19). In discussion, most delegates to the working group believed that the proposal raised more problems than it solved. As the report on the 1981 session put it:

> One speaker felt that the mass media does more good than harm and therefore the article should be phrased in a positive way, rather than in terms of protecting children from the mass media. States parties should ensure freedom of information, so that children can take advantage of a diversity of opinion concerning all matters. The speaker also stated that his delegation would urge deletion of the article unless it could be reformulated to take a positive approach, acknowledging the educational role of the mass media, the need for reciprocity in the free flow of information across international borders, and the importance of guaranteeing children access to information from a diversity of sources. (UN CHR, 1981:19)

This criticism of the Polish draft article, which was most probably made by a U.S. delegate, effectively blocked its adoption, and the working group then turned its attention to different Article 17 proposals that were submitted by governmental delegations, the Baha'i International Community, and the Informal NGO Ad Hoc Group (UN CHR, 1982:55 – 56, 1984:11 – 16). Throughout the discussions, delegates and NGOs made strong appeals on issues of special interest to them. Article 17(c), for example, which calls for the production and dissemination of children's books, was adopted as a result of the initiative taken by the International Board on Books for Young People (UN CHR, 1987:7). The United States made a strong case that Article 17 "should take into account the concerns of States where the private sector was involved in the mass media." It acknowledged, however, that "the State should and could guarantee the free flow of information" (UN CHR, 1984:12). Thus, according to the United States, the introductory paragraph of Article 17 should state, "Recognizing the important educational function performed by the mass media, States Parties shall ensure that the child has access to information from a diversity of sources, in particular by not impeding the free flow of information across international borders and the availability of such information, as well as by assuring freedom of expression and opinion for all" (UN CHR, 1984:11).

In view of all the different proposals that were being introduced in connection with Article 17, the working group established an informal "working party" in 1984, consisting of a variety of governmental representatives, to see if a compromise text could be drafted. It was clear that one of the most vexing problems was the U.S. insistence on a statement that there should be a free flow of information across international borders. In 1984, the U.S.-Soviet relationship in the working group was still characterized by ideological and political disputes that were typical of cold war international politics. Consequently, the report on the session indicated that on the subject of the free flow of information across international borders, "delegations continued to manifest divergent views," with some considering it a question "worthy of separate consideration" and others seeing "its inclusion as a recognition of the importance of the concept of free flow of information" (UN CHR, 1984:14). In a spirit of compromise, the working group agreed on the introductory paragraph and the other elements of Article 17, which essentially addressed all of the U.S. interests. With minor modifications, the article was adopted in its final form in 1989, by which time the U.S. and Soviet delegates were in agreement on many important issues regarding the substantive provisions of the convention (UN CHR, 1989b:53−55).

FREEDOM OF THOUGHT, CONSCIENCE, AND RELIGION

The freedom of thought, conscience, and religion raised a number of important issues when the Convention on the Rights of the Child was drafted, and substantial controversy surrounded their resolution. In fact, it could be said that these issues were among the most difficult to resolve when the convention was drafted (Cantwell, 1992:26). The reason for the controversy is not hard to find. Parents the world over have traditionally exercised, or claimed the right to exercise, considerable control over the religious beliefs, practices, and affiliations of their children. They have at least expected to be able to give guidance and provide education to their children in these matters. Their "right" to do so has sometimes resulted in highly emotional debates over how to balance religious freedom with other rights. For example, in recent years, laws regarding some educational standards and requirements in various European countries have come into conflict with certain Islamic religious beliefs and practices. Thus, state laws establishing compulsory elementary education, including physical education or education in biology, have clashed with the desire of parents to provide guidance regarding the religious education of their young daughters (Cantwell, 1989:15). It was probably inevitable, therefore, that the drafters of the Convention on the Rights of the Child would encounter serious difficulties in dealing with the issue of freedom of thought, conscience, and religion.

The Polish draft convention did not expressly address the issue, although its general nondiscrimination provision aimed to ban discrimination against children on religious grounds, and other articles referred to the moral and spiritual well-being of children (UN CHR, 1978a:2–3). But this was one of the most important respects in which the Polish draft appeared, to many delegates in the open-ended working group, to resemble more a declaration than a convention. On very important matters such as freedom of thought, conscience, and religion, the draft's provisions were much too brief, providing few if any details regarding the meaning of the rights and thus failing to provide sufficient guidance to states in what would be expected of them regarding the realization of the rights. Therefore, efforts to draft a more specific article that would affirm the right to freedom of thought, conscience, and religion began early during the negotiations on the convention. In fact, the United States proposed a draft article on the subject as early as 1982, and other states, including the Nordic group of countries and Canada, quickly followed suit (UN CHR, 1984:4–8). By 1989, a consensus had been reached on Article 14 of the convention, which provides:

> 1. States Parties shall respect the right of the child to freedom of thought, conscience and religion.
> 2. States Parties shall respect the rights and duties of the parents and, when applicable, legal guardians, to provide direction to the child in the exercise of his or her right in a manner consistent with the evolving capacities of the child.
> 3. Freedom to manifest one's religion or beliefs may be subject only to such limitations as are prescribed by law and are necessary to protect public safety, order, health or morals, or the fundamental rights and freedoms of others.

As a whole, Article 14 makes it clear that the exercise of the right to freedom of thought, conscience, and religion is not unlimited.

In fact, Article 14(3) reiterates the well-known principle that the exercise of the right is limited by the rights of others individually and collectively, among other things. This principle is so widely accepted that it was included in Article 14(3) with no controversy. The same was not true, however, regarding the terms of Article 14(1) and (2). As we will see below, although a consensus was eventually achieved on those provisions as well, their terms were not entirely satisfactory to some delegations.

The Scope of the Freedom of Thought, Conscience, and Religion

According to Article 14(1), the states that ratify the Convention on the Rights of the Child "shall respect the right of the child to freedom of thought, conscience and religion." At first glance, this statement seems quite laudable and seems to establish an important obligation of the states parties. However, many drafters were very dissatisfied with the statement. In fact, they divided into two main groups on the issue. Some would have preferred a stronger and more detailed statement, one that would have followed the precedents set in previously adopted human rights instruments, particularly the Universal Declaration of Human Rights and the International Covenant on Civil and Political Rights. Both instruments affirm the basic principle that states must recognize the freedom of thought, conscience, and religion, but they go on to expand on the scope of that freedom. Article 18 of the Universal Declaration, for example, provides: "Everyone has the right to freedom of thought, conscience and religion; this right includes freedom to change his religion or belief, and freedom, either alone or in community with others and in public or private, to manifest his religion or belief in teaching, practice, worship and observance." Article 18(1) of the International Covenant on Civil and Political Rights provides: "Everyone shall have the right to freedom of thought, conscience and religion. This right shall include freedom to have or to adopt a religion or belief of his choice, and freedom, either individually or in community with others and in public or private, to manifest his religion or belief in worship, observance, practice and teaching."

Many of the drafters of the Convention on the Rights of the Child wanted to follow these precedents. In 1984, for example, the Nordic countries proposed a draft of Article 14 that contained the following: "These rights [to freedom of thought, conscience, and religion] shall include in particular the right to have or to adopt a religion of whatsoever belief of his choice, and freedom, either individually or in community with others and in public or private, to manifest his religion or belief, and the right to have unimpeded access to education in the matter of religion and belief of his choice" (UN CHR, 1984:4). The Canadian delegation proposed an article that provided in part: "The States Parties to the present Convention undertake to ensure the freedom of thought, conscience and religion of the child in accordance with the Universal Declaration of Human Rights and other international instruments that relate to this freedom" (UN CHR, 1984:4).

During the earlier stages of negotiations on the convention, the Nordic and Canadian proposals enjoyed broad support. However, the situation changed dramatically when a group of Islamic states began participating in earnest during the last two years of negotiations. This group was very strongly opposed to adopting an article that would affirm a right of the child to choose or to change his or her religion or belief (Cohen, 1992:63). As a Moroccan observer in the working group argued, the notion that a child could freely choose his or her religion "ran counter to the principles of Muslim law: the child of a Muslim was bound to be a Muslim, and in order to renounce that fact, he had to conform to the rules of Muslim law on the matter" (UN CHR, 1988:12). Representatives and observers of other Islamic states supported this viewpoint (see UN CHR, 1989b:46–48). In fact, the representatives of Islamic states made it very clear that they considered the substance of Article 14 of the convention to be a matter of great importance; to reach a consensus, the working group would have to drop statements, such as those proposed by Canada and the Nordic countries, regarding the freedom of choice in religion.

The compromise was not actively supported by all drafters of the convention, however. In fact, some were very disappointed with it and expressed their displeasure in meetings of the Commission on Human Rights and the Third Committee of the General Assembly. A representative of the United States, for example, was especially critical of the compromise, stating, "It would have been desirable for the convention to include specific references, as did other international instruments, to such supplementary rights for children as the freedom to have or change a religion, the right to worship according to their beliefs alone or with others, and the right to teach, learn and practice their religion in public or in private" (UN GA C.3, 1989a:7; see also DCI, 1983:i, 1988:2). Some delegates were more conciliatory. A representative of Sweden, for example, indicated that his delegation had joined in the consensus that had developed on Article 14 with the understanding that the right to freedom of thought, conscience, and religion included precisely those supplementary rights that the U.S. delegation wished had been expressly recognized (UN CHR, 1989b:48).

But representatives of some Islamic states, which had been successful in imposing their views on the working group, adhered to the most strict construction of Article 14, specifically rejecting the notion that anything might be read into the article. In fact, representatives of Algeria, Jordan, and Yemen emphasized their strict construction of the article in the Third Committee and in the plenary session of the General Assembly when the convention was adopted, claiming that the freedom of religion means that a child has the right to practice his or her religion but not to choose it (UN GA C.3, 1989f:16; UN GA, 1989c:4−7).

Some Islamic states have followed up on this interpretation by making declarations or reservations to the convention when they ratified it. Jordan, for example, ratified with a reservation (UN LS,

1993:192) indicating that it does not consider itself bound by Article 14, which it interprets as granting "the child freedom of choice of religion," on the ground that such a freedom is "at variance with the precepts of the tolerant Islamic Shariah." Bangladesh ratified with a reservation (UN LS, 1993:189) to Article 14(1), without indicating precisely what its reservation was and apparently having a reservation not only to the right to freedom of religion but also to the right to freedom of thought and conscience. The Republic of Maldives made a reservation (UN LS, 1993:192) to Article 14(1) when signing the convention because its constitution and laws "stipulate that all Maldivians should be Muslims"; on ratification, it made a reservation to Article 14 and did not reiterate the basis for its reservation. Some other Islamic states made general reservations based on religious precepts that presumably cover Article 14.

In contrast to the Islamic states, Belgium (alone among the parties to the convention) ratified with a statement that it called an "interpretive declaration" (UN LS, 1993:189) indicating that it understands Article 14(1) in a manner consistent with the provisions of the International Covenant on Civil and Political Rights and the European Convention on Human Rights and that, therefore, "the right of the child to freedom of thought, conscience and religion implies also the freedom to choose his or her religion or belief." Thus, in contrast to its position on freedom of expression, where it seems to have invoked the provisions of the European Convention on Human Rights as a reason for not strictly applying Article 13 of the Convention on the Rights of the Child, the Belgian government, through its "interpretive declaration" regarding Article 14, is expanding the meaning of the freedom of thought, conscience, and religion by reference to the terms of other human rights treaties it has ratified. This more expansive interpretation is not prohibited; in fact, in view of Article 41 of the convention, which calls for the application of domestic or international laws that are more conducive to the realization of the rights of the child, the Belgian declaration was not necessary.

More broadly, it is interesting that *any* of the declarations or reservations that the states parties have made to Article 14 were perceived as necessary. This is especially so regarding the statements made by the Islamic countries, in view of the important concessions that the Western states made to them regarding the freedom of thought, conscience, and religion. That they still believed the reservations were necessary even after the concessions says much about the cultural diversity of the member states of the United Nations and about its impact on the interpretation and acceptance of human rights norms.

The Rights of Parents

Article 14(3) deals with the issue of the rights of parents regarding the religious upbringing of their children. According to this provision, the states parties to the convention must respect the rights of parents and legal guardians to provide guidance to the child in the exercise of his or her right to religious freedom, "in a manner consistent with the evolving capacities of the child."

The drafters had some difficulty with Article 14(3) because, even though they wanted to follow tradition and recognize parental rights regarding the child's right to religious freedom, they did not want to overemphasize parental rights at the expense of the rights of the child. Thus, the issue they faced was really how to strike a balance between the rights of the child and those of the parents. The compromise that was reached, recognizing parental rights "in a manner consistent with the evolving capacities of the child," was widely accepted (UN CHR, 1984:4–8). The Holy See, which had actively participated in discussions of these issues in the working group, ratified the convention with a reservation (UN LS, 1993:191) to the effect that it interprets Article 14, as well as other articles in which parental rights are concerned, "in a way which safeguards the primary and inalienable rights of the parents." Similarly, Poland ratified the convention with a declaration (UN LS, 1993:193) stating that it considers that the exercise of such freedoms as the freedom of religion, expression, and association "shall be exercised with respect for parental authority."

FREEDOM OF ASSOCIATION AND ASSEMBLY

The freedom of association and assembly is another important empowerment right. The Convention on the Rights of the Child contains an article on this right, an article that, like the others discussed above, is also based on the relevant article in the International Covenant on Civil and Political Rights. Article 15 of the convention provides:

> 1. States Parties recognize the rights of the child to freedom of association and to freedom of peaceful assembly.
> 2. No restrictions may be placed on the exercise of these rights other than those imposed in conformity with the law and which are necessary in a democratic society in the interests of national security or public safety, public order (*ordre public*), the protection of public health or morals or the protection of the rights and freedoms of others.

Article 15 also originated in a proposal that the United States introduced in the open-ended working group. Like other proposals concerning empowerment rights and introduced by the United States, it reflected the U.S. delegates' preoccupation with civil and political rights. According to the United States, the freedom of association and assembly was especially important because the "child," as defined by the convention, "included adolescents who had often acquired the skills needed to participate fully and effectively in society." Moreover, the United States believed that the freedom of association and assembly should be recognized because it would be a good complement to the freedom of thought, conscience, and religion and because it was recognized in the Universal Declaration of Human Rights and the International Covenant on Civil and Political Rights (UN CHR, 1987:26 – 27). Thus, the United States was motivated to push for the adoption of an article on freedom of association at least in part because of the need to draft a convention that would be normatively consistent with other general-purpose international human rights instruments.

Unlike the other U.S. proposals, however, its proposal regarding freedom of association and assembly engendered intense opposition from many states. Representatives of Algeria, China, Iraq, Poland, and the Soviet Union spoke against the article, giving various reasons for their opposition (UN CHR, 1986a:17). Even Western states, including Australia, Norway, Sweden, and the United Kingdom, found issues of concern in the U.S. proposal, especially in the fact that the draft article did not refer to the exercise of the right in terms of the "evolving capacities of the child" (UN CHR, 1987:27). The Chinese delegation was more blunt, stating that the freedom of association and assembly "could not be enjoyed by children in the same way as they are enjoyed by adults because the intellect of a child was not as developed as that of an adult, and therefore a child could only engage in activities commensurate with its intellect" (UN CHR, 1987:27).

There is something to be said in defense of the criticisms of the U.S. proposal, especially since the other articles that affirmed empowerment rights recognized that these rights are to be enjoyed in terms of the evolving capacities of the child. Why, then, should the same not be said of the freedom of association and assembly? In fact, the article was adopted amid some confusion as to how it was to be interpreted. Representatives of the United States as well as of other countries seemed to recognize that "older" children should have the right to join some organizations, for example, labor unions, whereas "younger" ones would not (UN CHR, 1988:13 – 15). Thus, they seemed to expect that governments would be able to restrict the exercise of the right in some circumstances. Nonetheless, they declined to adopt an amendment proposed by China, one that would have made the exercise of the rights expressly conditional on the "child's age and maturity" (UN CHR, 1988:13).

Some concern about the implications of the provisions of Article 15 lingers. Austria made the same reservation (UN LS,

1993:188–89) to Article 15 that it made in connection with Article 13 on freedom of expression; Belgium's "interpretive declaration" (UN LS, 1993:189) regarding Article 13 also applies to Article 15. The Holy See also made a reservation to the article (UN LS, 1993:191), again indicating that it understood the article as safeguarding the "primary and inalienable rights of parents" in the exercise of the right. Myanmar (formerly Burma), which has from time to time had problems with political demonstrations in recent years because of human rights abuses, ratified the convention in July 1991 with a reservation (UN LS, 1993:192) to Article 15 indicating that it "interprets the expression 'the law' in article 15, paragraph 2, to mean the Laws, as well as the Decrees and Executive Orders having the force of law, which are for the time being in force in the Union of Myanmar." Germany, Ireland, and Portugal objected to Myanmar's reservation for different reasons but with the same effects. Germany objected (UN LS, 1993:195) on the ground that it regarded the reservation as "incompatible with the object and purpose of the convention." Ireland and Portugal claimed in their objections that since the reservation invoked general principles of domestic law, it created doubts about Myanmar's commitment to the object and purpose of the convention. All three states, however, expressly indicated that they did not consider their objections as constituting obstacles to the entry into force of the convention between them and Myanmar.

THE RIGHT TO EDUCATION

As noted earlier, the right to education can be considered an important empowerment right because education contributes to the intellectual capacity of the person to think seriously and critically about his or her place in society and the world at large (Donnelly and Howard, 1988:235). The right is widely recognized. It is affirmed in a number of important international human rights instruments, including the Universal Declaration of Human Rights

(Article 26), the International Covenant on Economic, Social and Cultural Rights (Article 13), and the Declaration of the Rights of the Child (Principle 7). Moreover, it has frequently figured in discussions of human rights issues at international fora. It was discussed by the heads of state and government who attended the World Summit for Children at the United Nations in September 1990, and they adopted, as one of the goals for children and development in the 1990s, the provision of basic, primary education to at least 80 percent of primary school–age children, with emphasis on decreasing the "current disparities between boys and girls" (UN GA, 1990a:12–13, 22). The Vienna Declaration and Programme of Action, which was adopted at the World Conference on Human Rights in June 1993, urged all states to take measures, to the maximum extent of their available resources, to achieve the goals of the World Summit (World Conference, 1993:3.2.D).

For all practical purposes, to speak of a right to education is to speak of a right of the child. Adults too may be said to have a right to education, since the eradication of illiteracy has been a goal of many governments and organizations for many years. But ensuring that children have a right to education is the best place to begin. Indeed, discussions of the right usually take place in the context of the rights of the child.

The Polish draft of the Convention on the Rights of the Child gave prominence to the right to education. One full article of the draft (UN CHR, 1978a:3, 1980c:5) dealt exclusively with the right:

> 1. The child shall have the right to education which shall be free and compulsory, at least at elementary level. The parents and the State shall guarantee the child ample conditions for the realization of this right.
> 2. The States Parties to the present Convention shall develop various forms of secondary general and vocational education systems, and shall pursue gradual introduction of free education at this level, so as to enable all children to develop their talents and interests on a basis of equal opportunity.

Other articles of the draft affirmed that the states parties would be obliged to provide assistance to parents in seeing to the education of their children; the right to education for physically and mentally disabled children; and the responsibility of the state to provide education to children who were deprived of their natural family environment.

The drafters of the convention expanded on the provisions of the basic Polish draft article, dividing it into two articles that affirm the right to education (Article 28) and outline the goals toward which education shall be directed (Article 29). We shall deal with each of these articles separately.

The Nature of the Right to Education

Article 28 of the convention provides:

> 1. States Parties recognize the right of the child to education, and with a view to achieving this right progressively and on the basis of equal opportunity, they shall, in particular:
> (a) Make primary education compulsory and available free to all;
> (b) Encourage the development of different forms of secondary education, including general and vocational education, make them available and accessible to every child, and take appropriate measures such as the introduction of free education and offering financial assistance in case of need;
> (c) Make higher education accessible to all on the basis of capacity by every appropriate means;
> (d) Make educational and vocational information and guidance available and accessible to all children;
> (e) Take measures to encourage regular attendance at schools and the reduction of drop-out rates.
> 2. States Parties shall take all appropriate measures to ensure that school discipline is administered in a manner consistent with the child's human dignity and in conformity with the present Convention.
> 3. States Parties shall promote and encourage international co-operation in matters relating to education, in particular

with a view to contributing to the elimination of ignorance and illiteracy throughout the world and facilitating access to scientific and technical knowledge and modern teaching methods. In this regard, particular account shall be taken of the needs of developing countries.

According to Article 28(1), the states parties to the convention are to work toward the progressive realization of the right to education. Traditionally, of course, the right to education was perceived as falling within the category of economic, social, and cultural rights, and the realization of those rights was thought to be something that needed to be on the economic and social agenda of states — they were to be "progressively" realized. Indeed, the way in which the right to education is defined in Article 28 makes it most unlikely that its provisions are already realized in any country or that they could be realized in most countries in the world without great effort and determination. Therefore, the most that the convention could reasonably have done was to make the right to education a right that is to be progressively realized.

It is noteworthy that, according to Article 28(1)(a), the states parties assume the obligation to work toward making "primary education compulsory and available free to all." This provision is consistent with the relevant provisions of the Universal Declaration of Human Rights, the International Covenant on Economic, Social and Cultural Rights, and the Declaration of the Rights of the Child. In fact, it has been so widely accepted for such a long time that it seems odd that some drafters of the convention would have expressed misgivings about the provision. But some of them were concerned about the economic implications of saying that primary education should be free. The representative from China on the working group, for example, suggested that perhaps a clear qualifying statement be included in Article 28 to the effect that a free education had to be provided "as early as the circumstances permit" (UN CHR, 1985a:11). However, other drafters were concerned that such a qualification would undermine the enjoyment of the right.

The Soviet delegation, for example, believed that to make the qualifying statement too strong would be a "step backward," making Article 28 weaker than Article 13 of the International Covenant on Economic, Social and Cultural Rights (UN CHR, 1985a:11). The "stronger" commitment was adopted, but it remains a commitment to be progressively realized.

The drafters resisted efforts to include statements that would have committed the states parties to work toward making other levels of education free of charge. During the negotiations, some interest was expressed in including a statement in Article 28(1)(c) to the effect that the states parties would work toward the "progressive introduction of free education" at levels higher than the elementary level. However, a number of countries, including some, like the Netherlands, that have very advanced education policies, objected to such a proposal on the ground that it was their policy to provide financial assistance to students at higher levels of education but not necessarily to provide free education. Other wealthier countries, including Japan, the United Kingdom, and the United States, supported the Dutch viewpoint, and the proposal was dropped from discussion (UN CHR, 1989b:79–84).

If anything, normatively, Article 28 is somewhat weaker than other relevant international instruments that deal with the right to education. UNESCO participated in some of the discussions of Article 28, and it objected to the notion in Article 28(1)(b) to the effect that the states parties would be obliged to "encourage the development" of different forms of secondary education. The alternative would have been to say that the states parties would be obliged "to develop" different forms of secondary education. The United States and others preferred the softer obligation inherent in the language "encourage the development" of; UNESCO argued that the language made Article 28 weaker than the standard affirmed in the UNESCO convention on discrimination in education (UN CHR, 1989b:81–82).

Even if Article 28 may be found to be normatively weaker than other international instruments, it may actually be too ambitious when considered in the light of the prevailing situation. Despite the affirmations of the World Summit for Children discussed above, in a recent report UNICEF (1992:38), citing a study done by UNESCO, pointed out that the decade of the 1980s was "disastrous" for education. Two-thirds of the one hundred countries that were surveyed by UNESCO actually "saw a decline in expenditures per pupil and half saw a fall in the proportion of their children enrolled in primary school." The decline in expenditures was especially serious in the Third World, with Africa being particularly hard hit. The cause appears to have been the debt crisis that many of the Third World countries have faced. As a consequence, millions of children "have lost their opportunity to become literate and to acquire the basic skills necessary to themselves and their societies in the years ahead" (UNICEF, 1992:38). According to UNESCO, at least some of the most serious adverse consequences for young children could have been avoided if countries had not devoted a disproportionate share of their education resources to higher education, which is more expensive per pupil served.

The trends and difficulties suggest that the Committee on the Rights of the Child is likely to have to devote a good deal of its attention to the condition of educational systems in countries, especially poorer countries, when it examines reports they submit on the progress they have made in implementing the convention. In fact, the committee has already done so, and when it has, it has usually linked its concern about educational standards and goals to questions of discrimination on various grounds. For example, in the concluding observations and recommendations it issued on the report that the government of Bolivia submitted in 1992, the committee noted, "with concern," that "vulnerable groups of children, such as girl children, indigenous children and children living in rural areas," were "over-represented in the number of children not enrolled in school" (UN CRC, 1993i:3). In the case of Egypt, the committee stated that the "quality of education in schools" caused concern and could be an explanation for high dropout rates. The committee believed that the problem related to "pedagogical methods, curricula and the lack of adequate educational material" (UN CRC, 1993l:3). More advanced countries such as Sweden and the Russian Federation did not get the same kind of critical commentary on their educational systems and goals.

The Goals of Education

Article 29 of the convention expands on the basic right to education and outlines the basic goals toward which education will be directed. The article provides:

> 1. States Parties agree that the education of the child shall be directed to:
> (a) The development of the child's personality, talents and mental and physical abilities to their fullest potential;
> (b) The development of respect for human rights and fundamental freedoms, and for the principles enshrined in the Charter of the United Nations;
> (c) The development of respect for the child's parents, his or her own cultural identity, language and values, for the national values of the country in which the child is living, the country from which he or she may originate, and for civilizations different from his or her own;
> (d) The preparation of the child for responsible life in a free society, in the spirit of understanding, peace, tolerance, equality of sexes, and friendship among all peoples, ethnic, national and religious groups and persons of indigenous origin;
> (e) The development of respect for the natural environment.
> 2. No part of the present article or article 28 shall be construed so as to interfere with the liberty of individuals and bodies to establish and direct educational institutions, subject always to the observance of the principles set forth in paragraph 1 of the present article and to the requirements that the education given in such institutions shall conform to such minimum standards as may be laid down by the State.

The objectives of Article 29 are no less ambitious than those of Article 28. Obviously, the drafters must have believed that the schools are important agents of socialization and the transmission of values. In the main, the thrust of Article 29 is to emphasize that the child is to be the beneficiary of a liberal education in the best sense of that term. According to Article 29(2), which was advocated by the Dutch delegation, this education may be provided by the state or by private individuals and institutions, provided that the state shall have the authority to set the basic educational standards, with which the private institutions must comply (UN CHR, 1985a:12 – 13, 17 – 19). The drafters were in broad agreement on the provisions of Article 29, and a consensus on its terms was easy to achieve (UN CHR, 1989b:86 – 87).

PART THREE

The Committee on the Rights of the Child

≈

7 · Structure of the Committee

IN THE LAST several chapters, we were concerned mainly with how the international rights of the child have been formulated and defined. We shall now turn our attention to the problem of implementing those rights. In recent years, the word *implementation* has become key in discussions of human rights. Scholars, activists, and practitioners alike have argued that there has been enough standard-setting in the field and that priority must now be given to implementation (e.g., van Boven, 1991:3–10).

But what does it mean to speak of the implementation of human rights? There appears to be no consistent definition of the term. David Forsythe (1991:57–58), for example, suggests that implementation is a form of "protection" of human rights. It includes "passing nonbinding resolutions about specific problems or states, publishing lists of violative states or actions, engaging in diplomacy to try to solve specific problems, and providing goods or services helpful for the practice of human rights." *Implementation* is therefore weaker than *enforcement*, a term that Forsythe restricts to the issuance of a "command linked to the threat or application of sanctions," which, in the United Nations system, can come only from the Security Council or the International Court of Justice. Nonetheless, since both implementation and enforcement involve the "protection" of human rights, they are stronger measures than standard-setting or educational activities, which Forsythe argues relate merely to the "promotion" of human rights. Torkel Opsahl (1989:13–14), a Norwegian who has served on the Human Rights Committee, which functions under the International Covenant on Civil and Political Rights, takes a different view, providing a more all-inclusive definition of the word *implementation*. He suggests that it is more "neutral than enforcement, guarantee or protection of human rights," that it "refers, broadly, to all measures which aim at putting the substantive norms of human rights into operation."

However narrowly or broadly the concept is defined, everyone agrees that the implementation of human rights must be achieved through action at the national and international levels. In fact, as Forsythe, Opsahl, and others (e.g., Donnelly, 1989:250–58; Claude and Weston, 1989:184–228) have argued, action at the national level is extremely important in view of the fact that most of the existing international human rights mechanisms are very weak, reflecting many states' continuing concern with preserving their national sovereignty. Although few, if any, states would seriously argue today that their human rights policies and practices are *exclusively* matters of domestic concern (the simple fact that they have ratified the United Nations Charter, and thus accepted rudimentary human rights obligations, would make such a claim untenable), many would argue that they are *primarily* matters of domestic concern. For this reason, they oppose the creation of strong international mechanisms, preferring instead to rely primarily on national institutions such as legislatures, courts, and bureaucracies to implement human rights.

The fact that the international mechanisms are weak, however, does not mean that they do not have a vital role to play in the process of implementing human rights. To the contrary, it is generally assumed that international mechanisms can give greater meaning to the notion of the international accountability of states; one of the principal ways in which they can do this is by monitoring the extent to which states comply with their international human rights obligations (see, e.g., van Boven, 1991:7–10; UN GA, 1989b:44). As we shall see, some studies, including some done by the United Nations itself, raise doubts about how effectively international mechanisms have been able to perform this function, particularly at the global level. Nonetheless, broad agreement among statesmen and scholars still exists with the basic premise of the need for international action to implement human rights.

Several human rights bodies are involved in implementing rights of the child at the global and regional levels. This is because, as we discussed in the chapters of part 2, rights relevant to the child are affirmed in various general and child-specific human rights instruments. However, with the entry into force of the Convention on the Rights of the Child, there is now for the first time a child-specific international mechanism — the Committee on the Rights of the Child — that is designed to implement the provisions of the convention among the states that ratify it. The CRC is well positioned to become the key body in this field. For this reason, in this chapter and in chapter 8 we will focus on the CRC. More specifically, in this chapter we will focus on the structure of the committee; in chapter 8 we will focus on the functions of the committee.

The starting point for our discussion is Article 43 of the convention, the main article that deals with the structure of the CRC. It provides:

> 1. For the purpose of examining the progress made by States Parties in achieving the realization of the obligations undertaken in the present Convention, there shall be established a Committee on the Rights of the Child, which shall carry out the functions hereinafter provided.
> 2. The Committee shall consist of ten experts of high moral standing and recognized competence in the field covered by this Convention. The members of the Committee shall be elected by States Parties from among their nationals and shall serve in their personal capacity, consideration being given to equitable geographical distribution, as well as to the principal legal systems.
> 3. The members of the Committee shall be elected by secret ballot from a list of persons nominated by States Parties. Each State Party may nominate one person from among its own nationals.
> 4. The initial election to the Committee shall be held no later than six months after the date of the entry into force of the present Convention and thereafter every second year. At least four months before the date of each election, the Secretary-General of the United Nations shall address a letter to States Parties inviting them to submit their nominations within two months. The Secretary-General shall subsequently pre-

pare a list in alphabetical order of all persons thus nominated, indicating States Parties which have nominated them, and shall submit it to the States Parties to the present Convention.

5. The elections shall be held at meetings of States Parties convened by the Secretary-General at United Nations Headquarters. At those meetings, for which two thirds of States Parties shall constitute a quorum, the persons elected to the Committee shall be those who obtain the largest number of votes and an absolute majority of the votes of the representatives of States Parties present and voting.

6. The members of the Committee shall be elected for a term of four years. They shall be eligible for re-election if renominated. The term of five of the members elected at the first election shall expire at the end of two years; immediately after the first election, the names of these five members shall be chosen by lot by the Chairman of the meeting.

7. If a member of the Committee dies or resigns or declares that for any other cause he or she can no longer perform the duties of the Committee, the State Party which nominated the member shall appoint another expert from among its nationals to serve for the remainder of the term, subject to the approval of the Committee.

8. The Committee shall establish its own rules of procedure.

9. The Committee shall elect its officers for a period of two years.

10. The meetings of the Committee shall normally be held at United Nations Headquarters or at any other convenient place as determined by the Committee. The Committee shall normally meet annually. The duration of the meetings of the Committee shall be determined, and reviewed, if necessary, by a meeting of the States Parties to the present Convention, subject to the approval of the General Assembly.

11. The Secretary-General of the United Nations shall provide the necessary staff and facilities for the effective performance of the functions of the Committee under the present Convention.

12. With the approval of the General Assembly, the members of the Committee established under the present Convention

shall receive emoluments from the United Nations resources
on such terms and conditions as the Assembly may decide.

In broad strokes, Article 43 covers three major areas that will be
our main concern in this chapter. First, it situates the CRC within
the larger context of the United Nations as a whole. Second, it establishes guidelines regarding the nomination and election of the
committee members. And third, it prescribes the method that will
be used to finance the operations of the committee as well as other
activities related to the implementation of the convention. In dealing with the issues and problems that arose in connection with
each of these matters, the drafters of the convention could draw on
the experience that had been gained with the operation of committees established under other human rights conventions, including the CERD, CEDAW, and CAT. Therefore, we will put the CRC
into a broader, comparative perspective alongside these other
committees.

THE CRC IN THE UNITED NATIONS

The terms of Article 43 indicate that the CRC is an "uninstructed"
committee. As Article 43(2) states, the committee members are
elected in their "personal capacity," that is, they are not elected as
representatives of governments, as would be members of an "instructed" committee. They will therefore be expected to be impartial and objective in conducting committee business, even when
dealing with matters that concern their own governments (UN
CRC, 1992a:13–14).

The question is, of course, whether any formal mechanisms
could ever be devised to ensure that the committee members will
in fact conduct themselves in a truly impartial and objective manner. As one might expect, they are required to take oaths pledging
their impartiality and objectivity. They also promise not to participate in the examination of the periodic reports (discussed in
chapter 8) that their governments will be required to submit to the

CRC on the progress they have made in implementing the convention (UN CRC, 1992l:7–10). Moreover, the committee has to file
public reports and is subjected to the glare of publicity, both of
which can help to prevent bias in decision-making. Still, the fact
remains that committee members must be elected to their posts,
and the nomination and election processes are, as we shall see in a
moment, dominated by the governments of the states parties to the
convention. Political considerations are likely to weigh heavily in
the nomination and election processes. In the final analysis, therefore, although formal mechanisms such as requiring oaths may be
helpful in motivating the committee members to be objective and
impartial, their personal integrity will be the most important guarantee of their impartiality.

The committee also enjoys a degree of autonomy within the
overall structure of the United Nations. Among other things, it is
able to elect its own officers (Article 43[9]) and adopt its own rules
of procedure (Article 43[8]). These are important powers. As some
studies (e.g., Dormenval, 1990:35) have suggested, officers with
good diplomatic as well as administrative skills can be crucial to
the success of committees such as the CRC. Moreover, through the
adoption of its own rules of procedure, the committee can attempt
to set an agenda that may be more ambitious than had been intended by its creators. The CRC devoted its first session in 1991 to
the adoption of its rules of procedure (UN CRC, 1991d) and the general guidelines (UN CRC, 1991e) regarding the form and content of
the initial reports to be submitted by the states parties. In drafting
these instruments, the committee generally adopted the most liberal interpretations of the convention provisions. But none of this
is to say that the committee's autonomy cannot be checked; we
shall return to ways in which this can be done below.

Why an Uninstructed Committee?

In deciding to establish the CRC as an uninstructed committee,
the drafters of the convention followed in the footsteps of those

who had drafted other United Nations specialized human rights conventions. The CERD, CEDAW, and CAT were all established as uninstructed committees. It is noteworthy, however, that the initial proposals regarding the implementation of the Convention on the Rights of the Child did not call for the establishment of a committee of this type. To the contrary, according to the proposals prepared by the Polish government in 1978 and 1979 (UN CHR, 1980c:21–22), the states parties would have been required to submit periodic progress reports to the United Nations ECOSOC, an instructed body consisting of governmental representatives. In 1986 (UN CHR, 1986a:3.1–2), the Polish government revised its initial proposal and suggested that the ECOSOC establish a Group of Governmental Experts to assist it in examining the reports it received, but the need for such a group, its size, and the frequency of its meetings would all have been determined by the ECOSOC.

The drafters of the convention rejected the Polish proposals and decided to establish the CRC as an uninstructed committee in part because of their general dissatisfaction with the text of the Polish draft convention. As discussed in chapter 1, one of the criticisms of the Polish draft was that it resembled more a declaration than a convention, and most drafters wanted it revised to conform to the style of the other specialized human rights conventions, which prescribed the establishment of uninstructed committees. Another factor was the leadership of key states, especially Canada and Sweden. They introduced amendments to the Polish draft convention that eventually had a profound impact on the implementation system. Canada proposed a mixed system whereby the ECOSOC would be required to establish a Group of Experts that would be responsible for conducting a preliminary examination of the reports received from states. Sweden made more elaborate recommendations that called for the creation of an uninstructed committee similar to the CEDAW, CERD, and CAT (UN CHR, 1986a:3.1–2). These two sets of proposals became the focus of discussion among the drafters (UN CHR, 1987:36–37, 1988:21), and by 1989 a consensus was reached on all the important issues concerning the Committee on the Rights of the Child except, as discussed more fully later in this chapter, how its operations would be financed. Without the leadership of Canada and Sweden, it is doubtful that the consensus could have been reached so quickly.

Whatever their motives, the drafters' decision to establish the CRC as an uninstructed body is commendable. Many human rights scholars believe that uninstructed bodies are more effective in the promotion and protection of human rights than are instructed ones. As Forsythe (1989:52–53) has observed, instructed bodies "contain a built-in brake on effective protection of human rights. The foxes (states) are charged with protecting the chickens (human rights)." He argues that this arrangement is unsatisfactory because the states, which are "generally interested in protection of power and national sovereignty," are "in a position to elevate those interests over human rights." This is not to say that uninstructed bodies are necessarily more effective or that they are immune from political pressures. The CEDAW, CERD, and CAT have all been subjected to political pressures at one time or another, and they have depended largely on voluntary cooperation by states in complying with their recommendations. Nonetheless, the theory, at least, suggests that uninstructed bodies are likely to be more effective in the promotion and protection of human rights, and on balance, practice suggests that they are more effective even if they face certain limitations on their autonomy.

Limitations on the Autonomy of the CRC

The CRC meets as often as the need arises and for as long as necessary and needs to have sufficient secretariat services to be able to successfully fulfill its mandate. In fact, the importance of adequate time and staff can hardly be emphasized enough. As will be discussed in chapter 8, the states parties are obliged to report to the CRC on the progress they have made in implementing the provisions of the convention. If the states parties are faithful in submitting their reports—and this, as we will see, is by no means ensured—the committee will need all the assistance it can get to examine the reports efficiently. Yet, experience with other human rights bodies suggests that a lack of time and staff is likely to be among the most serious challenges that the CRC will face in the years to come.

According to Article 43(10), the meetings of the committee "shall normally be held at United Nations Headquarters or at any other convenient place as determined by the Committee." Normally the committee meets at the Geneva headquarters of the United Nations, which is the ideal setting because the Centre for Human Rights is located there and provides secretariat services to the committee. Most human rights bodies also meet in Geneva. The CEDAW is the major exception; it is based in Vienna, a location that many observers consider undesirable because it situates the committee on the fringe of United Nations human rights activities (UN GA, 1990f:90; UN CEDAW, 1988a:2–3).

But it is not the location of the meetings of the CRC that is likely to be a problem. Rather, it is the frequency and duration of its sessions (groups of meetings). According to Article 43(10), the committee shall "normally meet annually," and the "duration of the meetings . . . shall be determined, and reviewed, if necessary," by the states parties, "subject to the approval of the General Assembly." The drafters took into account the experience of other committees when they adopted this provision. The CERD, CEDAW, and CAT all have somewhat different rules regarding the frequency and duration of their sessions, and they have all experienced difficulties of one sort or another (see Burgers and Danelius, 1988:112; Dormenval, 1990:26; Jacobson, 1992:448–49; Partsch, 1992:346–47; UN CERD, 1990:1–2). The CEDAW is subject to the most restrictive conditions, "normally" being able to "meet for a period of not more than two weeks annually." This restriction has left the committee with insufficient time to adequately consider the reports it has received from states (UN GA, 1989a:13), thus necessitating that it hold presessional working groups consisting of a few of its members to do preliminary screening of reports (UN GA, 1990e:7–8, 95–96, 1990f:91–93). Since the drafters of the Convention on the Rights of the Child were aware of the difficulties that other committees such as the CEDAW had faced, they decided to allow for flexibility in Article 43(10).

When the states parties met for their first session in February 1991, they authorized the CRC to meet for three weeks in 1991 to adopt its rules of procedure, draft guidelines for the initial reports that the states parties would submit, organize its work program, and work out relations with specialized agencies and other entities involved in advancing the rights of the child (UN CRC, 1990:1–2). The committee met for its first session in October 1991, at which time it adopted a liberal interpretation of Article 43(10), deciding that it would "normally" hold two regular sessions each year and special sessions if necessary (UN CRC, 1991f:5–9). The committee's rules of procedure do not specify the length of the sessions that it plans to hold but merely indicate that it "shall hold meetings as may be required for the effective performance of its functions." In nonbinding "notes" reflecting its understanding of its rules of procedure, however, the committee indicated that its two regular sessions would "normally" last two weeks each and that, when necessary, it would request special meetings (UN CRC, 1991g:3). The rules also indicate that the CRC will appoint subcommittees when appropriate and that its plenary sessions at which it will consider reports of states parties will normally be prepared by a presessional subcommittee session.

The committee members were well aware that the terms of Article 43(10) require that the CRC get approval from the General Assembly to meet in two regular sessions each year and for a presessional working group (UN CRC, 1991h:4–7). In fact, the committee adopted a resolution at its first session (UN CRC, 1991c:3), formally requesting such authorizations from the General Assembly. The need to get the approval of the General Assembly means that states that have not ratified the convention have a voice and vote on matters of great importance to the operation of the committee. But it was necessary to make this allowance because, as we will see later, the committee's work is financed from the regular budget of the United Nations, on which all member states can vote.

The General Assembly can use its "power of the purse" to force the CRC to accept less than the committee would like so far as the frequency and duration of its sessions are concerned. In the initial stages of the committee's operations, however, the General Assembly has been generous. It has accepted the states parties' recommendations that the CRC be authorized to meet in two sessions per year, each of two or three weeks' duration, and that it be able to establish presessional working groups to do preliminary examinations of reports received from states parties. Actually, the General Assembly authorized the secretary-general to schedule the sessions and working groups, making them contingent on the availability of funds (UN CRC, 1992d:1–2). The committee plans its long-range schedule of meetings on the assumption that it will continue to meet in two sessions each year of three weeks each and that these sessions will be preceded by shorter meetings of its presessional working groups (UN CRC, 1993a:10–11). However, the states parties and the General Assembly were motivated to approve the committee's requests in large measure because of the unprecedented speed with which states were ratifying the convention and, consequently, the unusually large number of reports the committee would have to examine if the states parties submitted them on time. The committee faced a potential work load that was incredibly heavy. But, as we shall see in chapter 8, few reports have been received, and it remains to be seen if the General Assembly or the secretary-general will continue to allow the committee to hold such frequent and lengthy sessions.

The secretariat services that the CRC will receive — or, as the case may be, not receive — could also prove to be a problem, affecting the degree to which it will be able to function efficiently. According to Article 43(11) of the convention, the United Nations Secretariat will provide the staff and facilities necessary for the performance of the committee's functions. In practice, this means that the committee will be dependent on the Centre for Human Rights, which is based in Geneva. The centre constitutes the focal point of the human rights activities of the United Nations (see, e.g., van Boven, 1992:549–79). Its work is organized into several main sections. The International Instruments Section, which is responsible for providing the substantive and technical support needed by the human rights bodies established under various treaties, will be the most important one for the CRC (UN ECOSOC, 1990a:3–9).

The efficiency and the quality of the work of the International Instruments Section have been affected by two factors in recent years. First, the number of treaty bodies that it is required to serve has increased. At the end of 1990, it was serving the CERD, the CAT, the Human Rights Committee, and the Committee on Economic, Social and Cultural Rights. The secretary-general estimated that the creation of this last committee in 1987 and the CAT in 1988 had roughly doubled the volume of documentation handled by the section. The establishment of the CRC will put additional stresses and strains on the section. These will increase even more when the Convention on the Protection of the Rights of All Migrant Workers and Members of Their Families enters into force, since it will result in the establishment of a Committee on Migrant Workers (UN ECOSOC, 1990a:3–4). Should the CEDAW be relocated to Geneva, which some of its supporters would like to see, or should simply the servicing of the committee be taken over by the Centre for Human Rights, as the chairs of the treaty bodies have recommended (UN GA, 1992b:8, 22), the demand for services from the section will surely exceed its capacity given its historically low funding levels (UN GA, 1990b:6–7, 1990g:2).

The efficiency and the quality of the work of the International Instruments Section have also been affected by the steady increase in the number of states that have become parties to the human rights conventions. Since they are normally required to submit reports to committees, an increase in the number of parties means an increase in the reports that have to be processed, even allowing for nonsubmission of reports by many states parties (UN ECOSOC, 1990a:4–5). The volume of the documentation work load of the section has therefore increased dramatically (UN ECOSOC, 1990a:14). In addition, the section has had to provide assistance to the committees in drafting their own reports, and the complexity of this work too has increased as the reporting requirements have become more specific and sophisticated (UN ECOSOC, 1990a:4–5).

All indications are that the demands on the staff of the Centre for Human Rights are likely to increase in the future. Yet there is a widespread feeling that its staff and resources are already inadequate (Schmidt, 1990:374–79). In 1990 the chairs of the treaty bodies argued that they were without an adequate level of secretariat services. Accordingly, they urged the secretary-general and the General Assembly to "do their utmost to ensure that more resources are provided specifically" to enable the treaty bodies to function effectively (UN GA, 1990b:14). But the secretary-general has warned that the growing demands on the secretariat have become increasingly difficult to meet and that anticipated demands cannot be met without staff increases (UN GA, 1990g:1). At their fourth meeting in 1992, the chairs of the treaty bodies again called attention to the need for adequate secretariat services, claiming that, despite some improvements, the staff of the Centre for Human Rights remained "grossly inadequate" to "enable it to fulfil the manifold and constantly growing number of tasks entrusted to it." The chairs also claimed, "The existing working conditions of the secretariat, especially in terms of the facilities and information technology available at Geneva, can best be described as primitive" (UN GA, 1992b:15). The problems of the centre have, of course, affected the efficiency of the operation of the treaty bodies. The problems have been discussed in other fora, including the World Conference on Human Rights in June 1993, which adopted a number of recommendations regarding the need to increase funding for United Nations human rights programs and to strengthen the Centre for Human Rights (World Conference, 1993:3). The fact remains, however, that the United Nations continues to spend less than 1 percent of its regular budget on human rights activities, and a dramatic change in the operations of the Centre for Human Rights would be difficult to achieve because of the overall financial difficulties of the United Nations.

Since substantial staff increases for the centre are unlikely, alternative ways of increasing its efficiency have been considered. A task force established by the secretary-general—itself a model of efficiency given the speed with which it produced its report—recommended increasing the electronic data-processing capability of the centre, particularly in the area of word-processing (UN CHR, 1990:8–10). The task force reasoned that computerization of the system would help to maximize the utilization of available staff resources and help the centre provide other forms of support to its various constituencies, including states and the treaty bodies. The task force also suggested that a "committee resource room" be established within the Centre for Human Rights to house the documentation of various committees along with other information. But again, financial problems have stood in the way of making progress on these proposals (UN GA, 1990b:12). The secretary-general issued an appeal to states to contribute to the start-up costs of computerizing the system, but the contributions that have been received have fallen far short of the projected initial cost of the system; and the committee resource room, despite repeated appeals by the chairs of the treaty bodies, was not established (UN GA, 1992b:8, 15; UN CRC, 1992a:12–13).

More drastic proposals have sometimes been made to completely overhaul the United Nations human rights program. These proposals include transforming the United Nations Trusteeship Council, which is widely perceived to have lost its usefulness, into a Human Rights Council; transforming the present Human Rights

Commission into an uninstructed body composed of independent experts; establishing a United Nations Court of Human Rights and an international criminal court; and establishing a special or high commissioner for human rights (see Nowak, 1993). Some of these proposals have merit. In fact, the World Conference on Human Rights endorsed a U.S. proposal to create a post of High Commissioner for Human Rights, urging the General Assembly to give priority consideration to the idea (*New York Times*, 1993). Nonetheless, fundamentally transforming the United Nations human rights system in these ways would require substantial financial outlays and considerable political will on the part of the member states. Meanwhile, the CRC and other human rights bodies must function with inadequate staff and resources.

NOMINATING AND ELECTING COMMITTEE MEMBERS

The second important set of structural issues addressed in Article 43 of the convention concerns the procedures that will be followed in nominating and electing the members of the CRC. According to Article 43(2), the committee has a fixed membership of ten members. A larger committee, or one that would have varied in size depending on the number of states that ratified the convention, might in the long run have been preferable, especially if the states parties take their reporting responsibilities, which will be discussed in chapter 8, seriously. But the drafters decided not to create a larger committee or one with a variable membership mainly because of financial considerations: they realized that a smaller, fixed-membership committee would be cheaper to operate, and this was a very important consideration in light of the financial difficulties the United Nations has faced since the early 1980s (UN CHR, 1988:20–41). Some thought has, however, already been given to the possibility of expanding the CRC to eighteen members (UN CRC, 1993a:63); the idea could be given further, more serious, consideration if the committee's work load should substantially increase. Article 43(2) would have to be amended to effect such a structural change.

Nominating Members of the CRC

Only states that have ratified the Convention on the Rights of the Child can nominate people for election to the CRC. Moreover, they can nominate only one person, who must be from among their nationals (Article 43[3]). The convention thus makes legally impossible what was already politically improbable. It is not unprecedented for states that ratify multilateral conventions to nominate nationals other than their own for election to implementation organs; states have even been known to nominate nationals of states that have not ratified the convention in question. One of the best-known examples of this occurred when Costa Rica nominated the distinguished U.S. international lawyer Thomas Buergenthal for election to the Inter-American Court of Human Rights. Buergenthal was elected even though the United States was not a party to the American Convention on Human Rights under which the court functions. But such instances have been very rare. In the main, states nominate only their own nationals for election to human rights bodies. In the case of the CRC, however, the convention leaves no room for discretion in the matter.

The parties submit their nominations to the secretary-general, who has the responsibility of compiling the list of nominees and submitting it to the states parties two months before the election. The secretary-general's role in this process is purely administrative—he has no discretion in deciding whether nominees have or do not have the requisite qualifications for election (Article 43[4]). With the advance notice, the states parties have time to study and reflect on the qualifications of the nominees before the election. In the past, many if not most of the nominees for election to the CERD, CEDAW, and CAT have had extensive professional experience and substantial publication records. As we shall see in a moment, the first election of the members of the CRC produced a similar list of nominees. Ideally, these backgrounds should be carefully studied, and a timely response to the secretary-general's request for nominations would make that possible.

Service on human rights committees carries a certain amount of prestige for the committee member as well as for his or her state. One might therefore expect that eligible states would nominate their nationals and that there would be intense competition in the elections. Unfortunately, we have no systematic, comprehensive body of literature on the "recruitment" of members of human rights committees — certainly nothing comparable to the body of literature on the recruitment of national and subnational political elites — so we cannot generalize about how states have nominated people for election. Margaret Galey (1984) has shown in a study of the CEDAW that many committee members have, or have had, close ties to their governments, and she suggests that this raises questions about their objectivity and impartiality, especially when considering data about their own countries (see also Jacobson, 1992:472). But many aspects of the recruitment process of the human rights committees, including nominations and elections, remain obscure. It may be helpful, therefore, to look at what happened in the first election of the members of the CRC in February 1991. Table 7.1 provides some insight into this matter.

Table 7.1 takes into account only those states that had ratified the convention by January 31, 1991 (UN CRC, 1991a:3 – 6). These were the only states that could nominate candidates or vote in the election. As table 7.1 shows, 35 of the 70 states parties (50 percent) at that time nominated one of their nationals. Clearly, interest in the election was substantial across most of the regions, although there were some variations. The states parties in the West Europe region were more likely than those in any other region to nominate candidates, which one might have expected given their important role in drafting the convention. Four (France, Portugal, Spain, and Sweden) of the six parties (66.67 percent) in the West Europe region nominated a candidate. The East Europe region also ranked very high, with three (Czechoslovakia, Romania, and the USSR) of the five parties (60.00 percent) nominating candidates.

Perhaps the most striking feature of the data in table 7.1 is that states in regions that participated very little in drafting the Convention on the Rights of the Child but that have been very much

Table 7.1

NOMINATIONS FOR ELECTION TO THE CRC
IN FEBRUARY 1991

Region	Number of States Parties	Number of States Parties Making Nominations	%
Africa (52 states)	26	12	46.15
Asia and Pacific (27 states)	9	5	55.56
Europe — East (10 states)	5	3	60.00
Europe — West (19 states)	6	4	66.67
Latin America (21 states)	17	10	58.82
Middle East (16 states)	0	0	0
North America and Caribbean (14 states)	5	1	20.00
Others (4 observers/states)	2	0	0
Total	70	35	50.00

SOURCE: The table is based on data contained in UN CRC, 1991a, and on documents prepared for the first meeting of the states parties to the convention: "Election of the Ten Members of the Committee on the Rights of the Child in Accordance with Article 43 of the Convention" (UN CRC, 1991v–z).

NOTE: The regions in this table consist of the states listed in tables 2.1 and 2.3. The states parties in this table are the same as those listed in table 2.3.

inclined to ratify it, such as the states of Africa and Latin America, nominated the largest number of candidates (12 and 10 respectively). In fact, these two regions showed up very well in terms of the percentage of states parties in the regions nominating candidates (46.15 percent for Africa and 58.82 percent for Latin America). The Asia and Pacific region also ranked very high in the number of states parties nominating candidates (55.56 percent).

Article 43 also specifies some conditions of service on the CRC. For example, Article 43(2) states that the members of the CRC are to be "experts of high moral standing and recognized competence in the field covered by this Convention." This is a standard provision for conventions of this sort; similar statements can be found in the conventions that established the CERD, CEDAW, and CAT. The criteria seem entirely reasonable considering that the members of the CRC are to be *experts* who act in their personal capacity. Table 7.2 sheds some light on the background and experiences of the nominees in the first election of the CRC in February 1991. The table is based on data gleaned from the résumés of the nominees that were submitted by the governments. As the table shows, females were well represented among the nominees, with 54.3 percent of the total (6 of the women were elected). The nominees were also very highly educated, with 22 of the 35 (62.9 percent) having received graduate training in their home countries or abroad, principally in the United States and Western Europe. It is noteworthy that people with legal training (12 of the 35 nominees, or 34.3 percent) tended to be nominated more than people with any other professional specialty. This pattern has been observed in the membership of other human rights committees as well and suggests that human rights work is perceived as being essentially "legal" work. This perception may be unfounded, but it seems powerful nonetheless. Of the ten persons elected to the CRC in the first election, 4 had law degrees: Marta Santos Pais of Portugal; Youri Kolosov of the USSR; Akila Belembaogo of Burkina Faso; and Sandra Mason of Barbados.

It is also noteworthy that people with training in the important fields of medicine and social work were nominated for election to the CRC. Both fields seem especially appropriate for service on a committee primarily concerned with children; one physician (Maria de Fatima Borges de Omena of Brazil) and two persons with extensive training and experience in social work (Hoda Badran of Egypt and Flora Eufemio of the Philippines) were elected.

The data in table 7.2 also show that most of the nominees had practical experience in dealing with children and children's rights issues. Most of them had experience with NGOS and IGOS concerned with children. Thomas Hammarberg of Sweden, for exam-

Table 7.2

CHARACTERISTICS OF NOMINEES IN
FIRST ELECTION OF THE CRC

Characteristic	Number of Nominees	% of Total Nominees (35)
Sex		
Male	16	45.7
Female	19	54.3
Education		
Graduate Level	22	62.9
Legal	12	34.3
Medicine	6	17.1
Social Work	3	8.6
Other	10	28.6
N/A	4	11.4
Employment		
Govt. Service	21	60.0
Teaching	13	37.1
ngo/igo	21	60.0
Relevant Publications		
Books and Articles	20	57.1

SOURCE: "Election of the Ten Members of the Committee on the Rights of the Child in Accordance with Article 43 of the Convention" (UN CRC, 1991v-z).

ple, was secretary-general of Radda Barnen (the Swedish Save the Children) at the time of his election and had served as secretary-general of Amnesty International from 1980 to 1986. Virtually all the nominees who were elected listed publications in the field of children's rights and welfare or related human rights publications.

Finally, the data in table 7.2 show that many of the nominees (21 of the 35, or 60.0 percent) had previous experience in government service or were serving in government positions when nominated. Swithun Mombeshora of Zimbabwe, for example, was minister of state for local government, rural, and urban development at the time of his election; in 1990 he had served as his president's personal representative on a planning committee for the World Summit for Children and then served as a delegate to the summit in September 1990. Several nominees were members of parliament, and some had been active in representing their governments as delegates, or serving them as consultants and in other capacities, in United Nations bodies. In fact, four of the nominees had represented their governments in the working group that drafted the Convention on the Rights of the Child, and one of them (Marta Santos Pais of Portugal) was elected to the committee. Some researchers (e.g., Galey, 1984) have suggested that close government connections of this sort may be incompatible with election to a human rights committee. More research should be done on this issue. What we can say on the basis of the data presented in table 7.2 is that, in the case of the CRC, government service or connections seem to have been a good stepping stone to nomination when the first election was conducted in 1991.

Electing Members of the CRC

The members of the CRC are elected by secret ballot at states parties meetings that are convened by the United Nations secretary-general for that purpose (Article 43[3]). Only states that have ratified the convention can vote in the election (Article 43[2]). The fact that they alone can also nominate candidates makes the selection process of the committee members a completely "closed" system. Yet, as we shall see below, all the member states of the United Nations will contribute to the expenses incurred in implementing the convention.

The committee members are elected for four-year terms, and they may be reelected (Article 43[6]). Their terms are staggered so that the entire committee will not be changed at once, which could disrupt the continuity of its work. This was achieved by setting the terms of five of the members elected in the first election in February 1991 at two years. Henceforward, all members of the committee will be elected for four-year terms, but elections will be conducted every two years. In these respects, the CRC is similar to the CERD, CEDAW, and CAT. Their members are elected for four-year terms, terms of the members are staggered, and members are eligible for reelection.

Since we have no comprehensive study of the recruitment of members of human rights bodies, we cannot say with confidence what the practice of states has been regarding reelection. Available studies and evidence suggest that members are almost routinely reelected. For example, the CAT's records show that all of the members who were slated for two-year terms at the first election in 1988 were reelected to four-year terms in 1990 (UN CHR, 1989e:1–2, 1989f:1–3). In the first decade of the CERD's existence, 1970 to 1980, only forty-three experts from twenty-nine states had been elected (Lerner, 1980:151–53; see also Partsch, 1992:346). In the case of the CRC, four of the five members whose terms ended in 1993 (Hodra Badran of Egypt, Flora Eufemio of Philippines, Swithun Mombeshora of Zimbabwe, and Marta Santos Pais of Portugal) were renominated by their governments. Only Antonio Carlos Gomes da Costa of Brazil was not renominated, though the Brazilian government nominated another candidate (UN CRC, 1992b, 1993b-e). Given these experiences, it appears that the major hurdle to overcome in getting elected to a human rights committee is the initial election. Once elected, one stands a good chance of continuing to serve as long as one wants to do so.

The convention says nothing about the removal of committee members under any circumstances, although the matter was discussed by the drafters (UN CHR, 1989b:121–22). However, the CRC discussed this issue (UN CRC, 1991i:7–8) at its first session in October 1991 and adopted as one of its rules of procedure the following provision: "If, in the unanimous opinion of the other members, a member of the Committee has ceased to carry out his functions for any cause other than absence of a temporary character, the Chairman of the Committee shall notify the Secretary-General, who shall then declare the seat of that member to be vacant" (UN CRC, 1991d:3). The issue was discussed in the context of any member being suspected of "wilful or consistent absenteeism" (UN CRC, 1991i:5) and was apparently intended to apply only in such circumstances.

All vacancies that occur on the committee for whatever reason will be filled in accordance with a special procedure. In such instances, the state that nominated the member "shall appoint another expert from among its nationals to serve for the remainder of the term, subject to the approval of the Committee" (Article 43[7]) (UN CHR, 1988:23; UN CRC, 1991j:7). This procedure is not entirely satisfactory given the emphasis that the convention places on the competence of the committee members and their status as impartial experts. Nonetheless, it was strongly supported by most drafters of the convention because it was perceived as the best way to maintain equitable geographical distribution in the composition of the committee, which is required under the terms of Article 43. The CRC has already had experience with the procedure. Maria de Fatima Borges de Omena of Brazil, who was elected in the first election, resigned soon after her election and never participated in the committee's work. In keeping with the terms of the convention and the committee's rules of procedure, the Brazilian government proposed that Antonio Carlos Gomes da Costa serve out Borges de Omena's term. He was approved by the CRC in a secret 8–1 vote (UN CRC, 1992a:8, 1992c:2–3).

Article 43(2) requires the states parties to the convention give "consideration . . . to equitable geographical distribution, as well as to the principal legal systems," in conducting elections to the CRC. These essentially political criteria are well established in United Nations practice; in fact, they are commonly found in instruments such as the Convention on the Rights of the Child. However, neither criterion makes sense by itself. The need for equitable geographical distribution, for example, raises the question, equitable in relation to what? To the number of states in any given geographical region? To the number of states parties to the convention in any geographical region? Similarly, the notion of "principal legal systems" is vague and potentially misleading. Normally, it would seem to refer to the principal types of legal systems in the world and, in this respect, might be very closely related to, but not necessarily the same as, the principle of equitable geographical distribution. However vague, these concepts are commonly found in instruments of this type; they apply also in the election of members of the CEDAW, CERD, and CAT.

Again, since we have no comprehensive study of the recruitment of members of human rights bodies, we cannot say how states have interpreted and applied such principles in conducting elections. We know that among the states parties to the Convention Against Torture an informal agreement was reached concerning the composition of the CAT and that subsequently complaints were expressed about the results (Burgers and Danelius, 1988:110–11). We also know that during the CERD's early years, concern was expressed that its composition was "heavily loaded" against the West, although Natan Lerner (1980:152) found that the work of the committee had been "remarkably harmonious." Generally, it seems that the principle of equitable geographical distribution is too politically important to ignore, but it is vague enough to allow for considerable flexibility in its application. In any event, political considerations are likely to weigh heavily in the conduct of all elections. In fact, competition among states in the election process is clearly evident; five ballots were required to elect the ten members of the CRC at the first election in February 1991 (UN CRC,

1991k:1–5). The question, therefore, is how well competing inter-ests can be balanced so that the principle of equitable geographical distribution can be given due regard at the same time that people who are genuine experts in their field are elected.

Table 7.3

DISTRIBUTION OF MEMBERS OF THE CRC
AT FIRST ELECTION

Region	Number of States in Region (% of Total)	Number of States Parties in Region (% of Total)	Number of Committee Members (% of Total)
Africa	52 (31.90)	26 (37.14)	3[a] (30.00)
Asia and Pacific	27 (16.56)	9 (12.86)	1[b] (10.00)
Europe — East	10 (6.13)	5 (7.14)	1[c] (10.00)
Europe — West	19 (11.66)	6 (8.57)	2[d] (20.00)
Latin America	21 (12.88)	17 (24.29)	2[e] (20.00)
Middle East	16 (9.82)	0 (0)	0 (0)
North America and Caribbean	14 (8.59)	5 (7.14)	1[f] (10.00)
Others	4 (2.45)	2 (2.86)	0 (0)
Total	163 (100.00)	70 (100.00)	10 (100.00)

SOURCE: UN CRC, 1991a; "Election of the Ten Members of the Committee on the Rights of the Child in Accordance with Article 43 of the Convention" (UN CRC, 1991v-z).

[a] Akila Belembaogo of Burkina Faso, Hoda Badran of Egypt, and Swithun Mombeshora of Zimbabwe.
[b] Flora Eufemio of the Philippines.
[c] Youri Kolosov of the USSR.
[d] Marta Santos Pais of Portugal and Thomas Hammarberg of Sweden.
[e] Maria de Fatima Borges de Omena of Brazil and Bambaren Gastelumende of Peru.
[f] Sandra Mason of Barbados.

Table 7.3 shows how the states parties to the Convention on the Rights of the Child dealt with the principle of equitable geographical distribution in the composition of the CRC in the first election, held in February 1991. Overall, the data suggest that consideration was given to the principle but that other factors were also taken into account. Note that three of the members came from the African region and that this percentage of the total membership of the committee closely corresponds to the percentage of states in that region that ratified the convention and the percentage of states in the total United Nations membership that come from that region. The Asia and Pacific and the Latin America regions were also treated equitably, especially in relation to the percentage of states in those regions that ratified the convention. The East Europe and the West Europe regions were treated favorably inasmuch as the numbers of committee members elected from those regions were generous when compared with the numbers of states in those regions that had ratified the convention and in terms of their total membership in the United Nations at that time. By these standards, the West Europe region was especially well treated, with two committee members. But, as we have seen, the states in that region were the most active and constructive in drafting the Convention on the Rights of the Child. In addition, they carry the heaviest financial burdens in supporting the United Nations. These considerations could be legitimate reasons for overriding a strict application of the principle of equitable geographical distribution in the election of the committee members. They were certainly politically important enough to warrant doing so.

FINANCING THE CRC

Had the Convention on the Rights of the Child been adopted in the form initially proposed by the Polish government, the question of how to finance its implementation would not have been a serious issue during the drafting stage. As we have seen, the Polish proposal simply called for the states parties to the convention to submit periodic reports to the ECOSOC. This would not likely have required any substantial outlay of funds beyond what was already being spent on ECOSOC activities. But once the decision was made to establish a more elaborate implementation mechanism, the issue of funding was raised.

The ways and means of financing the operations of the CRC were first discussed in the 1987 meetings of the working group that drafted the convention. Taking into account methods that had been used to finance the operations of other human rights bodies, the drafters considered four options: voluntary funding; funding partly by states parties to the convention and partly by the United Nations as a whole; funding exclusively by the states parties to the convention; and funding entirely from the general United Nations budget. As discussed more fully below, each of these options carried advantages and disadvantages. Not all of them were realistic, nor were they all discussed seriously by the drafters. But the question of finance per se was very important; the discussion of the various options took place against the background of the financial problems that have been a major preoccupation of the United Nations since the early 1980s. In fact, the question of how best to finance the operations of the CRC was so contentious that it was the *only* issue on which the drafters of the convention could not reach a consensus. Accordingly, they left it up to the General Assembly to choose the method that would be used to finance the operations of the CRC. We shall return to this point below.

Voluntary Funding

Voluntary funding, or funding entirely on the basis of the willingness rather than the ability of states to pay, is commonplace in the United Nations, especially in the economic development and technical assistance fields. It is not unknown in the field of human rights as well. In fact, the Centre for Human Rights has established several voluntary funds. The Voluntary Fund for Victims of Torture, for example, was established in 1981 to provide legal and humanitarian aid to individuals whose human rights have been violated as a result of torture (UN GA, 1990h:1). The Voluntary Fund for Advisory Services and Technical Assistance provides assistance to states for setting up or improving national infrastructures for the promotion and protection of human rights. Its assistance ranges from educational programs (e.g., seminars and fellowships) to concrete action (e.g., technical assistance in translating basic human rights instruments into local languages) (UN ECOSOC, 1990a:12; Schmidt, 1990:373–74).

One of the main advantages of voluntary funding is that it is noncoercive; states can pick and choose what they wish to contribute to. But this would not have been an appropriate way to fund the activities of the Committee on the Rights of the Child for several reasons and, in fact, was not seriously considered as an option. In the first place, it is often argued that human rights are, as a matter of principle, everyone's concern, so everyone should be required to contribute to the costs of promoting and protecting them. A system of voluntary funding runs contrary to this basic principle. Second, none of the implementation organs of the other United Nations human rights treaties, such as the CERD, CEDAW, and CAT, rely on voluntary contributions for their funds. This suggests that if voluntary funding was considered when those treaties were being drafted, it was deemed inappropriate either for reasons of principle or for practical reasons. Third, experience with the already existing voluntary funds within the Centre for Human Rights suggests that voluntary funding functions inadequately as a method of financing human rights activities. For example, the Voluntary Fund for Advisory Services and Technical Assistance (UN GA, 1990b:10– 11) has apparently achieved positive results: the capabilities of some states in meeting their reporting obligations under some human rights instruments have been improved; and national human rights commissions have been formed and/or strengthened in some states. However, the demand for assistance from the fund has far exceeded the supply of funds, and large numbers of requests cannot be met because of the lack of funds (UN ECOSOC, 1990a:12). The other voluntary funds have also been underfunded because few states have made contributions. This experience suggests that when funding is voluntary, funds are not likely to be forthcoming. Since voluntarily funded entities appear to be at the mercy of domestic budgetary considerations, profound uncertainty and instability characterize their results (UN GA, 1989b:34).

Funding Partly by the United Nations and Partly by States Parties

The second method that the drafters could have used to finance the operations of the CRC is the one that has been used to finance the operations of the Committee on the Elimination of Racial Discrimination, namely, to rely on contributions partly from the states parties to the convention and partly from the general budget of the United Nations. According to the Convention on the Elimination of Racial Discrimination, the states parties are responsible for the "expenses of the members of the Committee while they are in performance of Committee duties." Other expenditures, such as the provision of secretariat services, are, according to the convention, financed through the general United Nations budget.

It has been argued that this method of financing the operations of the CERD was selected to emphasize and maintain the committee's independence (UN GA, 1989a:12). If this was truly the intention, it has had disastrous consequences in practice. Some states parties have failed to pay their assessed contributions, causing financial difficulties for the CERD. The problem has been exacerbated by the fact that some states parties that have made their contributions have not paid on time. These arrearages are not as serious a problem as an outright failure to pay, since the parties do eventually make their contributions, but the result of the two problems has been that the CERD has experienced severe cash-flow problems. The worst problems were avoided until the end of 1985 because the secretary-general was able to advance funds to the committee from the United Nations General Fund pending the receipt of contributions due from states parties (UN GA, 1989b:28–29; UN CERD, 1988:1–2). However, the United Nations financial crisis forced the secretary-general to abandon this practice. Consequently, the CERD had to cancel its 1986 summer session (UN GA, 1989b:28).

In 1987, the secretary-general convened an emergency meeting of the states parties to the Convention on the Elimination of Racial Discrimination in the hope of finding a solution to the CERD's financial problems, but the meeting revealed the extreme reluctance of the parties to take any effective measures. The United Nations comptroller announced that the CERD would not be able to meet unless the minimum amount required to cover the expenses of the committee members was received by the end of June 1987. Despite the seriousness of this situation, the states parties responded to the ultimatum by merely asking the states in arrears to pay (UN CERD, 1988:5). The relatively small sum of $110,000 had to be raised before the established deadline in order for the CERD to meet as scheduled. Although some states pledged to pay, the actual contributions fell short of expectations, and the August 1987 meeting of the committee had to be canceled; a one-week session was later held. Therefore, since 1986, the committee, which is supposed to meet in two annual sessions of three weeks each, has been forced to cancel some of its sessions and drastically curtail others (CERD, 1988:1–2; UN GA, 1988a:1). In 1989, for example, it was able to hold only one extended session of four weeks' duration; its spring session had to be canceled entirely (UN GA, 1990i:1).

The financial problems of the CERD have taken their toll on the time and energy of its members. At the curtailed 1987 meeting, for example, some members complained about the lack of funds, correctly diagnosing the situation they faced. As Mario Jorge Yutzis of Argentina noted, the "Committee was confronting not a financial crisis but a crisis of values with financial implications." He pointed out that if the United Nations budget had not been drawn on in the past, "the Committee would have had to cease its work long be-fore." As he saw it, the "crisis affecting the readiness of States par-ties to discharge their obligations predated the current financial crisis of the United Nations" (UN CERD, 1988:5). Other members of the committee also believed that the crisis was really a political one. Mahmoud Aboul-Nasr of Egypt complained that the "General As-sembly should be informed that fund-raising was not the Com-mittee's function and that the Committee's continued existence was a matter for the Assembly" (UN CERD, 1988:7). Others, like Karl Josef Partsch of the Federal Republic of Germany, believed that the long-term solution was probably to amend the convention so that all of the CERD's activities would be funded out of the United Nations regular budget (UN CERD, 1988:7–10). His view was shared by others, and as we shall see in a moment, an amend-ment is now under consideration by the states parties.

At subsequent meetings, the members of the CERD have had to deal with persistent financial problems. In August 1988, for exam-ple, they discussed the refusal of the General Assembly to allow funds to be advanced from the regular budget of the United Na-tions. When that possibility had been discussed, the representa-tives of some member states had objected on the ground that it "would be unfair to those Member States that paid their contribu-tions regularly" (UN CERD, 1989:97). Some committee members again referred to the "political" crisis affecting the financing of their work. Yutzis of Argentina suggested that the committee should consider resigning. As he said, "The time for half-way mea-sures was over, unless the Committee's work was to continue to be crippled" (UN CERD, 1989:99). But not all committee members fa-vored this course of action. Isi Foighel of Denmark, for one, was not in favor of resigning. As the report of the committee meeting so eloquently put it, "He knew from his experience as a member of the Government that ministers reacted with indifference when bodies they had created went on strike" (UN CERD, 1989:102).

In 1989, the CERD tried to pressure the states parties to make their contributions, and to do so on time, by publishing a list of assessments outstanding as of August 1989. The list showed that 74 of the 128 parties (57.8 percent) were in arrears. Of these, 45 still owed contributions from previous years, and 29 were late in making their contributions for 1989. The total of arrears was $172,560. Many of the states that were substantially in arrears were among the poorer of the less developed countries. In fact, many of these states, especially in Africa, have never paid their assessments despite the fact that the contributions required of them are quite small—$550 per year. Yet, Burkina Faso, Burundi, Central African Republic, Gambia, Guinea, Liberia, Mali, Sierra Leone, Somalia, and Togo had all accumulated arrearages of at least $5,000. Some of the Western states that were assessed large contributions, such as Canada ($3,989) and the United Kingdom ($5,947), were late in making their contributions for 1989, which contributed to the committee's cash-flow problems. At least 8 of the 18 committee members (44.4 percent) came from states that were in arrears in making their contributions (UN GA, 1990i:99–100). This unfortunate circumstance suggests that a close link between the states parties to a convention and the committee that is entrusted with its implementation will not ensure greater responsibility on the part of the states parties when it comes to such matters as meeting their financial obligations on time.

The CERD's financial problems have continued to have an adverse effect on its operations. In 1989 it was able to hold only one extended session of four weeks' duration (UN GA, 1990i:1). Again in 1990 it was able to hold only one session. Nonetheless, it continued to plan on two three-week sessions, as its schedule of sessions for 1991 and 1992 showed (UN GA, 1990j:6–8). Its inability to meet, as we will see in chapter 8, has affected its processing of reports received from states parties.

If threats of resignation and exposure of states for failing to contribute in a timely fashion will not work, would anything else? In a report submitted to the United Nations Commission on Human

Rights in 1990, the secretary-general suggested that there appeared to be only two avenues that offered any hope of resolving the CERD's financial difficulties. One was to establish a voluntarily funded "contingency reserve fund" of approximately $200,000 to cover the expenses of the committee. The CERD's meetings could be financed out of the contingency fund, which would be reimbursed when the contributions of the states parties were received (UN GA, 1990g:4). This avenue, however, does not hold much promise considering the experience with other voluntarily funded operations, as discussed earlier. For one thing, it would require considerable political will on the part of the General Assembly and of the states that would make the voluntary contributions. At the same time, without the contingency fund, the CERD will continue to experience serious operational difficulties. So, it is not surprising that the chairs of the treaty bodies, concerned about how financial problems have crippled the operations of the CERD, have called for the creation of such a fund as an interim measure until an amendment of the Convention on the Elimination of Racial Discrimination, mandating the financing of the CERD's activities out of the regular United Nations budget, can be adopted and put into effect (UN GA, 1992b:14).

The second avenue proposed by the secretary-general was to finance the activities of the CERD entirely out of the United Nations regular budget (UN GA, 1990g:3). This would necessitate amending the Convention on the Elimination of Racial Discrimination. Any state party can propose such amendments, and Australia did so in 1992. The states parties agreed, and the General Assembly endorsed the amendments in December 1992 (UN LS, 1993:113). Some observers expect that it will take approximately two years before the necessary two-thirds of the states parties to the convention (133 as of December 31, 1992) will ratify the amendments. For this reason, the chairs of the treaty bodies have urged that the General Assembly and the secretary-general take appropriate action in the interim, including perhaps the creation of a contingency fund as discussed above, to ensure the continued operation of the CERD (UN GA, 1992b:7, 14).

Given the problems that have arisen in financing the operation of the CERD, it is fortunate indeed that the drafters of the Convention on the Rights of the Child did not adopt the same method for financing the work of the CRC.

Funding Entirely by the States Parties

The third option available to the drafters of the Convention on the Rights of the Child was to finance all aspects of its implementation entirely from contributions by the states parties. This is the method that has been used to finance the implementation of the Convention Against Torture. Articles 17(7) and 18(3) and (5) of that convention provide that the states parties are responsible for all of the expenses incurred in its implementation. This includes the expenses of holding the meetings of the states parties or the meetings of the Committee Against Torture, any expenses of the members of the committee while they are in the performance of their duties, and any expenses incurred by the United Nations in providing staff and facilities for what the convention calls "the effective performance" of the CAT's functions. Thus, constitutionally, the CAT was made even more dependent on the good graces of the states parties to the convention that led to its creation than was the CERD.

But the Convention Against Torture established only the principle of self-reliance in the financing of its implementation. It said nothing about precisely how this is to be done. According to Herman Burgers and Hans Danelius (1988:112–13), both of whom were key players in drafting the convention, the states parties reached important decisions regarding this matter at their first meeting in November 1987. The secretary-general had outlined several options: dividing the expenses equally among all the parties; dividing them proportionally on the scale of assessments utilized in the regular budget of the United Nations; and using a combination of equal and proportional sharing of the expenses.

Burgers and Danelius report that the states parties discussed these options informally before their first meeting and reached a consensus that they would pay in accordance with the scale of assessments of the regular United Nations budget, provided that no party would be required to pay more than 25 percent of the total expenses. The states parties also agreed on some guidelines regarding arrearages, that is, parties would be considered in arrears if they had not paid their assessed contributions within sixty days of receiving their assessment notices. Meetings of the CAT would not be held unless there were sufficient funds available.

The Convention Against Torture was adopted in December 1984, when the United Nations financial crisis was at a high point, so the General Assembly was not likely to have adopted any other financing method. The idea underlying the self-financing arrangement is that states should be prepared and willing to pay for any expenses incurred in the operation of a treaty from which they might benefit. The argument has been attractive to some states, especially to the United States during the administrations of Presidents Ronald Reagan and George Bush. In fact, as we shall see below, the Reagan and Bush administrations maintained that position in the negotiations on the Convention on the Rights of the Child, finally losing the battle in the General Assembly. At the moment, the question we want to explore is, how well does the self-financing system work in practice?

The CAT is a relatively new body, having come into existence in 1987, making experience with its operation very limited. Nonetheless, certain trends regarding its financial situation became apparent early on. In 1990, Agnes Dormenval reported that certain parties to the Convention Against Torture were in arrears in paying their assessments. As she put it, it was not "reassuring" to know that some Western European states (e.g., Portugal and Spain) were in arrears. Nonetheless, since most of the parties in arrears were less developed countries with small contributions, the total of arrearages was not large enough to threaten the operation of the system—at least not yet. But Dormenval (1990:28–29) suggested that the future financial situation might be more bleak: as ratifications increased, so did the arrearages!

The Committee Against Torture has also been concerned about its tenuous financial situation as a result of arrearages. In particular, it has been concerned that the lack of financial resources might threaten the effective operation of the reporting system. Since the states parties had decided in 1987 that the committee would not be able to meet unless it had sufficient funds, the CAT was not able to meet for its second session in 1988, which meant that the examination of the initial reports of some states parties had to be postponed until 1989 (UN GA, 1989a:14). When the states parties met again in 1990, they expressed concern that "the accumulation of arrears in the payment of assessed contributions might ultimately have a paralyzing effect on the monitoring of the Convention's implementation" (UN GA, 1990b:5). Now, they too, like the states parties to the Convention on the Elimination of Racial Discrimination, have decided that the convention should be amended to finance its implementation out of the regular United Nations budget (UN GA, 1992b:14).

Aware of the experiences of the CAT (and the CERD), the working group that drafted the Convention on the Rights of the Child began discussing, at its meetings in 1987, the method that should be used to finance the operations of the CRC (UN CHR, 1987:35–36). It continued its discussions into 1988 (UN CHR, 1988:25) and 1989 (UN CHR, 1989b:122–23). Throughout these years, the U.S. representatives were the most outspoken in favor of a self-financing system such as that used for the CAT. In fact, they indicated that they would support only a self-financing system for the CRC. They specifically rejected financing through the regular United Nations budget, which was the method supported by the great majority of other participants in the working group. According to the U.S. representatives, the regular budget was already strained beyond its capacity and could not absorb any additional burdens (UN CHR, 1988:25). Consequently, they refused to go along with a consensus to rely on the regular United Nations budget, and the question of how to finance the CRC was, therefore, passed on to the General Assembly (UN CHR, 1989b:122–23).

When the issue was discussed in the Third Committee (Economic and Social Issues) of the General Assembly in November 1989, the outcome already seemed certain. Earlier, in March 1989, the Human Rights Commission had discussed the impasse that had developed in the working group. Most of the commission delegates favored financing the implementation of the convention out of the regular United Nations budget. Representatives of countries throughout the world pointed to the financial difficulties that had affected the work of other treaty bodies, especially the CERD and the CAT (UN CHR, 1989b:6–14, 1989c:7–10). The discussion in the Third Committee of the General Assembly was essentially the same. Speaker after speaker expressed concern that states would be dissuaded from ratifying human rights treaties if they were expected to shoulder all or most of the expenses incurred in implementing them. These speakers favored the broadest possible acceptance of the human rights treaties among states, and they believed that one way to bring this about was to make the United Nations itself morally and financially responsible for the effective implementation of all such instruments (UN GA C.3, 1989b:11, 1989c:6, 1989a:3–15, 1989d:5–15, 1989e:8–12).

At the opposite extreme, the United States continued to insist that the expenses of the CRC "should be borne exclusively" by the states ratifying the convention. Its representative, David Bolton, emphasized that the CRC was to be "an instrument of the States parties to the convention; they alone had the right to nominate and elect its members and were bound to submit reports to it." Furthermore, he argued, "since the convention would enter into force once it had been ratified by 20 States, it was inappropriate for the entire United Nations membership to fund a body created to serve what would initially be a very small number of States" (UN GA C.3,

1989a:7 – 8). But the United States stood virtually alone on this matter and demanded that a vote be taken. The outcome was 137 in favor of financing the implementation of the convention through the regular United Nations budget, one against (United States), and one abstention (Japan) (UN GA C.3, 1989f:12 – 13). Interestingly, Japan's reasons for abstaining were essentially the same as those that led the United States to vote against the motion. The Japanese representative explained that he had abstained because, "as a matter of principle, an intergovernmental body to be established after the entry into force of an international agreement from which it derived should be financed by the States parties to that agreement" (UN GA C.3, 1989f:13).

This recorded vote was the only one taken during the entire period of negotiations over the terms of the Convention on the Rights of the Child. In view of the outcome, which seemed predictable from the tenor of the debates that had preceded the vote, the wisdom of pushing the issue so hard seems questionable. The total expenses of implementing the convention, including conference services and meetings of states parties and the CRC, had been estimated at approximately $1.2 million for 1991. Some of the expenses, such as those related to conference services, would have been incurred by the United Nations even if the CRC did not exist (UN GA C.5, 1989:1 – 7). In the future, of course, especially as the work of the committee becomes regularized and reports from states parties begin to come in, the expenses will increase. In the context of the ongoing financial problems of the United Nations, $1 million is not a negligible amount, and larger figures are bound to be of even greater concern. In the broader context of the possible good that could come out of the effective operation of the convention, however, the sums seem relatively small. In any event, adding a touch of humor to the proceedings, the day after the Third Committee voted, the U.S. representative pointed out that the machine that was supposed to record the vote had malfunctioned (UN GA C.3, 1989g:1)!

Notwithstanding its experience in this instance, during the Bush administration the United States continued to press the issue of finance in negotiations on other human rights instruments. In 1990, for example, during negotiations on the Convention on the Protection of the Rights of All Migrant Workers and Members of Their Families, the U.S. representatives insisted that the self-financing method employed under the Convention Against Torture was the most desirable way to finance the implementation of human rights instruments. Therefore, they declined to go along with a developing consensus that the implementation of the convention on migrant workers should be financed from the regular United Nations budget and demanded that the General Assembly again be required to resolve the issue by a vote (UN GA, 1990c:11). Like the Convention on the Rights of the Child, the Convention on the Protection of All Migrant Workers will be financed from the regular United Nations budget.

Funding through the Regular United Nations Budget
The decision of the General Assembly to finance the implementation of the Convention on the Rights of the Child from the regular United Nations budget is one that will be welcomed by scholars and practitioners alike (e.g., Fletcher School of Law and Diplomacy, 1988:33). It is widely believed that this method is preferable to all others for various reasons. Philip Alston, for example, has argued that the "principal beneficiaries of a human rights treaty regime are, first and foremost, the international community as a whole and secondly those individuals and groups whose human rights are promoted and protected as a result." To Alston it is the "principal beneficiary — the international community — that should bear the cost involved." He bases his position on several arguments, including the fact that "treaties are part of the cornerstone of the international human rights system"; the General Assembly "has a special responsibility to them" because it adopted them; and the United Nations Charter itself "mandates

the development of effective approaches to human rights, and the development of international law in that field is one of the ways in which this can be done" (UN GA, 1989b:30–31).

Alston cleverly reverses the arguments for fairness or equity in the financing of human rights treaty bodies, arguments typically made by the U.S. representatives. As he sees it, "any arrangement that imposes significant costs on States that become parties to a human rights treaty results in the creation of a disincentive to ratification and thus conflicts directly with the oft-stated goal of achieving universal ratification of the principal treaties"; and the "incongruous results of State party funding arrangements are that those States which strengthen the overall system by ratifying are penalized financially while those States which do not participate are in effect rewarded." Beyond this, there is a "free-rider" element to consider because "nationals of non-ratifying States can, at no cost to their own State, enjoy the protection offered by the various treaties whenever they are present in the territory of a State that is a party" (UN GA, 1989b:31).

Alston's arguments have much to commend them, but experience with the operation of the CEDAW, the implementation organ of the Convention on the Elimination of Discrimination Against Women, suggests that it is not finance per se that is at issue here but rather the political attitudes and priorities of the member states of the United Nations. According to Article 17(8) and (9) of the convention, the costs incurred in the operation of the CEDAW and the "necessary staff and facilities for the effective performance of its functions" are to be covered by the regular United Nations budget. Article 20 of the convention, as discussed earlier, stipulates that the CEDAW shall "normally meet for a period of not more than two weeks annually" to consider the reports that are submitted to it. From these provisions, it would seem that the CEDAW would not have the kinds of problems that the CERD has faced and that are beginning to loom for the CAT.

But by the time of its fifth session in 1986, the implications of the two-week limitation on the meetings of the CEDAW were already becoming clear. A backlog of reports from states parties was beginning to build up — even though, as will be discussed in chapter 8, large numbers of parties were late with their reports or were failing to report altogether. The committee, therefore, began to discuss the possibility of holding longer sessions. At that point, it ran into two interrelated problems: the Convention on the Elimination of Discrimination Against Women stipulated that the CEDAW would meet for "not more than two weeks annually"; and the United Nations financial crisis made it unlikely that the CEDAW would receive any additional funding even if it did not face a "constitutional" limitation on the length of its meetings. The committee was forced to consider alternatives, including extending its individual meeting times by one hour and holding night meetings (UN GA, 1986c:3–4).

At the sixth session of the CEDAW in 1987, the issue of finance came up again. The continuing financial crisis of the United Nations had taken its toll on programs, documentation, conferences, and meetings. The committee would continue to be allowed to have summary records of its meetings, but only in English and French and only on substantive matters such as the examination of reports it received from states parties (UN GA, 1987:1–2). Clearly, the committee was beginning to feel the squeeze of the financial crisis: its program budget for the 1988–89 biennium was the same as it had been for 1986–87; subsequently, for the 1990–91 biennium, the program budget reflected no real growth (UN GA, 1990e:1–2). In response, the committee has begun holding presessional working groups of only five of its members, who give preliminary consideration to the states parties reports that will be considered at the session. The cost of these presessional working groups is substantially less than a full-fledged meeting of all twenty-three members of the CEDAW and is one way in which economies have been achieved (UN GA, 1990e:7, 95–96). Nonetheless, many observers remain concerned about the security and efficient operation of the CEDAW. As Roberta Jacobson (1992:470) has observed, although the General Assembly cannot on its own authority completely abolish the CEDAW, it could use the budget process to "nickel and dime" the committee to death, that is, it "could so underfund and understaff the Committee as to completely undermine its work and effectiveness." For this reason, in the long run it may be necessary for the committee to seek alternative sources of funds.

So far as financing human rights activities is concerned, the trend is in the direction of depending on the regular United Nations budget. Once the amendments that have been proposed to the Convention on the Elimination of Racial Discrimination and the Convention Against Torture take effect, all of the human rights treaty bodies will be financed in this way. However, experience with the CEDAW suggests that this method of financing will not in itself solve all the important problems that can arise. The fact remains that only a small fraction of the United Nations budget is allocated to human rights activities. Financing more committee operations without substantially increasing the amount of funds that are allocated to human rights activities could actually do more harm than good. Therefore, unless the funds are increased, we can be skeptical of the long-range effectiveness of the arrangement that was adopted for the Convention on the Rights of the Child.

8 · Functions of the Committee

THE COMMITTEE ON the Rights of the Child was established for "the purpose of examining the progress made by States Parties in achieving the realization of the obligations" they have assumed by ratifying the Convention on the Rights of the Child (Article 43[1]). This statement identifies the main function of the committee. But how is the committee to examine the progress of the states parties? According to Articles 44 and 45 of the convention, the parties will submit periodic reports on the measures they have adopted to promote the rights affirmed in the convention and on the progress they have made toward the enjoyment of those rights. Among other things, the committee will examine these reports. Similar reporting systems have been established under a number of other United Nations human rights conventions, including those we have been using in this study for comparative purposes: the Convention on the Elimination of Discrimination Against Women, the Convention on the Elimination of Racial Discrimination, and the Convention Against Torture.

Those who support the establishment of reporting systems claim that they advance the cause of human rights in two ways: first, they help to build a body of jurisprudence for the interpretation of human rights treaties (e.g., Fletcher School of Law and Diplomacy, 1988:30–32); and second, they provide a basis for criticism of a state's policies and practices because governments must defend their reports before committees of experts (e.g., Nowak, 1993:158; Weissbrodt, 1988:9–10). In contrast, critics of reporting systems maintain that they have been ineffective for various reasons. Some critics say that governments use reports to create the impression that they are concerned about human rights when in fact they are inattentive or unconcerned. Others say that governments are inclined to report only that which puts them in a favorable light. Still others point to the poor quality of many reports and to the fact that many governments fail to submit the reports required under various United Nations human rights conventions (e.g., Nowak, 1993:158 – 59; Bernard-Maugiron, 1990; UN GA, 1989a, 1990b).

Whatever can be said for or against reporting systems, they are widely used, so it does not seem odd or unusual that the drafters of the Convention on the Rights of the Child would have followed well-established practice. In doing so, they had to reach a consensus on very important issues. How frequently should parties to the convention be required to submit reports? Should any standards regarding the content of the reports be established, and if so, what should they be? How should the reports be examined? Should the Committee on the Rights of the Child have to rely on its own resources in this regard, or could it call on other entities competent in the field of children's rights to provide advice and assistance? Some of these questions were addressed in Article 44 of the convention, which sets forth, among other things, the basic standards regarding the submission of reports to the CRC. Others were addressed in Article 45, which deals with the processing of reports by the committee, including the involvement in that process by intergovernmental and nongovernmental organizations. Because of the substantive differences between these two articles, we shall deal with them separately in the remainder of this chapter.

THE REPORTING OBLIGATION: ARTICLE 44

Article 44 of the convention provides:

> 1. States Parties undertake to submit to the Committee, through the Secretary-General of the United Nations, reports on the measures they have adopted which give effect to the rights recognized herein and on the progress made on the enjoyment of those rights:
> (a) Within two years of the entry into force of the Convention for the State Party concerned:
> (b) Thereafter every five years.

2. Reports made under the present article shall indicate factors and difficulties, if any, affecting the degree of fulfillment of the obligations under the present Convention. Reports shall also contain sufficient information to provide the Committee with a comprehensive understanding of the implementation of the Convention in the country concerned.

3. A State Party which has submitted a comprehensive initial report to the Committee need not, in its subsequent reports submitted in accordance with paragraph 1 (b), repeat basic information previously provided.

4. The Committee may request from States Parties further information relevant to the implementation of the Convention.

5. The Committee shall submit to the General Assembly, through the Economic and Social Council, every two years, reports on its activities.

6. States Parties shall make their reports widely available to the public in their own countries.

Periodicity of Reports

One of the basic issues addressed by Article 44 is the frequency, or periodicity, of the reporting requirement. In fact, this was one of the most important issues discussed by the drafters of the convention. They perceived it as being important because of the problems that have arisen in recent years with other human rights conventions that require the submission of reports. These problems have been on the agenda of the United Nations in one form or another since the early 1980s. The secretary-general provided his first report on the subject to the General Assembly in 1983 (UN GA, 1985a:2). Since then, the subject has been discussed in various forums, including four meetings (1984, 1988, 1990, and 1992) of the chairs of treaty bodies that rely on reporting requirements to monitor the human rights policies and practices of states.

One of the most serious problems affecting the operation of the reporting systems has been the very large and ever-increasing number of overdue reports, some of which have been overdue for many years. In 1985, the secretary-general reported to the General Assembly that for the five human rights conventions that had reporting requirements, a total of 384 reports were overdue (UN GA, 1985a:3–5). Approximately one-half of those reports involved a group of 27 countries, and most of them were parties to either four or all five of the conventions then in force: 14 from Africa; 4 from Asia; 1 from Eastern Europe; and 8 from Latin America (UN GA, 1985a:6, 1985b:1–36). Unfortunately, these figures continued to rise. By June 1988 there were 146 parties to one or more of six United Nations conventions that had reporting requirements (not including the Convention Against Torture, which entered into force in June 1987), and the number of overdue reports totaled 626 (UN GA, 1989b:21; see also UN GA, 1989a:7–13). By the time the chairs of the treaty bodies met for their third meeting in October 1990, the total of overdue reports had risen to 767 (UN GA, 1990b:5). A recent study by Agnes Dormenval (1990:30) focused on the Committee Against Torture and indicated that overdue reports were beginning to be a problem for that committee too: it had expected to receive 27 reports in 1988 but received only 17; it expected 10 in 1989 but received only 5.

The usual explanation for these incredibly high nonsubmission rates is that the reporting "burden" is too heavy, especially for Third World countries—by far the worst offenders—which lack trained personnel or have an already overburdened bureaucracy that cannot handle the demand for good and timely reports (e.g., Dormenval, 1990:30; Nowak, 1993:158). This explanation is undoubtedly valid for some countries, especially the poorest and least developed ones, but the nonsubmission rates are so high that they probably also reflect an unwillingness on the part of some governments to take their reporting obligations seriously. Indeed, it may be that even the poorer countries, if they were determined to do so, could prepare short but nonetheless adequate reports and send a well-informed representative to the meeting of the treaty body when their report is examined; the representative could supplement the content of the report by providing information orally (e.g., Fletcher School of Law and Diplomacy, 1988:32).

Whatever the cause of the nonsubmission problem, what is important for our purposes is that many analysts have argued that it is creating tensions in the human rights implementation system. From the perspective of the chairs of the treaty bodies in particular, the failure of many states to fulfill their reporting obligations has "significantly undermined the objectives of the treaties." Accordingly, the chairs have urged that "every effort should be made by the States parties concerned to fulfill their reporting obligations" (UN GA, 1989a:16–17; see also UN GA, 1992b:6, 19). The committees themselves have resorted to different tactics and strategies to encourage greater compliance with reporting obligations, including sending written reminders to states with overdue reports, inviting them to discuss their difficulties in preparing reports, and offering them assistance in the preparation of their reports (UN GA, 1989a:7). In particular, the Committee on the Elimination of Racial Discrimination, which has had an especially serious problem of nonsubmissions (see Partsch, 1992:347), has tried to pressure states into compliance by listing those states with overdue reports in its own reports to the General Assembly. It has also delegated some of its members to raise the issue of overdue reports with representatives of the states concerned, and it has permitted states with overdue reports to consolidate several reports into one (UN GA, 1989a:10–11).

To date, none of the various tactics and strategies have produced the desired results. The chairs of the treaty bodies continue to urge committees to establish a dialogue with states that do not submit reports in order to explore means of assisting them (UN GA, 1990b:14, 1992b:19). Others have suggested that the periodicity of the reporting requirement might be extended or made more flexible. This could be achieved by including convention provisions that permit some discretion on the part of the supervisory bodies in determining the periodicity of reports (UN GA, 1989a:22). In addition, as discussed more fully below, some have suggested that a consolidation of the reporting guidelines under various conventions might help to reduce the burden of reporting requirements for those states that are parties to more than one convention, thereby reducing, even if indirectly, the high nonsubmission rates of those states. Most recently, it has been suggested that states that are parties to more than one convention be permitted to submit a single but comprehensive report—a "global" report—which would satisfy their reporting obligations under all conventions (UN GA, 1992b:20). As Manfred Nowak (1993:158–59) has observed, however, such a consolidated report, which could be submitted perhaps every four or five years, would probably necessitate a major structural change in the present human rights committee system, namely, a merging of the various human rights bodies into one "super-body"—into "a semi-permanent or permanent Human Rights Committee with an enlarged number of individual expert members representing different regions and professions."

Whether such a major structural change in the existing human rights implementation system can be achieved without a significant change in the attitudes of the member states of the United Nations is extremely doubtful. For one thing, they would have to commit themselves to adequately financing the system, and the seemingly permanent financial crisis of the United Nations would be a major hindrance. In addition, structural changes in the system would require the adoption of amendments to those human rights treaties that call for the creation of treaty-specific implementation committees. Even if such changes could be brought about, in the meantime the various existing committees, including the CRC, would have to deal with nonsubmission problems.

Having observed the experience of other committees, the drafters of the Convention on the Rights of the Child discussed the periodicity of the reporting requirement. They considered two options. One was to adopt a flexible system whereby reports would be due at specified intervals or at longer intervals if the Committee on the Rights of the Child so decided. According to this proposal, the parties to the convention would be allowed to fulfill their reporting obligations in stages as prescribed by the committee (UN CHR, 1987:33). The second option was to follow the precedents set in the Convention on the Elimination of Racial Discrimination, the Convention on the Elimination of Discrimination Against Women, and the Convention Against Torture, all of which specify the intervals at which reports are due, though the intervals vary from one convention to the other.

Of these two options, the drafters of the convention decided to follow established practice and to specify the periodicity of the reporting obligations of the states parties, but they discussed several formulas, indicating their concern about the nonsubmission problems of other human rights bodies (UN CHR, 1987:31–34). Most drafters seemed to believe that five-year intervals between reports would be preferable to shorter periods, given the high nonsubmission rates (UN CHR, 1988:27–28), their assumption apparently being that if governments were given more time to report they would eventually do so, a questionable assumption in light of the experience of other committees. In any event, the compromise that the drafters reached is reflected in Article 44(1)(a) and (b) of the convention, under which the states parties are required to submit their initial reports to the Committee on the Rights of the Child within two years of the entry into force of the convention; thereafter, they will be required to submit reports every five years.

Obviously, since the reporting requirement lies at the heart of the implementation system of the Convention on the Rights of the Child, its importance can hardly be overemphasized (see, e.g., DCI, 1986). Yet, the experience of other human rights conventions made it virtually certain that the CRC could also expect to have serious problems with nonsubmission of reports, and as we shall see in a moment, that has already occurred. The committee therefore began to discuss various issues related to the reporting requirement at its first session in October 1991.

As a preliminary matter, the committee took the position that it saw the process of examining state reports as an opportunity to engage in a "dialogue" with the states parties to the convention (UN CRC, 1991g:6). In other words, the committee hoped that states would not see their reporting obligations as unpleasant burdens but rather as opportunities to take stock of their human rights policies and practices and make changes where necessary. But what should the committee do if states parties did not submit their reports? Should it simply notify the General Assembly? Should it try to identify the reasons for the nonsubmission? Should it offer to assist states in meeting their reporting requirements? Should it consider the status of the rights of the child in a particular country even in the absence of a report (UN CRC, 1991r:2−4)?

At one point during the discussion of these issues, the chair of the committee, Hoda Badran of Egypt, summed up the committee's sentiment by saying that the committee "did not intend systematically to take strong action in respect of States which did not submit their reports, thereby leaving open the possibility of a continuing dialogue with the States parties concerned." But at least one member, Thomas Hammarberg, argued that the committee "should be very firm with States parties which did not submit reports as requested." In his view, "anything resembling negotiation with Governments could only detract from the Committee's work," and in light of what we already know about the nonsubmission of reports to other committees, he expressed well-founded reservations as to whether "the Committee could establish a dialogue with States parties until they had submitted their reports" (UN CRC, 1991r:4).

Ironically, while the committee discussed the ways and means of dealing with states that fail to meet their reporting obligations, it might have shown more interest in what it would do if all the states parties actually submitted their reports on time. As the data in table 8.1 show, beginning in 1992 the committee faced a potential flood of reports, a situation that resulted from the record-breaking

Table 8.1

INITIAL COUNTRY REPORTS
DUE IN 1992, 1993, 1994, AND 1995
(BASED ON NUMBER OF STATES PARTIES
AT DECEMBER 31, 1992)

Region	Number of States Parties	Report Due in 1992	Report Due in 1993	Report Due in 1994	Report Due in 1995
Africa (52 states)	39	22	11	6	0
Asia and Pacific (31 states)	19	9	6	3	1
Europe — East (25 states)	16	3	8	5	0
Europe — West (20 states)	16	4	6	6	0
Latin America (21 states)	19	14	5	0	0
Middle East (16 states)	7	0	6	1	0
North America and Caribbean (14 states)	10	4	4	2	0
Others (3 states)	1	1	0	0	0
Total	127	57	46	23	1

SOURCE: UN LS, 1993:187–95; UN CRC, 1991aa, 1992e-g.

Reports Due 1992:
AFRICA (22): Benin; Burkina Faso; Burundi; Chad; Egypt; Gambia; Ghana; Guinea; Guinea-Bissau; Kenya; Mali; Mauritius; Namibia; Niger; Senegal; Seychelles; Sierra Leone; Sudan; Togo; Uganda; Zaire; Zimbabwe.
ASIA AND PACIFIC (9): Bangladesh; Bhutan; Democratic People's Republic of Korea; Indonesia; Mongolia; Nepal; Pakistan; Philippines; Vietnam.
EUROPE (EAST) (3): Belarus; Romania; Russian Federation.
EUROPE (WEST) (4): France; Malta; Portugal; Sweden.
LATIN AMERICA (14): Bolivia; Brazil; Chile; Costa Rica; Ecuador; El Salvador; Guatemala; Honduras; Mexico; Nicaragua; Paraguay; Peru; Uruguay; Venezuela.
NORTH AMERICA AND CARIBBEAN (4): Barbados; Belize; Grenada; Saint Kitts and Nevis.
OTHERS (1): Holy See.

speed with which a large number of states had ratified the convention. The convention entered into force in September 1990. Since the parties are obliged to submit their initial reports within two years of the entry into force of the convention for them (Article 44[1][a]), some reports were due beginning in September 1992. In fact, as table 8.1 shows, 57 reports were due in the last three months of 1992 alone (UN CRC, 1991s:1–3). Although the number of reports due then declined (to 46 in 1993 and 23 in 1994), over 100 reports were due from states in the two-year period of 1992 and 1993. How could the committee expect to handle such a large volume of reports? Under ideal conditions, the committee hoped to devote two days to the examination of each report. However, as Youri Kolosov, a committee member from Russia, pointed out, if 100 reports were received during a two-year period, and if each of these reports was discussed over a two-day period, "the consideration of 100 reports would take 200 working days or 40 weeks. If sessions lasted four weeks each year, the 100th report would be considered at the earli-

---

Reports Due in 1993:
AFRICA (11): Angola; Côte d'Ivoire; Djibouti; Ethiopia; Madagascar; Malawi; Mauritania; Nigeria; Rwanda; Sao Tome and Principe; United Republic Tanzania.
ASIA AND PACIFIC (6): Australia; Lao People's Democratic Republic; Maldives; Myanmar; Republic of Korea; Sri Lanka.
EUROPE (EAST) (8): Bulgaria; Croatia; Czechoslovakia; Estonia; Hungary; Poland; Ukraine; Yugoslavia.
EUROPE (WEST) (6): Denmark; Finland; Italy; Norway; San Marino; Spain.
LATIN AMERICA (5): Argentina; Colombia; Cuba; Dominican Republic; Panama.
MIDDLE EAST (6): Cyprus; Israel; Jordan; Kuwait; Lebanon; Yemen.
NORTH AMERICA AND CARIBBEAN (4): Bahamas; Dominica; Guyana; Jamaica.

Reports Due in 1994:
AFRICA (6): Cape Verde; Central African Republic; Equatorial Guinea; Lesotho; Tunisia; Zambia.
ASIA AND PACIFIC (3): Cambodia; China; Thailand.
EUROPE (EAST) (5): Albania; Azerbaijan; Latvia; Lithuania; Slovenia.
EUROPE (WEST) (6): Austria; Belgium; Germany; Iceland; Ireland; United Kingdom.
MIDDLE EAST (1): Bahrain.
NORTH AMERICA AND CARIBBEAN (2): Canada; Trinidad and Tobago.

Reports Due in 1995:
ASIA AND PACIFIC (1): India.

est in some 10 years' time" (UN CRC, 1991t:9). In the interim, of
course, the committee would have been receiving the second reports from some states. Obviously, the volume of information for
the committee to process would have been enormous (Cohen,
Hart, and Kosloske, 1992:216 – 31). Even if only one-half of the reports due were received, the committee would still have built up a
huge backlog if each report would be discussed over a two-day
period.

Of course, as the CRC began to discuss all of these issues, the
only reasonable assumption it could make was that all the states
parties would meet their reporting obligations on time; it would
surely not have wanted to concede in advance that many states
would not submit their reports on time. This being the case, the
committee realized that it should plan its work so that all reports
would be considered within a reasonable time. Specifically, the
committee agreed that its plans for its sessions "should be based on
the principle that each received State party report should be considered in substance within one year. If the regular sessions are too
short for that, the Committee would endeavour to hold special sessions or prolong the regular ones" (UN CRC, 1991g:6). Some committee members, such as Thomas Hammarberg, believed that one
day would be sufficient for a discussion of each report, but this still
meant that the committee could look forward to a substantial
work load in the coming years (UN CRC, 1991u:3).

The committee also decided that it would be essential to establish presessional working groups consisting of three or four members who would meet approximately two months to six weeks in
advance of the committee's sessions to give preliminary consideration to state reports (UN CRC, 1991g:8, 1991u:3). Theoretically,
these working groups would perform the very important function
of identifying the main questions that would have to be further
discussed with representatives of states parties when they presented their government's report (UN CRC, 1992a:15). It was the
committee's understanding that the working groups would be

Table 8.2

STATUS OF SUBMISSION OF INITIAL COUNTRY REPORTS
DUE IN 1992

Region	Number of Reports Due	Number of Reports Submitted	% of States Submitting
Africa	22	3	13.64
Asia and Pacific	9	3	33.33
Europe — East	3	1	33.33
Europe — West	4	1	25.00
Latin America	14	5	35.71
Middle East	0	0	0
North America and Caribbean	4	0	0
Others	1	0	0
Total	57	13	22.81

SOURCE: UN CRC, 1993a:annex 4.

assisted by a "technical advisory group" consisting of representatives of specialized agencies, UNICEF and other United Nations organs and that NGOs and other "competent bodies" would be asked to give expert advice when appropriate (UN CRC, 1991g:6).

As could have been expected, however, the CRC did not receive nearly the number of reports that it should have received in 1992. As table 8.2 shows, by the time the committee met for its third session in January 1993, when it had planned to begin examining the reports due in 1992, only 13 of the 57 (22.81 percent) reports due had been received (in addition, Rwanda's report, which was not due until February 1993 was received in September 1992). The substantial majority of states in every region had failed to submit their reports on time; the experience of other human rights committees suggests that many, if not most, of the late reports will never be submitted. And the actual situation was worse than the statistics indicated. When the committee met, it was prepared to examine only 6 of the 13 reports (those of Bolivia, Egypt, the Russian Federation, Sudan, Sweden, and Vietnam); the secretary-general informed the committee that the other seven reports (those of Costa Rica, El Salvador, Indonesia, Mexico, Namibia, Pakistan, and Peru) had been received, but the committee had not seen them, nor had it had an opportunity to do a preliminary evaluation of them. Although the committee had planned to examine Rwanda's report at its third session, on request of the government it agreed to postpone the examination until its fourth session (UN CRC, 1993a: 12 – 13, annex 4).

The committee has discussed what it should do if a state party does not submit a report on time (UN CRC, 1992c:4 – 5). According to its rules of procedure, the state would be sent a reminder (UN CRC, 1992a:11). However, some committee members have disagreed as to how vigorously the committee should apply its rules of procedure on this matter. Some members, such as Thomas Hammarberg, have argued in favor of swift action, preferring that the committee automatically send out reminders as soon as a deadline for the submission of a report has passed (UN CRC, 1992c:4 – 5). Others have been willing to be more flexible on the issue so as not to offend governments. In any event, the secretariat of the Centre for Human Rights, which actually sends out the reminders, informed the committee that its practice was to contact the United Nations missions of nonsubmitting states by telephone when their governments did not submit reports by established deadlines. Then, the the centre would wait for six months to one year before sending a written reminder to the government (UN CRC, 1993p:4). The issue is obviously considered a "sensitive" one. The lack of pressure to submit reports on schedule most probably contributes to the nonsubmission problem; but even with pressure, in all likelihood many states would not be able to comply with their reporting obligations for the reasons discussed earlier.

Content of the Reports

From the standpoint of the effectiveness of a reporting system, the content of the government reports is as important, if not more important, than faithfulness in meeting reporting obligations. Good reports can provide the substantive information that international bodies need to reach conclusions and formulate recommendations for future action. In this endeavor, quality is more important than quantity. But precisely what should reports contain? This is another important question that is addressed in Article 44 of the Convention on the Rights of the Child.

According to Article 44(1), the parties to the convention are to report on "the measures they have adopted which give effect to the rights recognized" in the convention "and on the progress made on the enjoyment of those rights." Article 44(2) expands on this point and states that the reports "shall indicate factors and difficulties, if any, affecting the degree of fulfillment of the obligations under" the convention; and they "shall also contain sufficient information to provide the Committee with a comprehensive understanding of the implementation of the Convention in the country concerned." Should the committee find that the information it receives is unsatisfactory or incomplete, under Article 44(4) it could "request from States Parties further information relevant to the implementation of the Convention." According to Article 44(3), the parties that have "submitted a comprehensive initial report . . . need not, in [their] subsequent reports, . . . repeat basic information previously provided." Clearly, the reports submitted to the CRC should be more than mere recitations of domestic legal rules and regulations, a characteristic of many of the reports that have been submitted to other human rights bodies (Dormenval, 1990:30). By giving some direction to the states parties, the terms of Article 44 were intended to overcome this problem.

It is noteworthy that several proposals were introduced during the drafting stage that would have given more precise direction to the states parties than Article 44 presently does. At the 1987 session of the working group that drafted the convention, some participants, including the Belgian, Holy See, and Italian representatives, supported by some NGOS, proposed an additional paragraph stipulating that the reports "shall pay special attention to the least protected children" (UN CHR, 1987:35). The representatives of India, Poland, and Norway wanted to add a provision that would have required the reports to contain sufficient information on "social, economic and institutional aspects, as well as on assistance required from the international community, to provide the Committee with a comprehensive understanding of the operation of the Convention in that country" (UN CHR, 1988:29). The provision regarding "assistance required from the international community" was initially suggested by UNICEF and some NGOS.

Various objections were made to the form and substance of these proposals, and consensus could not be reached on any of them. The main concern was that the proposals would have oriented the convention too much in the direction of Third World countries, although, officially, those who objected did not do so on that basis but rather on the ground that the proposals were vague or that it would be best to draft the convention in such a way as to cover *all* children. In the end, therefore, the drafters decided to let the Committee on the Rights of the Child decide on the details of what it would expect to be included in the reports it received (UN CHR, 1988:29 – 31). We shall return to the committee's deliberations on this matter in a moment.

Article 44 also aims to reduce, as far as possible, the volume of information that the states parties will be expected to include in their reports, particularly after they submit their first, or initial, report. This is the thrust of Article 44(3) in particular. The volume of documentation that must be processed by human rights bodies has greatly increased in recent years because of the proliferation of reporting requirements. The problem has been discussed extensively in various forums, including meetings of the chairs of the treaty bodies that utilize reporting systems (UN GA, 1990b:7 – 8), the Human Rights Commission (UN CHR, 1990:14–16), and the Third Committee of the General Assembly (UN GA C.3, 1989h: 9–10, 1989e:5).

One solution that has been suggested for this problem is to streamline and, where possible, harmonize and consolidate the reporting requirements that exist under various conventions. Some analysts have insisted, of course, that the integrity of each convention must be defended and that, therefore, the reports submitted by the states parties under each convention must be unique and convention-specific (UN GA, 1989b:23–24; Higgins, 1989). But others maintain that it would be possible to harmonize and consolidate at least some portions of the reporting requirements that exist under several conventions and thereby reduce the overall burden of the reporting requirement for the countries that have ratified several conventions. For example, the country profile sections of reports could be consolidated, such information being provided under only one convention. This proposal was endorsed by the chairs of the treaty bodies.

In fact, significant progress has been made in consolidating reporting requirements. In February 1991, the Human Rights Commission adopted some consolidated guidelines for the initial part of the reports that states parties submit under various human rights treaties. The consolidated guidelines include the following topics: the basic characteristics of the land and its people, including the ethnic and demographic features of a country and its population, and the main socioeconomic and cultural indicators; the general political structure of the country, including its political history and type of government; the framework within which human rights are protected, including the judicial and administrative structures that have jurisdiction in the field of human rights, the types of remedies that are available to individuals, and how international human rights obligations are integrated into the national legal system; and the efforts that are undertaken in the fields of information and publicity to promote awareness of human rights among the public and relevant authorities (UN CHR, 1991:1–2).

In addition, in 1991, the United Nations Institute for Training and Research (UNITAR) published a reporting manual designed to provide assistance to governments in the preparation of their reports. The manual is based on a series of five training courses on human rights reporting that were held for government officials who are responsible for the preparation of such reports. The Ford Foundation provided grants to the institute to fund the courses. The manual provides an overview of the system of international human rights reporting. It also contains analyses of reporting under six major United Nations human rights conventions and could be very helpful to government officials who are responsible for preparing reports for human rights bodies (UNITAR, 1991).

The extensive use of cross-referencing in reports has also been suggested as a way to reduce the burden of reporting requirements, especially for those states that have ratified several conventions (UN GA, 1989b:23–26; UN CHR, 1990:14–16). The chairs of the treaty bodies discussed this strategy at their third meeting in October 1990. They agreed that cross-referencing was necessary to reduce the reporting burden for some states, especially those that have to provide comprehensive information to several treaty bodies, as well as to avoid duplication in the submitted information (UN GA, 1990b:7). The need for cross-referencing is likely to become even stronger in light of the entry into force of new treaties, including the Convention on the Rights of the Child. Still, cross-referencing has certain limitations. As the chairs pointed out, a "methodology had to be found to avoid depriving treaty bodies of the information they needed in the overall context of the implementation of a particular instrument, especially where interrelated rights and inconsistencies could be at issue" (UN GA, 1990b:7). They believed that each committee could appoint members who would establish contact with each of the other committees in an effort to work out any problems that might arise because of cross-referencing in reports (UN GA, 1990b:8).

All of these proposals and suggestions would probably be most effective if more progress could be made in the computerization of human rights documentation at the Centre for Human Rights. Indeed, effective use of computerized techniques to store, retrieve, and process information contained in the reports that states submit to human rights bodies is well worth pursuing. The volume of information that governments have to provide is enormous, especially if they provide good and timely reports. The reason is that the substantive articles of the human rights conventions are usually quite extensive in their provisions. Thus, if governments are expected to provide information regarding most if not all of these provisions, the ability of the committees to effectively process so much information is doubtful. In the case of the Convention on the Rights of the Child, some independent efforts (Cohen, Hart, and Kosloske, 1992) to develop a computerized information model to gather, store, and retrieve information relevant to compliance with the convention are already under way and could prove to be very helpful to the Committee on the Rights of the Child.

This concern for improving the quality of the reports that states submit to human rights committees provided the background against which the CRC discussed the guidelines it wanted to establish regarding the content of the reports it expects to receive from states parties to the convention (UN CRC, 1991l:3). At its first session in October 1991, the committee adopted guidelines for the initial reports that it will receive under Article 44(1)(a) (UN CRC, 1991e:1–7); it will draft guidelines for the subsequent reports that states parties will submit under Article 44(1)(b) in due course (UN CRC, 1991e:3).

The overall tenor of the guidelines for the initial reports is to make the reporting process seem as nonthreatening to states as possible. The guidelines emphasize the CRC's belief that the process of preparing a report "offers an important occasion for conducting a comprehensive review of the various measures undertaken to harmonize national law and policy with the Convention and to monitor progress made in the enjoyment of the rights set forth in the Convention" (UN CRC, 1991e:2). In fact, as the committee sees it, the "reporting process should establish an open and constructive dialogue . . . for the purpose of improving the situation of children" (UN CRC, 1991c:11). The guidelines add, however, that the "process should be one that encourages and facilitates popular participation and public scrutiny of government policies" (UN CRC, 1991e:2). As we will discuss more fully below, this statement is consistent with the terms of Articles 42 and 44(6) of the convention, which suggest that the reports should not simply be prepared by government bureaucrats without any public participation or scrutiny.

More specifically, the guidelines state that the initial part of the report, which deals with such things as the country profile and type of government, should be prepared in keeping with the consolidated guidelines adopted by the Human Rights Commission in 1991 (UN CRC, 1991e:2). This should help to reduce the reporting burden, as the consolidated guidelines were intended to do all along. But apart from the initial part of the report, the guidelines seem to impose heavy burdens on the states parties. Under Article 4 of the convention, the states parties agree to undertake all appropriate legislative, administrative, and other measures to implement the rights affirmed in the convention. The committee has obviously taken this article very seriously, since its guidelines call on states to provide information that would make it possible for the committee to get a good sense of how well the states parties are fulfilling their obligations under the convention. Specifically, they call for information about eight principal areas of concern to the committee (UN CRC, 1991e:3−7):

> 1. General Measures of Implementation, including information about the measures that have been taken "to harmonize national law and policy with the provisions" of the convention; the existing or planned mechanisms at all levels "for coordinating policies relating to children and for monitoring the implementation" of the convention; and the measures that states have planned or are taking to publicize informa-

tion about the convention and to spread awareness of their reports to the committee.

2. Definition of the Child, including information concerning the attainment of majority and the legal age for such things as compulsory education, marriage, employment, imprisonment, etc.

3. General Principles, including information about the principal legislative, administrative, judicial and other measures that are in force or are planned for implementing the general principles of the convention, e.g., nondiscrimination, and the right to life, survival and development.

4. Civil Rights and Freedoms, including information about the principal legislative, administrative, judicial and other measures that are in force, and the difficulties encountered and progress achieved in implementing the civil rights and freedoms of the convention, e.g., the rights to a name and nationality, freedom of expression, thought, conscience, assembly, etc.

5. Family Environment and Alternative Care, including information about the principal legislative, administrative, judicial and other measures that are in force, and the difficulties encountered and progress achieved in implementing rights that are relevant to the family and alternative care, e.g., parental responsibilities, adoption, and illicit transfer of children.

6. Basic Health and Welfare, including information about the principal legislative, administrative, judicial and other measures that are in force, the institutional infrastructure for implementing policy in this area, and the difficulties encountered and progress achieved in implementing rights relevant to health and welfare, e.g., survival and development of the child, health and health services, social security, etc.

7. Education, Leisure and Cultural Activities, including information about the principal legislative, administrative, judicial and other measures that are in force, the institutional infrastructure for implementing policy in this area, and the difficulties encountered and progress achieved in implementing provisions of the convention regarding such things as education, leisure and cultural activities of children.

8. Special Protection Measures, including information about

the principal legislative, administrative, judicial and other measures that are in force, and the difficulties encountered and progress achieved in implementing provisions of the convention that relate to refugee children, children in armed conflicts, and children subjected to exploitation of various kinds.

The committee has claimed that this "thematic approach" to the preparation of the initial reports of the states parties "would facilitate the preparation of reports" (UN CRC, 1991c:11), but in fact its guidelines call for abundant quantitative and qualitative information that many governments will find difficult to assemble and analyze and that will make computerized gathering, storing, and retrieval of data all the more important in the years to come. Theoretically, the subsequent reports that the states parties will present at five-year intervals will be less demanding than the initial reports, but much of the information that the committee has requested be included in the initial reports will probably need significant updating with the passage of time.

Although few of the reports that were due in 1992 were actually submitted to the CRC, those that were submitted provide insight into how well states will be able to follow the committee's guidelines. In fact, most of the reports followed the guidelines in terms of their organizational structure, but they were uneven in quality. Of the six reports that were examined by the committee at its third session in January 1993, the reports of Sweden (UN CRC, 1992h) and the Russian Federation (UN CRC, 1992j) were the most comprehensive.

The Swedish report provided extensive and in-depth coverage of Swedish law and practice regarding the provisions of the Convention on the Rights of the Child in accordance with the themes outlined in the CRC's guidelines. In substance, the report was not merely a compilation of legal rules and principles; it tried to give the committee a good grasp of public policies and the philosophical underpinnings of those policies. Although, as we shall see later, the committee was critical of some Swedish policies and practices, and made suggestions for improvements, the country's previous achievements and future plans were recognized and praised (UN CRC, 1993j).

The Russian Federation report was remarkable for its frankness. It too adhered closely to the CRC's thematic guidelines. At the outset, however, it chronicled various effects of the prevailing economic and social situation on children and on family life: an appreciable decline in the number of marriages and a high divorce rate ("about half of all men and women divorce at some time in their lives"); a steady increase in children born out of wedlock, accounting for about 16 percent of all births in 1991; a relatively high (and increasing) level of infant mortality, which seems to be directly related to the mother's state of health; the fact that approximately "15–20 per cent of school-age children" were "suffering from chronic ailments," with surveys indicating that "no more than 11–14 per cent of schoolchildren" were "in truly good health"; "cuts in guaranteed State medical assistance to women and children," cuts that were "becoming a reality" because of a decline in financing of health care; and the deterioration that was occurring in "virtually all public welfare areas" during the early 1990s. In general, the introductory part of the report provided a glimpse into a society in economic and social disarray and decline. Recent economic and social changes had clearly taken a toll. The number of offenses committed by minors had risen about 50 percent, and minors were taking to crime at an increasingly early age. Delinquency was on the rise (UN CRC, 1992j:4–8). Not surprisingly, the CRC appreciated "the frank, self-critical and comprehensive manner" in which the report was prepared, and it stated that it was "encouraged by the [Russian] Government's willingness to define and appreciate the problems impeding the implementation of the rights" affirmed in the convention and "to search for adequate solutions to face them" (UN CRC, 1993k:1–2).

In contrast to the Swedish and Russian reports, the others that were submitted in 1992 were lacking in quality, but in varying degrees. The Sudanese report (UN CRC, 1992i), for example, consisted mainly of a recitation of laws and regulations and did not give the committee a good feel for what was actually being done in the area of children's rights or for progress being made in implementing the convention. In fact, the committee believed that so many of its questions could not be answered by the information provided that it decided to request additional information in writing in accordance with Article 44(1) of the convention and to postpone further consideration of the Sudanese report until a later session (UN CRC, 1993m:1). The committee also requested further information to supplement the Bolivian (UN CRC, 1993i, 1993q:7, 17, 1993r:2–12) and Vietnamese (UN CRC, 1993a:20–21, 1993n) reports, but in neither case did it judge the reports so deficient that it had to postpone their consideration until a future meeting.

Ideally, the Swedish and the Russian Federation reports might serve as models of good reports. However, in reality their utility as models may be limited. Not all states will have had as much experience in the preparation of reports, the bureaucratic infrastructure that would make the preparation of good reports in a timely fashion easier, or the seriousness of commitment to their international human rights obligations. In addition, differences in culture and political and social systems will affect how the rights affirmed in the convention should be dealt with domestically. Therefore, in many cases the quality of reports submitted by the states parties will be less, and even much less, than that of the Swedish and the Russian Federation reports.

Dissemination of Information and Reports

The last major issue that Article 44 addresses — one that we alluded to above — is the dissemination of information and reports among the public at large. In this connection, the article deals with two kinds of reports: those that the states parties will submit to the Committee on the Rights of the Child; and those that the committee itself will prepare and submit to the United Nations General

Assembly. The drafters of the convention believed that one of the best ways to increase public awareness of the principles enshrined in the convention was to make available to the public at large as much information as possible (UN CHR, 1988:33). The rationale behind this educational process is that it might stimulate both bureaucratic reflection within states and public debate over domestic policies and practices concerning children.

As far as the reports prepared by the states parties are concerned, Article 44(6) provides that they are to be made "widely available to the public." This paragraph reinforces the provisions of Article 42 of the convention, which provides:

> States Parties undertake to make the principles and provisions of the Convention widely known, by appropriate and active means, to adults and children alike.

Article 42 originated in a proposal made by the Informal NGO Ad Hoc Group in 1987 (UN CHR, 1987:24). In its original formulation, its terms were more precise. The NGOs had proposed that the article stipulate that the provisions and principles of the convention be made known "in the forms, terminology and language (including local language) accessible" to adults and children alike. Although this formulation was supported by a few delegations, it was opposed by a number of others, including the U.S. delegation, on the ground that in such matters more rather than less flexibility was desirable (UN CHR, 1989b:119). For this reason, the phrase was dropped in favor of the more flexible provisions of Article 42, which require only that the educational campaign be undertaken by "appropriate and active means." However vague, the article is perceived as important by the CRC (UN CRC, 1991m:2−4). In fact, one of the guidelines adopted by the committee for the initial reports calls for the states parties to "describe the measures that have been taken or are foreseen, pursuant to article 42, to make the principles and provisions of the Convention widely known, by appropriate and active means, to adults and children alike" (UN CRC, 1991c:19).

The terms of Article 44(6) were also the subject of different formulations during the drafting stage. The Swedish delegation, for example, proposed that the paragraph state expressly that the states parties would make their reports available to national non-governmental organizations, as though such organizations might act as agencies for the mobilization of public opinion in defense of the rights of the child (UN CHR, 1987:33). But a working party established to deal with the issue recommended instead the present provisions of the paragraph whereby the states parties shall make their reports available only to the "public," a concept that may include, though not expressly, NGOS.

The different points of view expressed over Articles 42 and 44(6) suggest that states are willing to accept obligations to disseminate reports that they prepare for human rights committees, or information that they include in those reports, to the public at large. But if they are willing to accept this obligation in principle, they are concerned about the extent of that obligation. And it seems clear that what they are willing to accept depends at least in part on the sorts of information that they will be expected to make available and to whom they will have to make the information available. The reaction of the representative of the Federal Republic of Germany to a provision that was virtually identical to Article 44(6) and that was included in the Convention on the Protection of the Rights of All Migrant Workers and Members of Their Families, the newest of the specialized human rights conventions, illustrates the point. He objected to the inclusion of the provision by citing the "special nature" of the convention on migrant workers, which set forth "not only fundamental human rights but also specific rights relating to such matters as alien residents and aliens engaging in remunerated activity" (UN GA, 1990c:14). Germany has experienced serious problems with aliens in recent years, and its representative characterized those issues as "politically far more sensitive" than those dealt with in any other human rights treaty. Consequently, his government was not prepared to accept any obligation beyond simply informing anyone who requested a report that the report was "published by, and could be obtained from, the United Nations" (UN GA, 1990c:14). In order not to block consensus on the matter, however, he offered to go along with the provision provided that his position was "duly reflected in the report" of the negotiating session (UN GA, 1990c:14).

Despite misgivings of this sort, which are probably shared even if not expressed by many other states, the principle affirmed in Article 44(6) enjoys broad support in human rights circles; many analysts and activists argue that states should be obliged to disseminate as widely as possible the reports they submit to human rights bodies. The chairs of the treaty bodies, for example, have taken this position on several occasions. At their third meeting in 1990, they discussed the feasibility of distributing state reports, press releases, and even summary records of the human rights committees through the United Nations Centre for Human Rights and the Department of Public Information, and they noted that consultations regarding this possibility had at one point been under way. However, little progress was made, and the chairs believed that individuals as well as NGOs did not benefit from a regular flow of information of this type. Accordingly, they urged that efforts be undertaken to disseminate such information through United Nations information centers and by the secretariats of the different human rights bodies (UN GA, 1990b:11–16).

By its actions the committee has demonstrated that it is serious about the need for the states parties to make the principles and provisions of the convention widely known and that the states parties also have an obligation to keep the public informed about the measures they are taking to fulfill their obligations under the convention, including the reports that they submit to the CRC. Thus, during its examination of the initial reports of some states parties, the committee emphasized the importance of NGO and public involvement in implementing the provisions of the convention in the broadest sense, including, where appropriate, their participation in the preparation of the reports that the states parties submit to the CRC. Sweden (UN CRC, 1993j:1–2) in particular was praised for its efforts in these respects. At the same time, the committee recommended that Bolivia (UN CRC, 1993i:3–4) take steps to translate the text of the convention into local languages and that it give broad publicity to the principles and provisions of the convention. The committee made the same recommendation to the government of Vietnam (UN CRC, 1993a:20). It urged the Egyptian government to disseminate the text of the convention (UN CRC, 1993l:4). And the Sudanese government assured the CRC that it would make available to the public both its report to and dialogue with the committee; the CRC considered this a "positive" development (UN CRC, 1993m:2). Thus the CRC has indicated that the problem of implementing international human rights obligations is truly one that needs to be attacked at both the national and the international levels.

But it is not only states parties that will prepare reports under Article 44. The CRC will also be required to submit a report to the General Assembly every two years. According to Article 44(5), these reports will cover the activities of the committee. Everyone who participated in drafting the convention recognized that the CRC should be expected to report on its activities, but they disagreed on the frequency, some arguing in favor of requiring annual reports and others in favor of permitting longer intervals. The CERD, CAT, and CEDAW all submit annual reports to the General Assembly. With the proliferation of reporting requirements of all sorts, however, the volume of reports now received by the General Assembly has apparently become as burdensome as has the volume of state reports submitted to the individual committees, and it was mainly for this reason that the drafters of the convention decided that the CRC should be required to report only every two years.

Although it has become standard practice for committees such as the CRC to report to the General Assembly, legitimate doubts can be raised about this practice. After all, the human rights conventions have been ratified by varying combinations of states and none by all of the member states of the United Nations. Why, then, should the committees report to the General Assembly? Should they not report only to the states parties to the conventions? Some argue that the states parties might develop a greater sense of responsibility to discuss substantive matters regarding the implementation of the conventions that they have ratified if the committees reported only to them. But the present practice of reporting to the General Assembly is defended on the ground that the conventions have been adopted by the General Assembly and that the issue of their effective implementation is, therefore, an issue for the entire assembly (Fletcher School of Law and Diplomacy, 1988:35 – 36).

Although Article 44(5) says nothing about the need to disseminate the information contained in the reports the CRC will submit to the General Assembly, this subject has been raised in various quarters just as it has been in the case of state reports. The chairs of the treaty bodies, for example, have argued in favor of more widespread dissemination of committee reports because press conferences and press releases issued at the end of sessions have not always been sufficiently covered by the media. Therefore, they have argued that it "would be helpful if the reports of committees could be synthesized from time to time and made available in more readable form for distribution to the general public." They have also agreed that information about the activities of the committees could perhaps be most effectively targeted "to the potentially most interested groups, such as lawyers, judges and teachers" (UN GA, 1990b:12). Some analysts, such as Philip Alston, have taken a more expansive view. He has argued for making the kind of information contained in committee reports available to people "outside the circle of the initiated," that is, to people other than specialists, and he suggests that this will be possible only if the reports are presented in a more readable form (UN GA, 1989b:52 – 53). Unfortunately, the shortage of financial and staff resources at the

Centre for Human Rights, a shortage that was discussed in chapter 7, will limit progress in this area.

PROCESSING REPORTS: ARTICLE 45

Once the Committee on the Rights of the Child receives reports from the states parties, what is it to do with them? Obviously, the committee will examine the reports with a view toward evaluating the progress the parties have made in meeting their obligations under the convention. But how is it to do this? Will the committee have to rely on its own resources? Or can it get help from entities such as international governmental and nongovernmental organizations? What role would the states play? Should the committee be able to make comments on the reports it receives? And should it be able to make recommendations to states regarding the steps they ought to take in meeting their obligations? These are among the issues addressed in Article 45 of the convention, which provides:

> In order to foster the effective implementation of the Convention and to encourage international co-operation in the field covered by the Convention:
> (a) The specialized agencies, the United Nations Children's Fund, and other United Nations organs shall be entitled to be represented at the consideration of the implementation of such provisions of the present Convention as fall within the scope of their mandate. The Committee may invite the specialized agencies, the United Nations Children's Fund and other competent bodies as it may consider appropriate to provide expert advice on the implementation of the Convention in areas falling within the scope of their respective mandates. The Committee may invite the specialized agencies, the United Nations Children's Fund, and other United Nations organs to submit reports on the implementation of the Convention in areas falling within the scope of their activities;
> (b) The Committee shall transmit, as it may consider appropriate, to the specialized agencies, the United Nations Children's Fund and other competent bodies, any reports from

States Parties that contain a request, or indicate a need, for technical advice or assistance, along with the Committee's observations and suggestions, if any, on these requests or indications.

(c) The Committee may recommend to the General Assembly to request the Secretary-General to undertake on its behalf studies on specific issues relating to the rights of the child;

(d) The Committee may make suggestions and general recommendations based on information received pursuant to articles 44 and 45 of the present Convention. Such suggestions and general recommendations shall be transmitted to any State Party concerned and reported to the General Assembly, together with comments, if any, from States Parties.

The Role of Governmental Representatives

Government officials will be at center stage when the CRC examines the reports it receives. In most cases, of course, government officials will have been instrumental in the preparation of the reports. Ideally, the CRC would like to meet with high-level government officials, preferably from ministries that are relevant to the implementation of the provisions of the convention. The committee believes that meetings with individuals of this sort would promote more effective and constructive dialogues with the state parties (UN CRC, 1992a:15). But it would be unreasonable to expect that all states would be able to send such high-level officials to Geneva to meet with the committee for one or two days. The expense alone would dissuade some states from doing so. It is likely, therefore, that at least some states will rely on diplomats attached to their United Nations mission office in Geneva to meet with the committee.

In any event, the committee makes its hopes and expectations clearly known to the states parties. As we shall see later in this chapter, after the committee completes its examination of a report, it issues "concluding observations," which touch on a number of subjects, including the type of dialogue that it had with the officials from the state party concerned. Thus, the committee congratulated Sweden for sending a high-level delegation, which "enabled a constructive dialogue to take place between the Committee and officials from those ministries directly responsible for the implementation of the Convention" (UN CRC, 1993j:1). The Russian Federation was also praised for the "high-level representation sent to discuss the report," which the committee took as an "indication of the importance attached by the Government of the Russian Federation to its obligations under the Convention"; the committee also praised the delegation for its open, comprehensive, and constructive approach in the dialogue with the committee (UN CRC, 1993k:1). Similarly, Vietnam was complimented for "engaging through a high-ranking delegation in a constructive and frank dialogue with the Committee" (UN CRC, 1993n:1). In the case of Bolivia, however, the committee took "note of the statement made by the delegation regretting that it had not been possible to include high-level representatives from the ministries concerned with the actual implementation of the Convention who could have benefited from direct dialogue with the Committee," but it praised the representatives who did participate for providing additional information and for endeavoring to answer all of the committee's questions (UN CRC, 1993i:1).

Before the meetings between the committee and the governmental officials, the reports are examined by the presessional working group. This group is assisted by a technical advisory group consisting of representatives of relevant United Nations bodies including specialized agencies and NGOs. The presessional working group draws up a list of questions, which is then sent to the governments through their permanent missions to the United Nations in Geneva. The governments are informed that the list of questions is not exhaustive and that the committee might ask additional questions, but the list is intended to facilitate a constructive dialogue between the committee and the government officials who will attend the meetings at which the report will be discussed

(UN CRC, 1993a:9 – 10). In practice, this has helped to save some time and to get the discussions going quickly with government officials of some states.

During the discussions of the reports with the government officials, members of the committee who are nationals of the country under review do not participate in the discussions. The committee decided that its members should not participate in such instances to ensure that there could be no question about the impartiality and objectivity of the results (UN CRC, 1992a:13).

The Role of Nonstate Actors

As indicated above, one of the important questions that the drafters of the convention had to address was whether and, if so, how nonstate actors, such as international governmental and nongovernmental organizations, could assist the Committee on the Rights of the Child in processing the reports it received from the states parties. The drafters' discussion of this matter was characterized by sharp philosophical disagreement. The representatives of several organizations, including UNICEF, the UNHCR, and various NGOs, argued that nonstate actors should be permitted to assist the CRC in the implementation of the convention. Basically, they argued that involvement by nonstate actors would make for a "dynamic" and "innovative" approach to the implementation of the convention (UN CHR, 1988:34). From their viewpoint, it was important for the CRC to have access to as much information as possible, and they saw themselves as suppliers of valuable information (UN GA, 1990b:16, 1989b:48).

The position that these organizations took on this issue is widely shared in the human rights community. The chairs of the treaty bodies, for example, have considered the contributions that specialized agencies of the United Nations could make in monitoring compliance with human rights treaties. In fact, they have noted the contributions made by agencies such as the ILO, the WHO, and UNESCO in supplying information to human rights committees, and they have endorsed the idea that "extensive co-operation with specialized agencies should continue to be encouraged through various means" (UN GA, 1990b:11).

The chairs of the treaty bodies have also urged each of the human rights committees to decide on means of cooperating with NGOS (UN GA, 1990b:11). NGOS are believed to make valuable contributions to the cause of human rights by pressuring governments to stop human rights abuses and even by acting on cases of abuse. But beyond that, some NGOS have played significant roles in assisting various human rights committees, providing information and stimulating public awareness of human rights treaties and conventions.

Perhaps a good role model in this regard is the Minneapolis-based International Women's Rights Action Watch (IWRAW), which has been especially interested in the CEDAW (UN GA, 1990b:11). In 1992, the IWRAW launched an ambitious experiment that, if effective, could be emulated by NGOS that are interested in the work of other human rights bodies. It prepared a report for the CEDAW's 1992 session in which it suggested specific questions that the committee members might ask about the reports they would be examining from seven states parties: Barbados, Czechoslovakia, El Salvador, Honduras, Spain, Sri Lanka, and Venezuela (IWRAW, 1992).

Calling its own report an "experimental new step in monitoring implementation" of the Convention on the Elimination of Discrimination Against Women, the IWRAW provided overall evaluations of the seven reports. It characterized the report of Barbados as "good" but added, "More information could have been given on the problems of women as single heads of households which are a large proportion of the country's population" (IWRAW, 1992:7). It criticized the El Salvador report for its "conspicuous absence of any reference whatsoever to the effects of the sixteen year civil war in which over 75,000 people" had died and for its failure to acknowledge "an economic crisis so profound that over 50% of the population is unemployed" (IWRAW, 1992:12). In the initial report of Honduras, it seized on what it called "a rather telling statement concerning the theory, policies and objectives of the National Health plan," which stated as follows: "It is inconceivable that the country could be developed without first developing the Honduran man. Man must be the supreme aim of our society. We have an inescapable mandate to transform him into a being capable of devoting his entire creative potential to productive work, which is the principal source of our wealth" (IWRAW, 1992:15). The IWRAW complimented Spain's report for its "self-critical honesty" but criticized it for being "somewhat difficult to read" (IWRAW, 1992:19). And it faulted the Venezuelan report as being "almost entirely abstract," which led to the conclusion that very little had been done for women between 1985 and 1988 (IWRAW, 1992:26). In addition to all of these criticisms, the IWRAW's report raised very specific questions about government policies and the status of women in each of the countries being reviewed.

Not everyone agrees, of course, that nonstate actors should be so extensively involved in "assisting" the human rights bodies to monitor the implementation of the conventions. In fact, when the Convention on the Rights of the Child was being drafted, the representatives of many governments disagreed with the specialized agencies and NGOs and argued that the responsibility for the implementation of the convention lay with the states parties. As they saw it, the convention was an agreement among states; therefore, only states were entitled to "control compliance." Although some governmental representatives were willing to allow the CRC to *invite* nonstate actors to assist it when appropriate, none seemed willing to concede nonstate actors a right even to be present during the examination of reports (UN CHR, 1988:34).

The different points of view on the matter were quite pronounced, so the working group that drafted the convention had to establish "working parties" in the hope of reaching a compromise that most drafters could accept (UN CHR, 1987:39–40, 1988:35).

Once agreement in principle had been reached in favor of permitting involvement by nonstate actors, specific questions arose concerning precisely how they would be able to assist the Committee on the Rights of the Child. What kinds of organizations, if any, should be permitted to be present when the committee considered the reports it received? What kinds of organizations should be allowed to provide advice to the committee? And what kinds of organizations should be permitted to submit reports containing information they had gathered on the status and rights of children (UN CHR, 1988:36, 1989b:126–27)?

The drafters addressed these questions in Article 45 of the convention. Although the article refers to specialized agencies, UNICEF, and "other United Nations organs" (understood broadly to include treaty bodies and nontreaty bodies, such as the Commission on Human Rights), it does not refer expressly to NGOs. However, it mentions "other competent bodies," and the drafters understood these words to refer especially, but not exclusively, to NGOs. In fact the drafters, who chose the words "other competent bodies" precisely because they were broad and all-inclusive, intended that the words would be understood in the "widest possible sense to include intergovernmental and non-governmental bodies" (UN CHR, 1988:36–37). For its part, the CRC adhered to this broad interpretation of the words when it adopted its rules of procedure at its first session in October 1991; to the committee, "other competent bodies" include "both intergovernmental organs outside the United Nations system and non-governmental organizations" (UN CRC, 1991g:10).

Article 45 makes a formal distinction between the specialized agencies, UNICEF, and "other United Nations organs" on the one hand and "other competent bodies" on the other. According to Article 45(a), the specialized agencies are "entitled to be represented at the consideration of the implementation" of those provisions of the convention that "fall within the scope of their mandate." They may also be invited by the CRC to "provide expert advice" and to "submit reports on the implementation of the Convention in areas falling within the scope of their activities." The "other competent bodies" are referred to mainly in the context of their providing expert advice to the CRC if invited to do so. In other words, from a strict interpretation of Article 45, it does not appear that NGOS would be entitled to participate at any stage in the processing of reports received by the committee. The rules of procedure adopted by the committee reaffirm this interpretation (UN CRC, 1991d: 7–16). In practice, however, this formal distinction may be of no great consequence. If anything, some members of the CRC expect more from NGOS than they do from specialized agencies or other organs. At the committee's first session, some members emphasized that the NGOS are likely to be especially important in providing information during the presessional stage of processing the reports received from states parties and that it will be important to maintain a two-way flow of information between the committee and the NGOS (UN CRC, 1991n:8–9).

According to Article 45(b), the CRC may transmit to any of the nonstate actors any reports that it receives from states parties that request, or indicate a need for, technical advice or assistance. The committee looks forward to such opportunities, seeing them as opening the way for it to play a catalyzing role in stimulating cooperation among specialized agencies and other United Nations bodies (UN CRC, 1991g:8). The terms of Article 45(c), which authorizes the committee to request studies on specific issues regarding the rights of the child, also probably offer the committee an opportunity to stimulate cooperative contacts among various types of organizations.

In practice, the CRC has been open to the participation of specialized agencies and other United Nations organs in the implementation of the convention, and several of them were represented at the committee's first session in October 1991, including the United Nations Centre for Social Development and Humanitarian Affairs, UNICEF, the UNHCR, the ILO, the FAO, the WHO, and the

World Food Program (UN CRC, 19910:1). Their representatives discussed their interests in various aspects of the convention. For example, the UNHCR's representatives, which estimated that there are between seven and eight million refugee children in the world, emphasized their special interest in Article 22 of the convention, which pertains to refugee children, and discussed how the UNHCR could offer these children international protection and assistance (UN CRC, 1991p:5–6, 1991q:2–12). Representatives of UNICEF, which has the broadest mandate to deal with issues affecting children, took a leading role among the specialized agencies. It claimed to have initiated a process of using the normative provisions of the convention as the basis for developing its country programs. It also claimed to have begun supporting "information and education campaigns to promote knowledge and awareness of the rights of the child," especially among children and young people, offering "training . . . to ensure that Governments, the United Nations and non-governmental organizations, as well as its own staff, were familiar with the provisions of the Convention and could act to ensure that their programmes had a positive influence on progress [toward the] implementation of the Convention," and supporting "the organization of informal consultations and field visits in regional venues" that might bring the CRC closer to the situation of children throughout the world (UN CRC, 1991p:2–3).

NGOs have also shown a keen interest in the convention, and they are likely to continue to do so in the future. Some twenty-four NGOs were listed as represented at the CRC's first session, including Defense for Children International, International Catholic Child Bureau, International Save the Children Alliance, and Radda Barnen International (UN CRC, 19910:2). The NGOs that had organized themselves into an ad hoc group during the drafting of the convention now reorganized themselves into "thematic subgroups" to discuss specific issues that concern them, and they hoped to form a network of NGOs so that they could maximize their ability to provide appropriate information to the Committee and other United

Nations bodies. The NGOs hoped that through the subgroups, they would be able to "reach out to the national level and NGO community in general in terms of feeding information from the Committee and other United Nations bodies so that the non-governmental community could continue to be informed of developments within the United Nations system." At this stage, the NGOs argued for retaining the group structure that already existed rather than creating a new overall structure (UN CRC, 1991n:2–7).

Participation by various United Nations organs and other governmental and nongovernmental organizations in the sessions of the CRC has continued; many of them were represented at the second (UN CRC, 1992a:8–9) and third (UN CRC, 1993a:9) sessions of the committee. Although it seems clear that these bodies are willing and able to help, there are bound to be limitations on how much they can do. The ILO, for example, has been helpful in discussing with the committee a variety of issues related to child labor in the world, particularly in the developing world. As discussed in chapter 6, the ILO has programs and projects aimed at the eventual eradication of child labor. Since child labor has implications for the economic exploitation of children, which concerns the CRC, the interests of the ILO and the CRC are joined. One can easily imagine how the interests of other organizations, such as the World Health Organization, and of the CRC would also coincide. But could any of these organizations be more helpful, for example, in research on child labor or health standards issues that may be of particular interest to the CRC? On this matter the organizations have made it clear that they cannot permit their own agendas to be determined by some other body such as the CRC (UN CRC, 1992m: 2–10, 1992n:2–8).

However, the committee could rely on its own resources and scholarly work to supplement the kind of information that would ordinarily be provided by governments and organizations. In fact, it has already taken such actions under Article 45(c) of the convention. Recognizing the importance of scholarly research, it has urged the secretariat to build a bibliographic network of materials on the rights of the child (UN CRC, 1992a:20). It has also undertaken special studies on its own, setting aside some of its meetings for a discussion of specific topics. As discussed in chapter 5, the committee devoted two of its meetings at its second session in October 1992 to a discussion of children in armed conflicts. Representatives of various IGOS and NGOS participated in the discussions, and the committee even adopted a preliminary draft protocol to the convention that would prohibit states from recruiting people under the age of eighteen into their armed forces (UN CRC, 1992a:19 – 21, 1993a:annex 7). It has also undertaken a special study of children subjected to economic exploitation, a broad and complex subject that is covered by several articles of the convention (UN CRC, 1993a:annex 3).

Comments and Recommendations

Most people would probably expect that human rights committees like the CRC would be able to make some specific comments on the reports received from states and to recommend appropriate courses of action if corrective measures seem warranted. After all, the committees supposedly examine the reports with a view to determining how well states are complying with their human rights obligations. The committees may find the reports inadequate to make a proper judgment regarding compliance, and they can usually request additional information. The CRC is authorized to make such requests under Article 44(4) of the convention, and it has adopted rules of procedure pertaining to that provision of the article (UN CRC, 1991d:15 – 17). In fact, as we have seen, the committee has already requested supplementary information from several states, notably Sudan but also Bolivia and Vietnam. But what if the committee believes that a state is not making sufficient progress in implementing the convention? Can it make comments on why it has reached such a conclusion? Can it go further and make recommendations regarding measures it feels the state should take?

The drafters of the convention discussed these questions during the later stages of their negotiations (UN CHR, 1988:40). Their conclusions are reflected in the terms of Article 45(d), which authorizes the CRC to "make suggestions and general recommendations" based on all the information it receives in accordance with Articles 44 and 45 of the convention. This means that the suggestions and general recommendations could be based on the content of the reports received from states and on information provided by the variety of nonstate actors we discussed above. The committee would notify the states of its suggestions and general recommendations, which it would include in its reports to the General Assembly, along with any responses it may have received from the states concerned. But the terms of Article 45(d) remain unclear on whether the committee can make specific suggestions to individual states, general recommendations to individual states, or only general recommendations to all the states parties together.

The CRC discussed the terms of Article 45(d) when it drafted its rules of procedure at its first session in October 1991. One viewpoint advanced what might be called a strict construction of the words "suggestions and general recommendations," maintaining that they meant that the CRC "might wish, on the basis of its consideration of a number of reports by States, to make comments on specific articles of the Convention." In other words, the suggestions or general recommendations would not be addressed to any particular state but rather would be addressed to all the parties as a group in the hope of assisting them "in the preparation of their reports and the implementation of the Convention" (UN CRC, 1991j:3).

The committee did not adopt this strict construction of its competence but rather decided that Article 45(d) authorizes it to make general comments on articles of the convention and general recommendations in the field of the rights of the child (UN CRC, 1991j:4). Moreover, it decided that after it examines the reports received from states parties, it will issue its "concluding observations," which will be an "authoritative comment with the purpose of defining outstanding problems and discussing remedies." It anticipates that these "observations will form the basis for discussions about technical advice or assistance" (UN CRC, 1991g:6).

The committee's intentions are commendable, and it has carved out an ambitious agenda for itself. In fact, after adopting its rules of procedure, the committee developed more specific guidelines for the preparation of its concluding observations. It did so because it believed that it should provide the states parties with an authoritative statement of its views regarding their progress in implementing the convention. The observations would "serve as a starting point for the periodic reports" that the states parties would submit at five-year intervals. The committee believed that it should follow a common pattern in issuing its concluding observations, and it decided to follow the same five-point scheme that is used by the Human Rights Committee, which functions under the International Covenant on Civil and Political Rights: (1) an introduction with general comments; (2) a section on progress achieved; (3) a section on factors and difficulties impeding the application of the convention; (4) a section on the principal subjects of concern; and (5) a final section including suggestions and recommendations to be addressed by the state party (UN CRC, 1992a:15–16, 1993h).

The committee has adhered strictly to this scheme, since all the concluding observations it has issued have followed the same pattern. In general, the committee seems to have tried to offer as much praise to governments as possible, but it has also offered straightforward criticisms of their policies and practices when it has believed it necessary to do so. Thus, the committee has complimented all the governments that have submitted reports for their early ratification of the Convention on the Rights of the Child and for timely submission of their reports. It has also specifically complimented some governments (e.g., Egypt and Vietnam) for their efforts to implement the convention throughout their territories.

But when more measures have been taken by governments, the committee has been more praiseworthy. For example, the committee was pleased to see that the government of the Russian Federation was "willing to define and appreciate" the problems that impeded the implementation of the convention and that the government continued to search for solutions to those problems, expand legislation, involve government at all levels, train social workers, allocate more resources, and invite the participation of NGOS in the implementation of the convention (UN CRC, 1993k:2). The government of Sweden was complimented for recognizing the need to take an active approach to implementing the convention, for trying to harmonize its national laws with the convention, for its openness to NGOS, and for its work as well as that of its NGOS to improve the situation of children worldwide (UN CRC, 1993j:1−2).

At the same time, the committee has recognized the genuine difficulties that some states have faced in implementing the convention. In the case of Vietnam, for example, the committee recognized the difficulties that have occurred in the "transition from a centrally planned to a market oriented economy," which "produces new, or aggravates old, social problems which have a negative impact on the situation of children" (UN CRC, 1993n:2). Similarly, it recognized economic difficulties in Egypt (UN CRC, 1993l:2) and Bolivia (UN CRC, 1993i:2) and noted the impact that these difficulties could have, especially on the implementation of those convention articles that deal with economic, social, or cultural rights. Nonetheless, it emphasized that Article 4 of the convention requires states to implement provisions that pertain to economic, social, and cultural rights to the maximum extent of their available resources.

The committee has also been quite blunt in expressing its principal areas of concern: the negative impact of recent economic and social reforms on children and child prostitution and pornography (Vietnam); the status of children in rural areas, child labor, the status of children in detention, and the "reality" of inequality between the sexes even if the law guarantees equality—an inequality that can be seen in the "pattern of disparity between boys and girls," particularly in the field of education (Egypt); the incompatibility of some areas of domestic legislation with the convention, for example, forced labor, slavery, and flogging as a form of punishment (Sudan); the effects of economic troubles on children, the serious problems of family life, and the increasing crime rate (Russian Federation); the gap between the less fortunate and the fortunate, especially in the areas of health and education (Bolivia); and the fact that the law does not appear to protect children against all forms of discrimination (Sweden).

Finally, the committee has made suggestions and recommendations to all the states that submitted reports. These ranged from the expected to what might seem novel or unusual. Most countries were urged to expand knowledge and awareness of the convention and the rights of the child as broadly as possible and to expand the involvement of NGOs in the implementation of the convention. Other recommendations were tailored to a country's specific situation. Thus, Vietnam was urged to take all necessary steps, including making use of all assistance available, to reduce the negative impact of economic reforms on children. Egypt was encouraged to take specific steps regarding discrimination and to seek the assistance of the ILO in undertaking studies on child labor. The Russian Federation was urged to monitor the effects of economic reforms on children; to improve family life, education, and health care; and to take "determined steps" to combat child prostitution. Overall, the committee showed a deep interest in especially vulnerable children in all countries, such as children who are economically and culturally disadvantaged, rural, and disabled. In some cases, the committee recommended that a state ratify other international human rights instruments. For example, it recommended that the Egyptian government consider ratifying ILO Convention No. 138 and others that pertain to such subjects as minimum ages of employment and the protection of children and young people at work. And it recommended that the government of Bolivia consider ratifying the Convention Against Torture.

The concluding observations already issued by the CRC indicate that the committee is off to a good start in trying to hold states accountable to the obligations they have assumed by ratifying the Convention on the Rights of the Child. It has found something to criticize in the policies and practices of all states, highly developed or underdeveloped. This strategy has undermined—though probably not eliminated—any arguments that the committee has been insensitive to the legitimate problems that states face in trying to fully implement the convention.

Nonetheless, the experience of other human rights bodies indicates that the committee will have to exercise some restraint, and be realistic and cautious, in issuing its concluding observations. On some occasions, higher political organs of the United Nations have reacted to the recommendations made by human rights committees, and these reactions have had a chilling effect on how the committees have gone about doing their work. The CERD and the CEDAW are both authorized to make suggestions and general recommendations based on the examination of the reports and information they receive from states. In its early years, the CERD interpreted its competence as allowing it to comment on the adequacy of the reports it received, but this practice was not well received by the General Assembly (UN GA, 1989a:11). In fact, the CERD's work was criticized by powerful and influential members of the Third Committee of the General Assembly during the early 1970s, including the United States, the United Kingdom, Canada, and France. These members objected to some of the committee's practices, including its "incursions into fields not within its competence, as when it requested information concerning relations between States Parties and racist regimes" (Lerner, 1980:146–47). The criticisms took their toll, curtailing the activism of the committee, which eventually discontinued its practice of commenting on the adequacy of the reports it received (UN GA, 1989a:11).

The CEDAW has also experienced negative reactions from states. During its early years, the committee was divided over how to interpret its authority to make suggestions and general recommendations, although a majority favored a broad interpretation (UN CEDAW, 1986a:4–7, 1986b:7–9, 1986c:6–7, 1986d:2–9, 1986e:7–11). The CEDAW makes what it calls "general recommendations" and "decisions," and its experience with both has been mixed. At its sixth session in 1987, for example, it adopted a "decision" in which it called on the "United Nations system as a whole, in particular the specialized agencies . . . and the Commission on the Status of Women, to promote or undertake studies on the status of women under Islamic laws and customs and in particular on the status and equality of women in the family on issues such as marriage, divorce, custody and property rights and their participation in public life of the society, taking into consideration the principle of *El Ijtihad* in Islam" (UN GA, 1987:80). The committee was motivated to request these studies because some of its members, lacking knowledge of Islam, felt uncomfortable dealing with reports that came from Islamic countries (UN GA, 1988b:17–18). But the committee was rebuked by the ECOSOC and the Third Committee of the General Assembly; the representatives of some Islamic states apparently misunderstood the committee's request and presumed it to be an attack against alleged discriminatory practices regarding women under Islam (UN GA, 1988b:18). The committee also had to move slowly in formulating and adopting a "general recommendation" on the eradication of female circumcision (UN CEDAW, 1988b:2–3; UN GA, 1990f:73). The acceptance of the general recommendation it eventually adopted in 1990, which contained specific recommendations regarding what states could do to eradicate the practice, was helped by the fact that organizations such as the WHO and UNICEF had developed an interest in the practice because of its serious health and other consequences for women and children (UN GA, 1990e:10, 80–81).

These experiences suggest that the human rights bodies' interest in maintaining a dialogue with states while monitoring their compliance with human rights obligations limits how far they can go in making specific suggestions and recommendations. It may, indeed, be impossible for these bodies to maintain a dialogue in some instances. But some analysts argue that the function of proposing corrective measures is perhaps better left to policy-making bodies such as the United Nations Commission on Human Rights or even the General Assembly (UN GA, 1989b:48 – 49). Although this may be true, it is difficult to imagine how the human rights committees can avoid getting into the fray in all instances if they are to engage in a true dialogue in examining the progress made by states in meeting international obligations on human rights.

Conclusion

MANY NONGOVERNMENTAL and intergovernmental organizations concerned with the rights of the child, and many specialists in the field, have hailed the adoption of the Convention on the Rights of the Child as a major achievement in the field of children's rights. Whatever its shortcomings or weaknesses, the convention's widespread ratification by states throughout the world, and its recognition in all serious debate about children's rights in important international fora, such as the World Summit for Children in 1990 and the World Conference on Human Rights in 1993, have made the convention the most authoritative standard-setting international instrument on the rights of the child. In fact, borrowing from Jack Donnelly (1986:599–642), one could say that the convention forms the centerpiece of an evolving international "regime"—defined loosely as a system of "norms and decision-making procedures that regulate an issue area"—on the rights of the child. The convention is the centerpiece of this regime because of its authoritative status. The regime is an evolving one in the sense that the convention is not the first, nor will it be the last, international instrument to proclaim or affirm rights of the child. In fact, as we have seen, some provisions of the convention have already been the subject of further elaboration, as in the case of Articles 20 and 21, which pertain to adoption. These articles set the basic framework for the negotiations on the new Hague Convention on intercountry adoptions.

The effort to further elaborate the norms affirmed in the Convention on the Rights of the Child is understandable, since some of its provisions are vague and require fuller definition if they are to be effectively implemented. This effort also reflects the dynamic rather than static nature of human rights norms and implementation procedures. The development of these norms and procedures has been an ongoing process throughout the post–World War II period. Some of the instruments adopted have been in the form of nonbinding declarations or resolutions; others have been in the form of conventions or treaties. Some have been global in application; others have been regional. Some have been general-purpose; others have been specific to certain groups of people. Ideally, in this dynamic process of the development of international human rights law, the norms and implementation procedures of the different instruments will complement and reinforce rather than contradict each other. In any event, the process of expansion and growth is not yet—and may never be—completed.

What can we conclude more specifically about the development of the Convention on the Rights of the Child as an exercise in the treaty-making process of the United Nations? Did the experience more or less conform to what we already know about that process? And what about the significance of the adoption of the convention? Is it likely to have any impact on the status and treatment of children?

The United Nations treaty-making process, as we discussed in chapters 1 and 2, has been the subject of intensive study in recent years by a number of scholars and practitioners, and many of them have criticized the process for its shortcomings and inefficiencies, which have affected the corpus of human rights law. Most critics have argued that there has been relatively little quality control in the conclusion of human rights instruments: proposals to draft treaties have originated in various forums at different levels of diplomatic interaction; they are oftentimes very poorly thought-out, lacking the kind of compelling rationale that would seem necessary in view of their lofty objectives; they raise problems of normative inconsistencies between and among related international instruments; and they have resulted in the proliferation of human rights implementation bodies that are insufficiently staffed and underfinanced, that are confined mainly to monitoring state compliance with international norms, and that lack any real supervisory or enforcement powers.

During the last two decades or so, the United Nations has tried to address these problems. For example, the General Assembly has urged the member states to concentrate more on effecting the implementation of existing human rights instruments than on adopting new ones. This recommendation has been reiterated on several occasions, most recently at the World Conference on Human Rights in June 1993. But the system as a whole manifests the tendencies for which it has been so thoroughly criticized, and change will be difficult.

The experience with the development of the Convention on the Rights of the Child reflected many of the shortcomings of the United Nations human rights lawmaking process. As we discussed in chapters 1 and 2, the initial proposal to draft the convention provided insufficient reasons for moving ahead with the project. In particular, no plausible criticisms of then existing international norms regarding the status and treatment of children were provided. Nor was the proposal itself put forward with sufficient clarity so as to give the member states of the United Nations a good sense of why they should proceed further with it. In every respect, the initial proposal bore the stamp of hasty improvisation rather than systematic craftsmanship. It was as though the main proponents of the proposal believed that the need for a convention was self-evident in the General Assembly's declaration of 1979 as the International Year of the Child. The adoption of a convention would have been a concrete achievement of the celebrations of that year.

Furthermore, at no time during the early deliberations was there ever an express decision by any United Nations body to move ahead with the drafting of a convention. Even though many states, particularly Western states, had serious reservations about proceeding with the project, the reservations were couched in such vague and weak terms that they were to no effect. In the main, rather than addressing squarely the question of the need or desirability of a new convention on the rights of the child, those who

had reservations about the project concentrated on what they argued were technical weaknesses of the initial Polish draft. This
strategy reflected the importance of political considerations in the
early stages of the deliberations over whether a convention on the
rights of the child was necessary or desirable. Many states, perhaps
concerned about offending another state, showed a distinct reluctance to oppose the initiative that the Polish delegation had taken
in proposing the drafting of the convention. Those states that were
closely aligned to Poland at that time on ideological grounds,
namely, the East European members of the Soviet bloc, were the
most reluctant to speak out against the conclusion of a convention.
In fact, they spoke in favor of the project. But, overall, it was probably more important that the proposal to draft a convention was
not actively opposed by any states, even though it was not actively
supported by many states. In this way, the convention developed a
life of its own. The Western states' strategy of raising questions of
an essentially technical nature could not stop the momentum that
was building for the conclusion of a convention.

It is arguable that the convention looks at the child in a dual perspective, that is, in a more traditional perspective as an object of
protection and in a more progressive perspective as a possessor of
rights in his or her own right. But although much has been made
of this by the most ardent admirers of the convention, the perspective is perhaps less progressive and more protective than many
of them might have hoped for. The convention is progressive in the
sense that it aims to empower children in some important respects,
for example, in the areas of freedom of expression and thought,
conscience, and religion. Nonetheless, as we discussed in chapters
3 through 6, the convention is actually quite weak in the area of
empowerment rights, conceding substantial control and discretion to parents and guardians or the state. The convention is traditional in the sense that it reflects a very strong concern for the protection of children from the economic and social conditions that
define their lives and that are the breeding grounds for various
forms of abuse and maltreatment.

The reasons for the stronger tendency toward traditionalism in the convention are not hard to find. In the first place, the negotiations on the convention were being conducted and brought to a close at a time when the situation of children worldwide was at or near a crisis point. Reports of the abuse and exploitation of children have become commonplace in recent years. The drafters of the convention would have found it difficult if not impossible to ignore these reports. It was only natural, therefore, that the drafters would have been drawn more to the protection than to the liberation of children. Second, the fact that the traditional approach to children's rights has been to protect rather than to liberate also contributed to the preoccupation of the drafters. The historical perception of children as vulnerable to societal forces beyond their control has made the impulse to protect them very strong. In other words, historically, there has been more concern about the impact that such things as economic forces have on the lives, well-being, and sense of security of children than about whether they are able freely to exercise such rights as freedom of expression, freedom of association or assembly, or freedom of thought, conscience, and religion. Third, the drafters faced the reality of the tension that exists between the rights of the child and the rights of parents to control their children. Nor could they avoid emphasizing the responsibilities of the state in attending to issues that affect the welfare of children. The drafters did not stand alone in defense of this traditionalism. There are still strong, articulate, and thoughtful advocates (e.g., Purdy, 1992) of the view that the main concern for children *should* be to protect rather than liberate them.

Several trends characterized the negotiations on the convention and affected the character of its norms and implementation mechanism. First, although nonstate actors were involved in the drafting process, governmental representatives were dominant. In this connection, it is noteworthy that the Western states, which had the most serious reservations about the drafting of a new convention on the rights of the child, took the lead in the negotiation process and had a great impact on the final form and content of the convention. They were assisted in this process mainly by some states in the East European region. As a result of the efforts of these states, the convention "grew" substantially from a document with a handful of articles to a lengthy, detailed, and complex instrument that contains many articles pertaining to the survival, membership, protection, and empowerment rights of the child and that includes an implementation mechanism to monitor state progress toward the realization of those rights.

Although the states in the West and East European regions were the main participants in the negotiating process, no single state, or small group of states, dominated the shaping of all the major provisions of the convention. Instead, individual states and groups of states took strong stands on different articles and managed to get their way in some circumstances. The United States, for example, maintained very strong positions on a range of traditional civil and political rights and, for the most part, prevailed. But some other Western states, for example, Canada and Sweden, introduced proposals that were instrumental in shaping the implementation mechanism of the convention. Some Western states had special, more narrow interests. For example, the French delegation to the drafting group lobbied aggressively and with some success on the convention provisions that deal with the abduction of children (Article 35), a problem that has been important to the French government in its relations with some Arab states.

In contrast to the West and East European states, Third World states, with so much at stake because of their enormous populations of children, showed relatively little interest in the convention during the drafting stage and, indeed, did not become actively involved until the final stages, undoing the consensus that had been previously reached on a number of issues that were vitally important to them. The conventional explanation for this behavior is that Third World countries lack the financial resources or personnel to participate in such activities to the same extent as the more developed states of West and East Europe. Yet, they have been quick to ratify the convention even if its effective implementation would call for substantial outlays of financial resources, which they presumably lack. In all probability, there is more at work here than simply a lack of resources or personnel; there are different perceptions of international law and its place in the further development and strengthening of human rights norms and procedures.

Nonstate actors such as international governmental and nongovernmental organizations, as well as specialized agencies and other United Nations bodies, participated in the drafting of the Convention on the Rights of the Child with varying degrees of intensity and effectiveness. The interests of the IGOs, specialized agencies, and other United Nations bodies tended to be narrow, generally confined to issues and problems that fall more precisely within their mandates. Given their historical experiences and vulnerability to political pressures from states, this is probably the most that could have been expected from these organizations and agencies.

The NGOs were more active, even organizing themselves into a group to increase the effectiveness of their lobbying activities, and their interests were much broader than those of the IGOs, specialized agencies, and other United Nations bodies. Just as some regional groups of states emerged as the most important states in the drafting process, a core group of NGOs took the lead. The question for the future, as far as the NGOs are concerned, is whether they will be able to maintain high visibility in the implementation of the convention, in which they will have a role to play. Like other nonstate actors, NGOs can be subjected to political pressures, and they have been attacked from various quarters when they have been perceived as being too active or have been suspected of bias (see, e.g., Chiang Pei-heng, 1981). Such attacks can limit the potential effectiveness of NGOs, but it is clear that states continue to assert their own primacy, and one manifestation of this may be occasional attacks against NGOs. At the World Conference on Human Rights, NGOs were excluded from participating in the preparation of the final act or declaration, which some criticized as a "flawed document." They also expressed concern about what they perceived as a failure of the conference to take a forward-looking approach to human rights problems and about some statements in the final declaration, which they considered condescending toward the proper role of NGOs in the human rights field (*New York Times*, 1993).

The second major point that should be emphasized about the negotiation of the Convention on the Rights of the Child concerns the norms of the convention. Although the drafters did a good job of integrating what have traditionally been considered civil and political rights and economic, social, and cultural rights into one instrument, the convention is not, at least as far as the definition of its norms is concerned, a very innovative instrument. In principle, there is no reason why an international agreement cannot go beyond standards that are already accepted in international or domestic law—that it cannot be used to *advance* the expansion of human rights norms. There are many who dispute this as a real possibility, however. They argue that the most that can be hoped for is that international instruments will *reflect* the most expansive view of a given subject that is already accepted by the international community of states.

Whatever can be said for either viewpoint, the result in the case of the Convention on the Rights of the Child was a general lack of innovation in defining the norms. In other words, for the most part, rather than affirming new rights or defining well-established rights more broadly than they have been in other international instruments, the convention reaffirms rights that have already been affirmed in other instruments. Article 38 of the convention, which pertains to the participation of children in armed conflicts, provides one of the best examples of this lack of innovation. Although some drafters wanted to go beyond the present standards of international humanitarian law, under which states can recruit people as young as fifteen years of age into their armed forces, and to establish a new, higher threshold figure of eighteen years of age, the proposals to do so were met with very strong resistance from powerful and influential states such as the United States.

In part, the lack of innovation may have been caused by the decision-making procedure that was used, namely, consensus. The need to reach a consensus forced the delegates to the working group to more often than not take the path of least resistance. Indeed, whenever they faced serious difficulties with specifying details of rights, the drafters usually abandoned the effort altogether and adopted a watered-down formula that would be acceptable to all concerned. In some cases, such as issues related to intercountry adoptions and abductions of children, the drafters left very important issues unresolved and, therefore, left them to future determination in other international instruments. But in addition to the decision-making procedure, the lack of innovation seems to have been due to the attitude of many delegates. The arguments that surrounded the adoption of Article 38 on the participation of young people in armed conflicts — that the convention was not the proper place to rewrite international humanitarian law — reflects the importance of attitudes.

This point can be carried further. In the negotiations, it was evident that the drafters of the convention were primarily concerned with making the provisions compatible with their own domestic laws and not the other way around. Thus, on several occasions during the negotiations, the representatives of Germany, the Netherlands, and the United Kingdom, among others, spoke out against proposals that would have affected their immigration laws and policies. Aware of their states' recent problems with immigrants, they wanted to maintain maximum flexibility and discretion in adopting and enforcing their own laws.

Third, the norms of the convention were very much affected by such things as different cultural and religious values and legal and political systems of peoples and states throughout the world. Compromise was the order of the day and was necessary in order to conclude a convention that would be acceptable to the largest number of states. As Adam Lopatka, the chair of the drafting group, pointed out in the Human Rights Commission and the Third Committee of the General Assembly before the convention was formally adopted, it had been "necessary to reconcile numerous differences relating to traditions, cultures, religions, levels of economic development, legal systems and, indeed, political attitudes" during the negotiations. Hence, the text of the convention represented a "broad consensus on what should be the obligations of the family, society and the international community towards children." In his view, the convention was "realistic," but he conceded that it could have been more "ambitious" (UN CHR, 1989g:2; UN GA C.3, 1989a:2–3).

As discussed in chapters 3 through 6, some of the most significant compromises based on cultural and religious considerations were reached in connection with Article 14, on freedom of thought, conscience, and religion, and Articles 20 and 21, on adoption. For each of these articles, several Islamic states were able to force the adoption of provisions, resisted in varying degrees by Western and other states, that they argued made the convention's terms more acceptable to them given their religious precepts.

Article 24, on the right to an adequate standard of health care, provides another illustration of the importance of cultural values. In this case, the issue was "traditional practices" that are injurious to the health of women and young girls in particular, practices such as female circumcision, a tradition mainly in Africa. Of course, other harmful traditional practices exist, such as son preference, but the one that most drafters seemed to be especially concerned about was female circumcision. The vague provision that was eventually adopted in Article 24—which merely obliges the states parties to the convention to take "all effective and appropriate" measures to abolish traditional practices prejudicial to the health of children—fell short of what the representatives of some Western states would have liked to see. However, the issue may be effectively addressed, even if over a longer period of time, by concerted action at the national level. At least one United Nations study of the practice of female circumcision has shown that some African heads of state and government have come out strongly against the practice, and national organizations have been working to make advances against the tradition. In this way, a strong, new international consensus could eventually emerge. It might have been helped along, however, by being specifically mentioned in Article 24.

Differences in political systems too had an effect on the norms of the convention, but mainly in the earliest stages of the negotiations. The Convention on the Rights of the Child is the first major international human rights instrument to have been negotiated over the years that witnessed the end of the cold war between East and West and the beginning of a new era of cooperation. Indeed, as one looks back over the ten years during which the negotiations on the convention took place, it is remarkable how much progress was made in overcoming sharp ideological differences between East and West. During the early 1980s, the representatives of the United States and the Soviet Union clashed over such matters as the proper role of the state in providing material assistance in the care of children and the extent to which the convention could affirm rights of an essentially civil and political nature. In the later 1980s, however, dramatic changes occurred, and the U.S. and Soviet delegates, and others from Eastern Europe as well, more easily agreed on issues that would previously have been taboo. One of the most notable examples of this was the recognition in Article 10 of the right of the child and his or her parents to leave and return to their country. The extraordinary degree of cooperation that these previously adversarial states were able to achieve on this and other issues made it possible for the drafting group to reach a consensus more quickly than would otherwise have been possible. It also reflected how changes in international relations outside the United Nations can affect relations within the organization on matters of "low" politics, such as human rights, and on matters of "high" politics, such as security (e.g., the Persian Gulf War).

Since the convention has been ratified by such a large number of states with different cultures and political systems, the compromises that were reached seem to have had the desired effect. In some very sensitive matters, the states parties have been able to "read" into the convention what they want to see without undermining or negating its express terms. Perhaps the best example of this is the effect of the compromise reached on the very sensitive issue of abortion. The wording of Article 1 of the convention — that a "child" is every human being below eighteen years of age — has made it possible for some predominantly Roman Catholic countries and the Holy See to say that they understand life as beginning at the moment of conception. At the same time, the United Kingdom's government can say that it understands the convention to be applicable following a live birth.

Yet, despite the compromises, some of the parties, as we have seen, ratified the convention with reservations even to articles that they had helped to shape to their own liking. Very few states have objected to the reservations made by the states parties to the convention, and those that have objected have not gone so far as to indicate that they do not consider themselves in treaty relations with the reserving state. In general, experience with the reservations to the Convention on the Rights of the Child suggests that the reservation regime of the Vienna Convention on the Law of Treaties does not work very well in practice. Although it seems to foster universal acceptance, as reflected in the large number of parties to the convention, its ability to check for abusive interpretations that could undermine the integrity of the convention provisions is very weak.

Fourth, the drafters of the convention often expressed concern about maintaining its normative consistency with the provisions of other general-purpose as well as specific, including child-specific, human rights instruments. Among the most frequently mentioned, and of greatest concern, were the International Covenants on Civil and Political Rights and on Economic, Social and Cultural Rights. In addition, provisions of other specialized human rights conventions such as the Convention on the Elimination of Racial Discrimination, the Convention on the Elimination of Discrimination Against Women, and the Convention Against Torture were taken into account. In some instances, when very specific aspects of rights were being discussed, the drafters took into account the provisions of very specialized conventions adopted under the auspices of the ILO or UNESCO.

Fifth, and finally, the structure and functions of the implementation mechanism of the convention, the Committee on the Rights of the Child, also reflect the drafters' mixed attitude toward innovation. As discussed in chapters 7 and 8, the committee is patterned on human rights bodies that have been established under other specialized human rights conventions, including the Convention on the Elimination of Racial Discrimination, the Convention on the Elimination of Discrimination Against Women, and the Convention Against Torture. Like these other bodies, the CRC will be an uninstructed body, which should help to reduce, though not necessarily eliminate, the importance of political factors in its decision-making. The drafters were somewhat innovative in dealing with the monitoring powers of the committee in that they explicitly recognized the contributions that "other competent bodies," including NGOs, could make in monitoring compliance with the convention. The NGOs could indeed make significant, but nonetheless limited, contributions in this regard.

But there is nothing about the CRC's structure that is truly innovative. In fact, the same kinds of problems that have plagued other human rights bodies can be expected to affect the operations of the CRC as well. For example, none of the financing arrangements that have been utilized have worked well in practice. The CRC will be financed through the regular United Nations budget, which many analysts believe to be the best method of financing its work. But even though the states parties and the secretary-general have been generous so far in enabling the committee to hold sessions, the very serious overall financial problems of the United Nations, problems that are now, if anything, becoming more acute, will probably take their toll on the operation of the CRC, as they have on other committees, such as the CEDAW, that are financed through the regular budget. In addition, the effective operation of the committee is bound to be affected by the staff and resource shortages of the United Nations Centre for Human Rights, which will be primarily responsible for servicing the committee. Although both of these problems are, strictly speaking, financial in nature, they are fundamentally political problems with financial implications, that is, they reveal a lack of interest or will on the part of states to faithfully make their financial contributions to the United Nations or specific human rights programs on time.

Also, like other specialized human rights bodies, the committee will have to rely on the submission of reports by the states parties to assess their progress toward the implementation of the provisions of the convention. The primary responsibility for the implementation of the convention falls first and foremost to the legislative, administrative, and judicial institutions of the individual states that ratify it. The most that can be expected of the committee at the international level is that it will be able to monitor the application of the convention by the states parties through the examination of reports and through the formulation of recommendations on how the states parties might best go about implementing the convention. In this endeavor, the committee is off to a very good start in some respects. It has been aggressive in interpreting its mandate, and it has laid out an ambitious agenda for itself. It has taken a holistic approach to the convention, emphasizing the indivisibility of the civil, political, economic, social, and cultural rights of the child. It has also clearly indicated what it expects the reports of the states parties to contain and the format that it will use in specifying its suggestions and recommendations in its concluding observations and comments. But these are the most encouraging aspects of the committee's experience so far. On the negative side, the committee is already beginning to face — as have other committees of its type — serious problems with the nonsubmission of reports by many states parties.

Given the amount of time and energy that analysts have devoted to studying the problem of the nonsubmission of reports to other human rights bodies, and the failure of any of their recommendations to reduce the occurrence of nonsubmissions to any appreciable degree, it is tempting to think that a major restructuring of the United Nations human rights implementation system is necessary and that, among other things, greater efforts at consolidating the reporting requirements will increase the volume and quality of the reports received. But a restructuring would not address the major causes of the problem, and the most important of these causes is probably the attitude of many states. Some states are undoubtedly unable to meet their reporting requirements for legitimate reasons, such as a lack of resources or trained personnel. But most states that fail to report probably could do so if they were willing. To them, the ratification of human rights instruments is important for various reasons, including the image that they wish to project to other states, the image that they are concerned about — or at least not indifferent to — human rights. A restructuring of the human rights implementation system, however drastic, will not change their attitude. To effectively address the basic needs of children will require more than a legal commitment; it will require a political commitment on the part of governments to provide the resources necessary to deal effectively with those needs. Still, the legal commitment, such as that embodied in the Convention on the Rights of the Child, can provide the standard against which government actions and policies can be evaluated.

APPENDIX A

THE GENEVA DECLARATION OF
THE RIGHTS OF THE CHILD (1924)

By the present Declaration of the Rights of the Child, commonly known as the Declaration of Geneva, men and women of all nations, recognizing that mankind owes to the child the best that it has to give, declare and accept as their duty that, beyond and above all considerations race, nationality or creed:

I. The child must be given the means requisite for its normal development, both materially and spiritually.

II. The child that is hungry must be fed; the child that is sick must be nursed; the child that is backward must be helped; the delinquent child must be reclaimed; and the orphan and the waif must be sheltered and succored.

III. The child must be the first to receive relief in times of distress.

IV. The child must be put in a position to earn a livelihood and must be protected against every form of exploitation.

V. The child must be brought up in the consciousness that its talents must be devoted to the service of its fellowmen.

THE DECLARATION OF THE
RIGHTS OF THE CHILD (1959)

Preamble

Whereas the peoples of the United Nations have, in the Charter, reaffirmed their faith in fundamental human rights and in the dignity and worth of the human person, and have determined to promote social progress and better standards of life in larger freedom,

Whereas the United Nations has, in the Universal Declaration of Human Rights, proclaimed that everyone is entitled to all the rights and freedoms set forth therein, without distinction of any kind, such as race, color, sex, language, religion, political or other opinion, national or social origin, property, birth or other status,

Whereas the child, by reason of his physical and mental immaturity, needs special safeguards and care, including appropriate legal protection, before as well as after birth,

Whereas the need for such special safeguards has been stated in the Geneva Declaration of the Rights of the Child of 1924, and recognized in the Universal Declaration of Human Rights and in the statutes of specialized agencies and international organizations concerned with the welfare of children,

Whereas mankind owes to the child the best it has to give,

Now therefore,

The General Assembly

Proclaims this Declaration of the Rights of the Child to the end that he may have a happy childhood and enjoy for his own good and for the good of society the rights and freedoms herein set forth, and calls upon parents, upon men and women as individuals, and upon voluntary organizations, local authorities and national Governments to recognize these rights and strive for their observance by legislative and other measures progressively taken in accordance with the following principles:

Principle 1

The child shall enjoy all the rights set forth in this Declaration. Every child, without any exception whatsoever, shall be entitled to these rights, without distinction or discrimination on account of race, color, sex, language, religion, political or other opinion, national or social origin, property, birth or other status, whether of himself or of his family.

Principle 2

The child shall enjoy special protection, and shall be given opportunities and facilities, by law and by other means, to enable him to develop physically, mentally, morally, spiritually and socially in a healthy and normal manner and in conditions of freedom and dignity. In the enactment of laws for this purpose, the best interests of the child shall be the paramount consideration.

Principle 3

The child shall be entitled from his birth to a name and a nationality.

Principle 4

The child shall enjoy the benefits of social security. He shall be entitled to grow and develop in health; to this end, special care and protection shall be provided both to him and to his mother, including adequate pre-natal and post-natal care. The child shall have the right to adequate nutrition, housing, recreation and medical services.

Principle 5

The child who is physically, mentally or socially handicapped shall be given the special treatment, education and care required by his particular condition.

Principle 6

The child, for the full and harmonious development of his personality, needs love and understanding. He shall, wherever possible, grow up in the care and under the responsibility of his parents, and, in any case, in an atmosphere of affection and of moral and material security; a child of tender years shall not, save in exceptional circumstances, be separated from his mother. Society and the public authorities shall have the duty to extend particular care to children without a family and to those without adequate means of support. Payment of State and other assistance towards the maintenance of children of large families is desirable.

Principle 7

The child is entitled to receive education, which shall be free and compulsory, at least in the elementary stages. He shall be given an education which will promote his general culture and enable him, on a basis of equal opportunity, to develop his abilities, his individual judgement, and his sense of moral and social responsibility, and to become a useful member of society.

The best interests of the child shall be the guiding principle of those responsible for his education and guidance; that responsibility lies in the first place with his parents.

The child shall have full opportunity for play and recreation, which should be directed to the same purposes as education; society and the public authorities shall endeavour to promote the enjoyment of this right.

Principle 8

The child shall in all circumstances be among the first to receive protection and relief.

Principle 9

The child shall be protected against all forms of neglect, cruelty and exploitation. He shall not be the subject of traffic, in any form.

The child shall not be admitted to employment before an appropriate minimum age; he shall in no case be caused or permitted to engage in any occupation or employment which would prejudice his health or education, or interfere with his physical, mental or moral development.

Principle 10

The child shall be protected from practices which may foster racial, religious and any other form of discrimination. He shall be brought up in a spirit of understanding, tolerance, friendship among peoples, peace and universal brotherhood, and in full consciousness that his energy and talents should be devoted to the service of his fellow men.

THE CONVENTION ON THE
RIGHTS OF THE CHILD (1989)

Preamble

The States Parties to the Present Convention,

Considering that, in accordance with the principles proclaimed in the Charter of the United Nations, recognition of the inherent dignity and of the equal and inalienable rights of all members of the human family is the foundation of freedom, justice and peace in the world,

Bearing in mind that the peoples of the United Nations have, in the Charter, reaffirmed their faith in fundamental human rights and in the dignity and worth of the human person, and have determined to promote social progress and better standards of life in larger freedom,

Recognizing that the United Nations has, in the Universal Declaration of Human Rights and in the International Covenants on Human Rights, proclaimed and agreed that everyone is entitled to all the rights and freedoms set forth therein, without distinction of any kind, such as race, color, sex, language, religion, political or other opinion, national or social origin, property, birth or other status,

Recalling that, in the Universal Declaration of Human Rights, the United Nations has proclaimed that childhood is entitled to special care and assistance,

Convinced that the family, as the fundamental group of society and the natural environment for the growth and well-being of all its members and particularly children, should be afforded the necessary protection and assistance so that it can fully assume its responsibilities within the community,

Recognizing that the child, for the full and harmonious development of his or her personality, should grow up in a family environment, in an atmosphere of happiness, love and understanding,

Considering that the child should be fully prepared to live an individual life in society, and brought up in the spirit of the ideals proclaimed in the Charter of the United Nations, and in particular in the spirit of peace, dignity, tolerance, freedom, equality and solidarity,

Bearing in mind that the need to extend particular care to the child has been stated in the Geneva Declaration on the Rights of the Child of 1924 and in the Declaration of the Rights of the Child adopted by the United Nations in 1959 and recognized in the Universal Declaration of Human Rights, in the International Covenant on Civil and Political Rights (in particular in articles 23 and 24), in the International Covenant on Economic, Social and Cultural Rights (in particular in its article 10) and in the statutes and relevant instruments of specialized agencies and international organizations concerned with the welfare of children,

Bearing in mind that, as indicated in the Declaration of the Rights of the Child adopted by the General Assembly on 20 November 1959, "the child, by reason of his physical and mental immaturity, needs special safeguards and care, including appropriate legal protection, before as well as after birth",

Recalling the provisions of the Declaration on Social and Legal Principles relating to the Protection and Welfare of Children, with Special Reference to Foster Placement and Adoption Nationally and Internationally; the United Nations Standard Minimum Rules for the Administration of Juvenile Justice (The Beijing Rules); and the Declaration on the Protection of Women and Children in Emergency and Armed Conflict,

Recognizing that, in all countries in the world, there are children living in exceptionally difficult conditions, and that such children need special consideration,

Taking due account of the importance of the traditions and cultural values of each people for the protection and harmonious development of the child,

Recognizing the importance of international co-operation for improving the living conditions of children in every country, in particular in the developing countries,

Have agreed as follows:

PART I

Article 1

For the purpose of the present Convention, a child means every human being below the age of eighteen years unless, under the law applicable to the child, majority is attained earlier.

Article 2

1. The States Parties to the present Convention shall respect and ensure the rights set forth in the Convention to each child within their respective jurisdiction without discrimination of any kind, irrespective of the child's or his or her parent's or legal guardian's race, color, sex, language, religion, political or other opinion, national, ethnic or social origin, property, disability, birth or other status.

2. States Parties shall take all appropriate measures to ensure that the child is protected against all forms of discrimination or punishment on the basis of the status, activities, expressed opinions, or beliefs of the child's parents, legal guardians, or family members.

Article 3

1. In all actions concerning children, whether undertaken by public or private social welfare institutions, courts of law, administrative authorities or legislative bodies, the best interests of the child shall be a primary consideration.

2. States Parties undertake to ensure the child such protection and care as is necessary for his or her well-being, taking into account the rights and duties of his or her parents, legal guardians, or other individuals legally responsible for him or her, and, to this end, shall take all appropriate legislative and administrative measures.

3. States Parties shall ensure that the institutions, services and facilities responsible for the care or protection of children shall conform with the standards established by competent authorities, particularly in the areas of safety, health, in the number and suitability of their staff, as well as competent supervision.

Article 4

States Parties shall undertake all appropriate legislative, administrative, and other measures for the implementation of the rights recognized in this Convention. With regard to economic, social and cultural rights, States Parties shall undertake such measures to the maximum extent of their available resources and, where needed, within the framework of international co-operation.

Article 5

States Parties shall respect the responsibilities, rights and duties of parents or, where applicable, the members of the extended family or community as provided for by local custom, legal guardians or other persons legally responsible for the child, to provide, in a manner consistent with the evolving capacities of the child, appropriate direction and guidance in the exercise by the child of the rights recognized in the present Convention.

Article 6

1. States Parties recognize that every child has the inherent right to life.

2. States Parties shall ensure to the maximum extent possible the survival and development of the child.

Article 7

1. The child shall be registered immediately after birth and shall have the right from birth to a name, the right to acquire a nationality and, as far as possible, the right to know and be cared for by his or her parents.

2. States Parties shall ensure the implementation of these rights in accordance with their national law and their obligations under the relevant international instruments in this field, in particular where the child would otherwise be stateless.

Article 8

1. States Parties undertake to respect the right of the child to preserve his or her identity, including nationality, name and family relations as recognized by law without unlawful interference.

2. Where a child is illegally deprived of some or all of the elements of his or her identity, States Parties shall provide appropriate assistance and protection, with a view to speedily re-establishing his or her identity.

Article 9

1. States Parties shall ensure that the child shall not be separated from his or her parents against their will, except when competent authorities

subject to judicial review determine, in accordance with applicable law and procedures, that such separation is necessary for the best interests of the child. Such determination may be necessary in a particular case such as one involving abuse or neglect of the child by the parents, or one where the parents are living separately and a decision must be made as to the child's place of residence.

2. In any proceedings pursuant to paragraph 1, all interested parties shall be given an opportunity to participate in the proceedings and make their views known.

3. States Parties shall respect the right of the child who is separated from one or both parents to maintain personal relations and direct contact with both parents on a regular basis, except if it is contrary to the child's best interests.

4. Where such separation results from any action initiated by a State Party, such as the detention, imprisonment, exile, deportation or death (including death arising from any cause while the person is in the custody of the State) of one or both parents or of the child, that State Party shall, upon request, provide the parents, the child or, if appropriate, another member of the family with the essential information concerning the whereabouts of the absent member(s) of the family unless the provision of the information would be detrimental to the well-being of the child. States Parties shall further ensure that the submission of such a request shall of itself entail no adverse consequences for the person(s) concerned.

Article 10

1. In accordance with the obligation of States Parties under article 9, paragraph 1, applications by a child or his or her parents to enter or leave a State Party for the purpose of family reunification shall be dealt with by States Parties in a positive, humane and expeditious manner. States Parties shall further ensure that the submission of such a request shall entail no adverse consequences for the applicants and for the members of their family.

2. A child whose parents reside in different States shall have the right to maintain on a regular basis save in exceptional circumstances personal relations and direct contacts with both parents. Towards that end and in accordance with the obligation of States Parties under article 9, paragraph 2, States Parties shall respect the right of the child and his or her

parents to leave any country, including their own, and to enter their own country. The right to leave any country shall be subject only to such restrictions as are prescribed by law and which are necessary to protect the national security, public order (*ordre public*), public health or morals or the rights and freedoms of others and are consistent with the other rights recognized in the present Convention.

Article 11

1. States Parties shall take measures to combat the illicit transfer and non-return of children abroad.

2. To this end, States Parties shall promote the conclusion of bilateral or multilateral agreements or accession to existing agreements.

Article 12

1. States Parties shall assure to the child who is capable of forming his or her own views the right to express those views freely in all matters affecting the child, the views of the child being given due weight in accordance with the age and maturity of the child.

2. For this purpose, the child shall in particular be provided the opportunity to be heard in any judicial and administrative proceedings affecting the child, either directly, or through a representative or an appropriate body, in a manner consistent with the procedural rules of national law.

Article 13

1. The child shall have the right to freedom of expression; this right shall include freedom to seek, receive and impart information and ideas of all kinds, regardless of frontiers, either orally, in writing or in print, in the form of art, or through any other media of the child's choice.

2. The exercise of this right may be subject to certain restrictions, but these shall only be such as are provided by law and are necessary:

(a) For respect of the rights or reputations of others; or

(b) For the protection of national security or of public order (*ordre public*), or of public health or morals.

Article 14

1. States Parties shall respect the right of the child to freedom of thought, conscience and religion.

2. States Parties shall respect the rights and duties of the parents and,

when applicable, legal guardians, to provide direction to the child in the exercise of his or her right in a manner consistent with the evolving capacities of the child.

3. Freedom to manifest one's religion or beliefs may be subject only to such limitations as are prescribed by law and are necessary to protect public safety, order, health or morals, or the fundamental rights and freedoms of others.

Article 15

1. States Parties recognize the rights of the child to freedom of association and to freedom of peaceful assembly.

2. No restrictions may be placed on the exercise of these rights other than those imposed in conformity with the law and which are necessary in a democratic society in the interests of national security or public safety, public order (*ordre public*), the protection of public health or morals or the protection of the rights and freedoms of others.

Article 16

1. No child shall be subjected to arbitrary or unlawful interference with his or her privacy, family, home or correspondence, nor to unlawful attacks on his or her honor and reputation.

2. The child has the right to the protection of the law against such interference or attacks.

Article 17

States Parties recognize the important function performed by the mass media and shall ensure that the child has access to information and material from a diversity of national and international sources, especially those aimed at the promotion of his or her social, spiritual and moral well-being and physical and mental health. To this end, States Parties shall:

(a) Encourage the mass media to disseminate information and material of social and cultural benefit to the child and in accordance with the spirit of article 29;

(b) Encourage international co-operation in the production, exchange and dissemination of such information and material from a diversity of cultural, national and international sources;

(c) Encourage the production and dissemination of children's books;

(d) Encourage the mass media to have particular regard to the linguistic needs of the child who belongs to a minority group or who is indigenous;

(e) Encourage the development of appropriate guidelines for the protection of the child from information and material injurious to his or her well-being, bearing in mind the provisions of articles 13 and 18.

Article 18

1. States Parties shall use their best efforts to ensure recognition of the principle that both parents have common responsibilities for the upbringing and development of the child. Parents or, as the case may be, legal guardians, have the primary responsibility for the upbringing and development of the child. The best interests of the child will be their basic concern.

2. For the purpose of guaranteeing and promoting the rights set forth in the present Convention, States Parties shall render appropriate assistance to parents and legal guardians in the performance of their child-rearing responsibilities and shall ensure the development of institutions, facilities and services for the care of children.

3. States Parties shall take all appropriate measures to ensure that children of working parents have the right to benefit from child-care services and facilities for which they are eligible.

Article 19

1. States Parties shall take all appropriate legislative, administrative, social and educational measures to protect the child from all forms of physical or mental violence, injury or abuse, neglect or negligent treatment, maltreatment or exploitation, including sexual abuse, while in the care of parent(s), legal guardian(s) or any other person who has the care of the child.

2. Such protective measures should, as appropriate, include effective procedures for the establishment of social programmes to provide necessary support for the child and for those who have the care of the child, as well as for other forms of prevention and for identification, reporting, referral, investigation, treatment, and follow-up of instances of child maltreatment described heretofore, and, as appropriate, for judicial involvement.

Article 20

1. A child temporarily or permanently deprived of his or her family environment, or in whose own best interests cannot be allowed to remain in that environment, shall be entitled to special protection and assistance provided by the State.

2. States Parties shall in accordance with their national laws ensure alternative care for such a child.

3. Such care could include, *inter alia*, foster placement, *kafalah* of Islamic law, adoption, or if necessary placement in suitable institutions for the care of children. When considering solutions, due regard shall be paid to the desirability of continuity in a child's upbringing and to the child's ethnic, religious, cultural and linguistic background.

Article 21

States Parties that recognize and/or permit the system of adoption shall ensure that the best interests of the child shall be the paramount consideration and they shall:

(a) Ensure that the adoption of a child is authorized only by competent authorities who determine, in accordance with applicable law and procedures and on the basis of all pertinent and reliable information, that the adoption is permissible in view of the child's status concerning parents, relatives and legal guardians and that, if required, the persons concerned have given their informed consent to the adoption on the basis of such counselling as may be necessary;

(b) Recognize that inter-country adoption may be considered as an alternative means of child's care, if the child cannot be placed in a foster or an adoptive family or cannot in any suitable manner be cared for in the child's country of origin;

(c) Ensure that the child concerned by inter-country adoption enjoys safeguards and standards equivalent to those existing in the case of national adoption;

(d) Take all appropriate measures to ensure that, in inter-country adoption, the placement does not result in improper financial gain for those involved in it;

(e) Promote, where appropriate, the objectives of the present article by concluding bilateral or multilateral arrangements or agreements, and endeavour, within this framework, to ensure that the placement of the child in another country is carried out by competent authorities or organs.

Article 22

1. States Parties shall take appropriate measures to ensure that a child who is seeking refugee status or who is considered a refugee in accordance with applicable international or domestic law and procedures shall, whether unaccompanied or accompanied by his or her parents or by any other person, receive appropriate protection and humanitarian assistance in the enjoyment of applicable rights set forth in the present Convention and in other international human rights or humanitarian instruments to which the said States are Parties.

2. For this purpose, States Parties shall provide, as they consider appropriate, co-operation in any efforts by the United Nations and other competent intergovernmental organizations or non-governmental organizations co-operating with the United Nations to protect and assist such a child and to trace the parents or other members of the family of any refugee child in order to obtain information necessary for reunification with his or her family. In cases where no parents or other members of the family can be found, the child shall be accorded the same protection as any other child permanently or temporarily deprived of his or her family environment for any reason, as set forth in the present Convention.

Article 23

1. States Parties recognize that a mentally or physically disabled child should enjoy a full and decent life, in conditions which ensure dignity, promote self-reliance and facilitate the child's active participation in the community.

2. States Parties recognize the right of the disabled child to special care and shall encourage and ensure the extension, subject to available resources, to the eligible child and those responsible for his or her care, of assistance for which application is made and which is appropriate to the child's condition and to the circumstances of the parents or others caring for the child.

3. Recognizing the special needs of a disabled child, assistance extended in accordance with paragraph 2 shall be provided free of charge, whenever possible, taking into account the financial resources of the par-

ents or others caring for the child, and shall be designed to ensure that the disabled child has effective access to and receives education, training, health care services, rehabilitation services, preparation for employment and recreation opportunities in a manner conducive to the child's achieving the fullest possible social integration and individual development, including his or her cultural and spiritual development.

4. States Parties shall promote, in the spirit of international co-operation, the exchange of appropriate information in the field of preventive health care and of medical, psychological and functional treatment of disabled children, including dissemination of and access to information concerning methods of rehabilitation education and vocational services, with the aim of enabling States Parties to improve their capabilities and skills and to widen their experience in these areas. In this regard, particular account shall be taken of the needs of developing countries.

Article 24

1. States Parties recognize the right of the child to the enjoyment of the highest attainable standard of health and to facilities for the treatment of illness and rehabilitation of health. States Parties shall strive to ensure that no child is deprived of his or her right of access to such health care services.

2. States Parties shall pursue full implementation of this right and, in particular, shall take appropriate measures:

(a) To diminish infant and child mortality;

(b) To ensure the provision of necessary medical assistance and health care to all children with emphasis on the development of primary health care;

(c) To combat disease and malnutrition, including within the framework of primary health care, through, *inter alia*, the application of readily available technology and through the provision of adequate nutritious foods and clean drinking-water, taking into consideration the dangers and risks of environmental pollution;

(d) To ensure appropriate pre- and post-natal health care for mothers;

(e) To ensure that all segments of society, in particular parents and children, are informed, have access to education and are supported in the use of basic knowledge of child health and nutrition, the advantages of breast-feeding, hygiene and environmental sanitation and the prevention of accidents;

(f) To develop preventive health care, guidance for parents and family planning education and services.

3. States Parties shall take all effective and appropriate measures with a view to abolishing traditional practices prejudicial to the health of children.

4. States Parties undertake to promote and encourage international co-operation with a view to achieving progressively the full realization of the right recognized in the present article. In this regard, particular account shall be taken of the needs of developing countries.

Article 25

States Parties recognize the right of a child who has been placed by the competent authorities for the purposes of care, protection or treatment of his or her physical or mental health, to a periodic review of the treatment provided to the child and all other circumstances relevant to his or her placement.

Article 26

1. States Parties shall recognize for every child the right to benefit from social security, including social insurance, and shall take the necessary measures to achieve the full realization of this right in accordance with their national law.

2. The benefits should, where appropriate, be granted, taking into account the resources and the circumstances of the child and persons having responsibility for the maintenance of the child, as well as any other consideration relevant to an application for benefits made by or on behalf of the child.

Article 27

1. The States Parties recognize the right of every child to a standard of living adequate for the child's physical, mental, spiritual, moral and social development.

2. The parent(s) or others responsible for the child have the primary responsibility to secure, within their abilities and financial capacities, the conditions of living necessary for the child's development.

3. States Parties, in accordance with national conditions and within

their means, shall take appropriate measures to assist parents and others responsible for the child to implement this right and shall in case of need provide material assistance and support programmes, particularly with regard to nutrition, clothing and housing.

4. States Parties shall take all appropriate measures to secure the recovery of maintenance for the child from the parents or other persons having financial responsibility for the child, both within the State Party and from abroad. In particular, where the person having financial responsibility for the child lives in a State different from that of the child, States Parties shall promote the accession to international agreements or the conclusion of such agreements, as well as the making of other appropriate arrangements.

Article 28

1. States Parties recognize the right of the child to education, and with a view to achieving this right progressively and on the basis of equal opportunity, they shall, in particular:

(a) Make primary education compulsory and available free to all;

(b) Encourage the development of different forms of secondary education, including general and vocational education, make them available and accessible to every child, and take appropriate measures such as the introduction of free education and offering financial assistance in case of need;

(c) Make higher education accessible to all on the basis of capacity by every appropriate means;

(d) Make educational and vocational information and guidance available and accessible to all children;

(e) Take measures to encourage regular attendance at schools and the reduction of drop-out rates.

2. States Parties shall take all appropriate measures to ensure that school discipline is administered in a manner consistent with the child's human dignity and in conformity with the present Convention.

3. States Parties shall promote and encourage international co-operation in matters relating to education, in particular with a view to contributing to the elimination of ignorance and illiteracy throughout the world and facilitating access to scientific and technical knowledge and

modern teaching methods. In this regard, particular account shall be taken of the needs of developing countries.

Article 29

1. States Parties agree that the education of the child shall be directed to:

(a) The development of the child's personality, talents and mental and physical abilities to their fullest potential;

(b) The development of respect for human rights and fundamental freedoms, and for the principles enshrined in the Charter of the United Nations;

(c) The development of respect for the child's parents, his or her own cultural identity, language and values, for the national values of the country in which the child is living, the country from which he or she may originate, and for civilizations different from his or her own;

(d) The preparation of the child for responsible life in a free society, in the spirit of understanding, peace, tolerance, equality of sexes, and friendship among all peoples, ethnic, national and religious groups and persons of indigenous origin;

(e) The development of respect for the natural environment.

2. No part of the present article or article 28 shall be construed so as to interfere with the liberty of individuals and bodies to establish and direct educational institutions, subject always to the observance of the principles set forth in paragraph 1 of the present article and to the requirements that the education given in such institutions shall conform to such minimum standards as may be laid down by the State.

Article 30

In those States in which ethnic, religious or linguistic minorities or persons of indigenous origin exist, a child belonging to such a minority or who is indigenous shall not be denied the right, in community with other members of his or her group, to enjoy his or her own culture, to profess and practice his or her own religion, or to use his or her own language.

Article 31

1. States Parties recognize the right of the child to rest and leisure, to

engage in play and recreational activities appropriate to the age of the child and to participate freely in cultural life and the arts.

2. States Parties shall respect and promote the right of the child to participate fully in cultural and artistic life and shall encourage the provision of appropriate and equal opportunities for cultural, artistic, recreational and leisure activity.

Article 32

1. States Parties recognize the right of the child to be protected from economic exploitation and from performing any work that is likely to be hazardous or to interfere with the child's education, or to be harmful to the child's health or physical, mental, spiritual, moral or social development.

2. States Parties shall take legislative, administrative, social and educational measures to ensure the implementation of the present article. To this end, and having regard to the relevant provisions of other international instruments, States Parties shall in particular:

(a) Provide for a minimum age or minimum ages for admissions to employment;

(b) Provide for appropriate regulation of the hours and conditions of employment; and

(c) Provide for appropriate penalties or other sanctions to ensure the effective enforcement of the present article.

Article 33

States Parties shall take all appropriate measures, including legislative, administrative, social and educational measures, to protect children from the illicit use of narcotic drugs and psychotropic substances as defined in the relevant international treaties, and to prevent the use of children in the illicit production and trafficking of such substances.

Article 34

States Parties undertake to protect the child from all forms of sexual exploitation and sexual abuse. For these purposes, States Parties shall in particular take all appropriate national, bilateral and multilateral measures to prevent:

(a) The inducement or coercion of a child to engage in any unlawful sexual activity;

(b) The exploitative use of children in prostitution or other unlawful sexual practices;

(c) The exploitative use of children in pornographic performances and materials.

Article 35

States Parties shall take all appropriate national, bilateral and multilateral measures to prevent the abduction, the sale of or traffic in children for any purpose or in any form.

Article 36

States Parties shall protect the child against all other forms of exploitation prejudicial to any aspects of the child's welfare.

Article 37

States Parties shall ensure that:

(a) No child shall be subjected to torture or other cruel, inhuman or degrading treatment or punishment. Neither capital punishment nor life imprisonment without possibility of release shall be imposed for offenses committed by persons below eighteen years of age;

(b) No child shall be deprived of his or her liberty unlawfully or arbitrarily. The arrest, detention or imprisonment of a child shall be in conformity with the law and shall be used only as a measure of last resort and for the shortest appropriate period of time;

(c) Every child deprived of liberty shall be treated with humanity and respect for the inherent dignity of the human person, and in a manner which takes into account the needs of persons of their age. In particular, every child deprived of liberty shall be separated from adults unless it is considered in the child's best interest not to do so and shall have the right to maintain contact with his or her family through correspondence and visits, save in exceptional circumstances;

(d) Every child deprived of his or her liberty shall have the right to prompt access to legal and other appropriate assistance, as well as the right to challenge the legality of the deprivation of his or her liberty before a court or other competent, independent and impartial authority, and to a prompt decision on any such action.

Article 38

1. States Parties undertake to respect and to ensure respect for rules of international humanitarian law applicable to them in armed conflicts which are relevant to the child.

2. States Parties shall take all feasible measures to ensure that persons who have not attained the age of fifteen years do not take a direct part in hostilities.

3. States Parties shall refrain from recruiting any person who has not attained the age of fifteen years into the armed forces. In recruiting among those persons who have attained the age of fifteen years but who have not attained the age of eighteen years, States Parties shall endeavour to give priority to those who are oldest.

4. In accordance with their obligations under international humanitarian law to protect the civilian population in armed conflicts, States Parties shall take all feasible measures to ensure protection and care of children who are affected by an armed conflict.

Article 39

States Parties shall take all appropriate measures to promote physical and psychological recovery and social reintegration of a child victim of: any form of neglect, exploitation, or abuse; torture or any other form of cruel, inhuman or degrading treatment or punishment; or armed conflicts. Such recovery and reintegration shall take place in an environment which fosters the health, self-respect and dignity of the child.

Article 40

1. States Parties recognize the right of every child alleged as, accused of, or recognized as having infringed the penal law to be treated in a manner consistent with the promotion of the child's sense of dignity and worth, which reinforces the child's respect for the human rights and fundamental freedoms of others and which takes into account the child's age and the desirability of promoting the child's reintegration and the child's assuming a constructive role in society.

2. To this end, and having regard to the relevant provisions of international instruments, States Parties shall, in particular, ensure that:

(a) No child shall be alleged as, be accused of, or recognized as having infringed the penal law by reason of acts or omissions that were not prohibited by national or international law at the time they were committed;

(b) Every child alleged as or accused of having infringed the penal law has at least the following guarantees:

(i) To be presumed innocent until proven guilty according to law;

(ii) To be informed promptly and directly of the charges against him or her, and, if appropriate, through his or her parents or legal guardian, and to have legal or other appropriate assistance in the preparation and presentation of his or her defence;

(iii) To have the matter determined without delay by a competent, independent and impartial authority or judicial body in a fair hearing according to law, in the presence of legal or other appropriate assistance and, unless it is considered not to be in the best interest of the child, in particular, taking into account his or her age or situation, his or her parents or legal guardians;

(iv) Not to be compelled to give testimony or to confess guilt; to examine or have examined adverse witnesses and to obtain the participation and examination of witnesses on his or her behalf under conditions of equality;

(v) If considered to have infringed the penal law, to have this decision and any measures imposed in consequence thereof reviewed by a higher competent, independent and impartial authority or judicial body according to law;

(vi) To have the free assistance of an interpreter if the child cannot understand or speak the language used;

(vii) To have his or her privacy fully respected at all stages of the proceedings.

3. States Parties shall seek to promote the establishment of laws, procedures, authorities and institutions specifically applicable to children alleged as, accused of, or recognized as having infringed the penal law, and, in particular:

(a) The establishment of a minimum age below which children shall be presumed not to have the capacity to infringe the penal law;

(b) Whenever appropriate and desirable, measures for dealing with such children without resorting to judicial proceedings, providing that human rights and legal safeguards are fully respected.

4. A variety of dispositions, such as care, guidance and supervision orders; counselling; probation; foster care; education and vocational training programmes and other alternatives to institutional care shall be available to ensure that children are dealt with in a manner appropriate to their well-being and proportionate both to their circumstances and the offence.

Article 41

Nothing in the present Convention shall affect any provisions which are more conducive to the realization of the rights of the child and which may be contained in:

(a) The law of a State Party; or

(b) International law in force for that State.

PART II

Article 42

States Parties undertake to make the principles and provisions of the Convention widely known, by appropriate and active means, to adults and children alike.

Article 43

1. For the purpose of examining the progress made by States Parties in achieving the realization of the obligations undertaken in the present Convention, there shall be established a Committee on the Rights of the Child, which shall carry out the functions hereinafter provided.

2. The Committee shall consist of ten experts of high moral standing and recognized competence in the field covered by this Convention. The members of the Committee shall be elected by States Parties from among their nationals and shall serve in their personal capacity, consideration being given to equitable geographical distribution, as well as to the principal legal systems.

3. The members of the Committee shall be elected by secret ballot from a list of persons nominated by States Parties. Each State Party may nominate one person from among its own nationals.

4. The initial election to the Committee shall be held no later than six months after the date of the entry into force of the present Convention and thereafter every second year. At least four months before the date of each election, the Secretary-General of the United Nations shall address a letter to States Parties inviting them to submit their nominations within two months. The Secretary-General shall subsequently prepare a list in alphabetical order of all persons thus nominated, indicating States Parties which have nominated them, and shall submit it to the States Parties to the present Convention.

5. The elections shall be held at meetings of States Parties convened by the Secretary-General at United Nations Headquarters. At those meetings, for which two thirds of States Parties shall constitute a quorum, the persons elected to the Committee shall be those who obtain the largest number of votes and an absolute majority of the votes of the representatives of States Parties present and voting.

6. The members of the Committee shall be elected for a term of four years. They shall be eligible for re-election if renominated. The term of five of the members elected at the first election shall expire at the end of two years; immediately after the first election, the names of these five members shall be chosen by lot by the Chairman of the meeting.

7. If a member of the Committee dies or resigns or declares that for any other cause he or she can no longer perform the duties of the Committee, the State Party which nominated the member shall appoint another expert from among its nationals to serve for the remainder of the term, subject to the approval of the Committee.

8. The Committee shall establish its own rules of procedure.

9. The Committee shall elect its officers for a period of two years.

10. The meetings of the Committee shall normally be held at United Nations Headquarters or at any other convenient place as determined by the Committee. The Committee shall normally meet annually. The duration of the meetings of the Committee shall be determined, and reviewed, if necessary, by a meeting of the States Parties to the present Convention, subject to the approval of the General Assembly.

11. The Secretary-General of the United Nations shall provide the necessary staff and facilities for the effective performance of the functions of the Committee under the present Convention.

12. With the approval of the General Assembly, the members of the

Committee established under the present Convention shall receive emoluments from the United Nations resources on such terms and conditions as the Assembly may decide.

Article 44

1. States Parties undertake to submit to the Committee, through the Secretary-General of the United Nations, reports on the measures they have adopted which give effect to the rights recognized herein and on the progress made on the enjoyment of those rights:

   (a) Within two years of the entry into force of the Convention
   for the State Party concerned:

   (b) Thereafter every five years.

2. Reports made under the present article shall indicate factors and difficulties, if any, affecting the degree of fulfillment of the obligations under the present Convention. Reports shall also contain sufficient information to provide the Committee with a comprehensive understanding of the implementation of the Convention in the country concerned.

3. A State Party which has submitted a comprehensive initial report to the Committee need not, in its subsequent reports submitted in accordance with paragraph 1 (b), repeat basic information previously provided.

4. The Committee may request from States Parties further information relevant to the implementation of the Convention.

5. The Committee shall submit to the General Assembly, through the Economic and Social Council, every two years, reports on its activities.

6. States Parties shall make their reports widely available to the public in their own countries.

Article 45

In order to foster the effective implementation of the Convention and to encourage international co-operation in the field covered by the Convention:

   (a) The specialized agencies, the United Nations Children's Fund, and other United Nations organs shall be entitled to be represented at the consideration of the implementation of such provisions of the present Convention as fall within the scope of their mandate. The Committee may invite the specialized agencies, the United Nations Children's Fund and other competent bodies as it may consider appropriate to provide expert advice on the implementation of the Convention in areas falling within the scope of their respective mandates. The Committee may invite the specialized agencies, the United Nations Children's Fund, and other United Nations organs to submit reports on the implementation of the Convention in areas falling within the scope of their activities;

(b) The Committee shall transmit, as it may consider appropriate, to the specialized agencies, the United Nations Children's Fund and other competent bodies, any reports from States Parties that contain a request, or indicate a need, for technical advice or assistance, along with the Committee's observations and suggestions, if any, on these requests or indications.

(c) The Committee may recommend to the General Assembly to request the Secretary-General to undertake on its behalf studies on specific issues relating to the rights of the child;

(d) The Committee may make suggestions and general recommendations based on information received pursuant to articles 44 and 45 of the present Convention. Such suggestions and general recommendations shall be transmitted to any State Party concerned and reported to the General Assembly, together with comments, if any, from States Parties.

PART III

Article 46
The present Convention shall be open for signature by all States.

Article 47
The present Convention is subject to ratification. Instruments of ratification shall be deposited with the Secretary-General of the United Nations.

Article 48
The present Convention shall remain open for accession by any State. The instruments of accession shall be deposited with the Secretary-General of the United Nations.

Article 49

1. The present Convention shall enter into force on the thirtieth day following the date of deposit with the Secretary-General of the United Nations of the twentieth instrument of ratification or accession.

2. For each State ratifying or acceding to the Convention after the deposit of the twentieth instrument of ratification or accession, the Convention shall enter into force on the thirtieth day after the deposit by such State of its instrument of ratification or accession.

Article 50

1. Any State Party may propose an amendment and file it with the Secretary-General of the United Nations. The Secretary-General shall thereupon communicate the proposed amendment to States Parties, with a request that they indicate whether they favor a conference of States Parties for the purpose of considering and voting upon the proposals. In the event that, within four months from the date of such communication, at least one third of the States Parties favor such a conference, the Secretary-General shall convene the conference under the auspices of the United Nations. Any amendment adopted by a majority of States Parties present and voting at the conference shall be submitted to the General Assembly for approval.

2. An amendment adopted in accordance with paragraph (1) of the present article shall enter into force when it has been approved by the General Assembly of the United Nations and accepted by a two-thirds majority of States Parties.

3. When an amendment enters into force, it shall be binding on those States Parties which have accepted it, other States Parties still being bound by the provisions of the present Convention and any earlier amendments which they have accepted.

Article 51

1. The Secretary-General of the United Nations shall receive and circulate to all States the text of reservations made by States at the time of ratification or accession.

2. A reservation incompatible with the object and purpose of the present Convention shall not be permitted.

3. Reservations may be withdrawn at any time by notification to that

effect addressed to the Secretary-General of the United Nations, who shall then inform all States. Such notification shall take effect on the date on which it is received by the Secretary-General.

Article 52

A State Party may denounce the present Convention by written notification to the Secretary-General of the United Nations. Denunciation becomes effective one year after the date of receipt of the notification by the Secretary-General.

Article 53

The Secretary-General of the United Nations is designated as the depositary of the present Convention.

Article 54

The original of the present Convention, of which the Arabic, Chinese, English, French, Russian and Spanish texts are equally authentic, shall be deposited with the Secretary-General of the United Nations.

In witness thereof the undersigned plenipotentiaries, being duly authorized thereto by their respective Governments, have signed the present Convention.

BIBLIOGRAPHY

Alston, P. 1984. "Conjuring up New Human Rights: A Proposal for Quality Control." *American Journal of International Law* 78:607–21.

——. 1989. "Implementing Children's Rights: The Case of Child Labour." *Nordic Journal of International Law* 58:35–53.

——. 1990. "The Unborn Child and Abortion under the Draft Convention on the Rights of the Child." *Human Rights Quarterly* 12:156–78.

——, ed. 1992. *The United Nations and Human Rights: A Critical Appraisal.* Oxford: Clarendon Press.

Armstrong, J. D. 1986. "Non-Governmental Organizations." In *Foreign Policy and Human Rights*, ed. R. J. Vincent. Cambridge: Cambridge University Press.

Baehr, P. 1989. "The General Assembly: Negotiating the Convention on Torture." In *The United Nations in the World Political Economy*, ed. D. Forsythe. New York: St. Martin's Press.

Barsh, R. 1989. "The Draft Convention on the Rights of the Child: A Case of Eurocentrism in Standard-Setting." *Nordic Journal of International Law* 58:24–34.

Becker, M. J. 1989. "The Pressure to Abandon." In *Protecting Children's Rights in International Adoptions*, 24–25. Geneva: Defense for Children International.

Benedick, R. 1991. *Ozone Diplomacy: New Directions in Safeguarding the Planet.* Cambridge: Harvard University Press.

Bequele, A. 1991. "Towards a Strategy of Combatting Child Labour in Very Poor Countries." In *International Child Labour Seminar*, ed. M. Schaule Jullens. Delft: Netherlands Organization for Applied Scientific Research.

Bequele, A., and J. Boyden, eds. 1988. *Combating Child Labour.* Geneva: International Labour Organization.

Bernard-Maugiron, N. 1990. "20 Years After: 38th Session of the Committee on the Elimination of Racial Discrimination." *Netherlands Quarterly of Human Rights* 4:395–402.

Boonpala, P. 1991. "Working Children of Asia." In *International Child Labour Seminar*, ed. M. Schaule Jullens. Delft: Netherlands Organization for Applied Scientific Research.

Bourguignon, H. 1989. "The Belilos Case: New Light on Reservations to Multilateral Treaties." *Virginia Journal of International Law* 29:347–86.

Burgers, J. H., and H. Danelius. 1988. *The United Nations Convention Against Torture.* Dordrecht: Martinus Nijhoff Publishers.

Burra, N. 1991. "Child Labour in India: Poverty, Exploitation, and Vested Interest." In *International Child Labour Seminar*, ed. M. Schaule Jullens. Delft: Netherlands Organization for Applied Scientific Research.

Byrnes, A. 1992. "The Committee Against Torture." In *The United Nations and Human Rights: A Critical Appraisal*, ed. P. Alston. Oxford: Clarendon Press.

317

Cantwell, N. 1989. "The 'Headscarves' Affair." *International Children's Rights Monitor* (Special Issue) 6:15.

——. 1990. "Who Said 'Best Interests'?" *International Children's Rights Monitor 7* (1/2):1, 19.

——. 1992. "The Origins, Development, and Significance of the United Nations Convention on the Rights of the Child." In *The United Nations Convention on the Rights of the Child: A Guide to the 'Travaux Preparatoires,'* ed. S. Detrick. Dordrecht: Martinus Nijhoff Publishers.

Chiang Pei-heng. 1981. *Non-Governmental Organizations at the United Nations: Identity, Role, and Function.* New York: Praeger Special Studies.

Children's Defense Fund. 1991. *The State of America's Children 1991.* Washington, D.C.

Clark, B. 1991. "The Vienna Convention Reservations Regime and the Convention on Discrimination Against Women." *American Journal of International Law* 85:281–321.

Claude, R., and B. Weston, eds. 1989. *Human Rights in the World Community.* Philadelphia: University of Pennsylvania Press.

Coccia, M. 1985. "Reservations to Multilateral Treaties on Human Rights." *California Western International Law Journal* 15:1–51.

Cohen, C. P. 1990. "The Role of Nongovernmental Organizations in the Drafting of the Convention on the Rights of the Child." *Human Rights Quarterly* 12:137–47.

——. 1992. "The Relevance of Theories of Natural Law and Legal Positivism." In *The Ideologies of Children's Rights*, ed. M. Freeman and P. Veerman. Dordrecht: Martinus Nijhoff Publishers.

Cohen, C. P., and H. A. Davidson, eds. 1990. *Children's Rights in America: U.N. Convention on the Rights of the Child Compared with United States Law.* Chicago: American Bar Association/Defense for Children International-USA.

Cohen, C. P., S. Hart, and S. Kosloske. 1992. "The UN Convention on the Rights of the Child: Developing an Information Model to Computerize the Monitoring of Treaty Compliance." *Human Rights Quarterly* 14:216–31.

Cohen, C. P., and H. Naimark. 1991. "United Nations Convention on the Rights of the Child: Individual Rights Concepts and Their Significance for Social Scientists." *American Psychologist* 46:60–65.

Cook, R. 1986. "Human Rights and Infant Survival: A Case for Priorities." *Columbia Human Rights Law Review* 18:1–41.

——. 1990. "Reservations to the Convention on the Elimination of All Forms of Discrimination Against Women." *Virginia Journal of International Law* 30:643–716.

Danish Center of Human Rights/Netherlands Institute of Human Rights. 1991. *AIDS and Human Rights in the European Communities.* Copenhagen/Utrecht: Danish Center of Human Rights/Netherlands Institute of Human Rights.

Dao, H. T. 1989. "ILO Standards for the Protection of Children." *Nordic Journal of International Law* 58:54–67.

Davis, S., and M. Schwartz. 1987. *Children's Rights and the Law.* Lexington, Mass.: Lexington Books.

DCI (Defense for Children International). 1983. *The Draft Convention on the Rights of the Child: Report of Informal Consultations Among International Non-Governmental Organizations.* Geneva: Defense for Children International.

——. 1984. *The Draft Convention on the Rights of the Child: Informal Consultations Among International Non-Governmental Organizations.* Geneva: Defense for Children International.

——. 1985. *The Draft Convention on the Rights of the Child: Informal Consultations Among International Non-Governmental Organizations.* Geneva: Defense for Children International.

——. 1986. *Informal Consultations Among International Non-Governmental Organizations: Proposals and Recommendations on Implementation Provisions of the Draft Convention on the Rights of the Child.* Geneva: Defense for Children International.

——. 1987. *Summary Report of an Information Meeting for Representatives of Permanent Missions in Geneva on NGO Proposals on the Draft Convention on the Rights of the Child.* Geneva: Defense for Children International.

——. 1988. *Information Meeting for Representatives of Permanent Missions in Geneva on the Proposals of the NGO Ad Hoc Group on the Drafting of the Convention on the Rights of the Child.* Geneva: Defense for Children International.

——. 1989a. "An Organized Cross-Border Crime" and "A Case in Point." *Protecting Children's Rights in International Adoptions,* 7–10. Geneva: Defense for Children International.

——. 1989b. *Protecting Children's Rights in International Adoptions.* Geneva: Defense for Children International.

——. 1990. "Activity Report 1989." Geneva: Defense for Children International.

DCI et al. 1991a. *Preliminary Findings of a Joint Investigation on Independent Intercountry Adoptions.* Geneva: Defense for Children International.

——. 1991b. *Preliminary Findings of a Joint Investigation on the "Waiting Period" in Intercountry Adoptions.* Geneva: Defense for Children International.

Detrick, S. 1992. *The United Nations Convention on the Rights of the Child: A Guide to the 'Travaux Preparatoires'.* Dordrecht: Martinus Nijhoff Publishers.

Donnelly, J. 1986. "International Human Rights: A Regime Analysis." *International Organization* 40:599–642.

——. 1989. *Universal Human Rights in Theory and Practice.* New York: Cornell University Press.

Donnelly, J., and R. Howard. 1988. "Assessing National Human Rights Performance: A Theoretical Framework." *Human Rights Quarterly* 10:214–48.

Dormenval, A. 1990. "UN Committee Against Torture: Practice and Perspectives." *Netherlands Quarterly of Human Rights* 8:26–44.

Eide, A. 1989. "Realization of Social and Economic Rights and the Minimum Threshold Approach." *Human Rights Law Journal* 10:35 – 51.

Elahi, M. 1988. "The Rights of the Child under Islamic Law: Prohibition of the Child Soldier." *Columbia Human Rights Law Review* 19:259 – 79.

Flekkoy, M. G. 1992. "Attitudes to Children — Their Consequences for Work for Children." In *The Ideologies of Children's Rights*, ed. M. Freeman and P. Veerman. Dordrecht: Martinus Nijhoff Publishers.

Fletcher School of Law and Diplomacy. 1988. *Taking Stock of United Nations Human Rights Procedures*, comp. P. Alston and M. Rodriguez-Bustelo. Medford, Mass.: Fletcher School of Law and Diplomacy.

Forsythe, D. 1989. *Human Rights and World Politics*. Lincoln: University of Nebraska Press.

———. 1991. *The Internationalization of Human Rights*. Lexington, Mass.: Lexington Books.

Freeman, M. 1992. "The Limits of Children's Rights." In *The Ideologies of Children's Rights*, ed. M. Freeman and P. Veerman. Dordrecht: Martinus Nijhoff Publishers.

Freeman, M., and P. Veerman, eds. 1992. *The Ideologies of Children's Rights*. Dordrecht: Martinus Nijhoff Publishers.

Galenson, W. 1981. *The International Labor Organization*. Madison: University of Wisconsin Press.

Galey, M. 1984. "International Enforcement of Women's Rights." *Human Rights Quarterly* 6:463 – 90.

Graham, P. 1992. "The Child's Right to Health." In *The Ideologies of Children's Rights*, ed. M. Freeman and P. Veerman. Dordrecht: Martinus Nijhoff Publishers.

Grannes, E. A. 1990. CEDAW #9: Report on the Ninth Session of the Committee on the Elimination of Discrimination Against Women. Oslo: Institute of Women's Law.

Hague Conference (Hague Conference on Private International Law). 1990a. "Conclusions of the Special Commission of June 1990 on Intercountry Adoption." Preliminary Doc. No. 3, August.

———. 1990b. "Illustrative Draft Articles for a Convention on the Protection of Children and on International Co-operation in Respect of Intercountry Adoption." Preliminary Doc. No. 4, December.

———. 1991a. Special Commission on Intercountry Adoption, April 22 – May 3, 1991. "Report of Meeting No. 17." April.

———. 1991b. Special Commission on Intercountry Adoption, April 22 – May 3, 1991. "Document Submitted by the Delegation of Australia." Working Doc. 34, April.

———. 1991c. Special Commission on Intercountry Adoption, April 22 – May 3, 1991. "Report of Meeting No. 19." April.

———. 1991d. Special Commission on Intercountry Adoption, April 22 – May 3,

1991. "Document Submitted by the Delegation of Colombia." Working Doc. 72, April.

———. 1993. "Final Act of the Seventeenth Session." May.

Hammarberg, T. 1990. "The UN Convention on the Rights of the Child—and How to Make It Work." *Human Rights Quarterly* 12:97–105.

Higgins, R. 1989. "The United Nations: Still a Force for Peace." *Modern Law Review* 52:1–21.

Humphrey, J. 1989. *No Distant Millennium: The International Law of Human Rights*. Paris: United Nations Educational, Scientific and Cultural Organization.

Hunt, K. 1991. "The Romanian Baby Bazaar." *New York Times Magazine*. March 24.

Hyndman, P. 1989. "The Exploitation of Child Workers in South and South East Asia." *Nordic Journal of International Law* 58:94–109.

ICJ (International Commission of Jurists). 1979. "Warsaw Conference of the Legal Protection of the Child." *Review of the International Commission of Jurists* 22:63–66.

Interights. 1986. *Family, Marriage, and Children: Selected International Human Rights Instruments*. London: International Centre for the Legal Protection of Human Rights.

IWRAW (International Women's Rights Action Watch). 1992. *1992 Q & A: An Analysis of Country Reports to CEDAW and the Questions They Suggest*. Minneapolis: University of Minnesota, IWRAW.

Jacobson, R. 1992. "The Committee on the Elimination of Discrimination Against Women." In *The United Nations and Human Rights: A Critical Appraisal*, ed. P. Alston. Oxford: Clarendon Press.

Johnson, D. 1990. "The Convention—Off and Running!" *International Children's Rights Monitor* 71 (2):3.

———. 1992. "Cultural and Regional Pluralism in the Drafting of the UN Convention on the Rights of the Child." In *The Ideologies of Children's Rights*, ed. M. Freeman and P. Veerman. Dordrecht: Martinus Nijhoff Publishers.

Jupp, M. 1991. "The United Nations Convention on the Rights of the Child: An Opportunity for Advocates." *Howard Law Journal* 34:15–25.

Kaufmann, J. 1988. *Conference Diplomacy: An Introductory Analysis*. Dordrecht: Martinus Nijhoff Publishers.

Kent, G. 1992. "Little Foreign Bodies: International Dimensions of Child Prostitution." In *The Ideologies of Children's Rights*, ed. M. Freeman and P. Veerman. Dordrecht: Martinus Nijhoff Publishers.

Keohane, R., and J. Nye, Jr. 1989. *Power and Interdependence: World Politics in Transition*. Glenview, Ill.: Scott Foresman/Little Brown.

Krill, F. 1992. "The Protection of Children in Armed Conflicts." In *The Ideologies of Children's Rights*, ed. M. Freeman and P. Veerman. Dordrecht: Martinus Nijhoff Publishers.

Kubota, Y. 1989. "The Protection of Children's Rights and the United Nations." *Nordic Journal of International Law* 58:7 – 23.

Leary, V. 1979. "A New Role for Non-Governmental Organizations in Human Rights: A Case Study of Non-Governmental Participation in the Development of International Norms Against Torture." In *UN Law — Fundamental Rights: Two Topics in International Law*, ed. A. Cassese. The Netherlands: Sijthoff and Noordhoff.

———. 1992. "Lessons from the Experience of the International Labour Organisation." In *The United Nations and Human Rights: A Critical Appraisal*, ed. P. Alston. Oxford: Clarendon Press.

Lerner, N. 1980. *The U.N. Convention on the Elimination of All Forms of Racial Discrimination*. The Netherlands: Sijthoff and Noordhoff.

Limburg Principles. 1987. "The Limburg Principles on the Implementation of the International Covenant on Economic, Social and Cultural Rights." *Human Rights Quarterly* 9:122 – 35.

Livezey, L. 1988. *Nongovernmental Organizations and the Ideas of Human Rights*. Princeton: Center for International Studies.

Lopatka, A. 1992. "The Rights of the Child Are Universal: The Perspective of the UN Convention on the Rights of the Child." In *The Ideologies of Children's Rights*, ed. M. Freeman and P. Veerman. Dordrecht: Martinus Nijhoff Publishers.

Lubin, C. R., and A. Winslow. 1990. *Social Justice for Women: The International Labor Organization and Women*. Durham: Duke University Press.

Melton, G. B., and S. P. Limber. 1992. "What Children's Rights Mean to Children: Children's Own Views." In *The Ideologies of Children's Rights*, ed. M. Freeman and P. Veerman. Dordrecht: Martinus Nijhoff Publishers.

Meron, T. 1986. *Human Rights Law-Making in the United Nations: A Critique of Instruments and Processes*. London: Oxford University Press.

Miljeteig-Olssen, P. 1990. "Advocacy of Children's Rights — The Convention as More Than a Legal Document." *Human Rights Quarterly* 12:148 – 55.

Narvesen, O. 1989. *The Sexual Exploitation of Children in Developing Countries*. Oslo: Redd Barna.

New York Times. 1993. "Rights Forum Ends in Call for a Greater Role by U.N." International Section, June 26.

Nowak, M. 1993. "Proposals for Improving the UN Human Rights Programme." *Netherlands Quarterly of Human Rights* 11:153 – 62.

O'Donnell, D. 1989. "The Execution of Juvenile Offenders." *International Children's Rights Monitor* 6:23 – 26.

Opsahl, T. 1989. "Instruments of Implementation of Human Rights." *Human Rights Law Journal* 10 (1 – 2):13 – 34.

Pais, M. S. 1991. "The Committee on the Rights of the Child." *Review of the International Commission of Jurists* 47:37 – 43.

Partsch. K. J. 1992. "The Committee on the Elimination of Racial Discrimination." In *The United Nations and Human Rights: A Critical Appraisal*, ed. P. Alston. Oxford: Clarendon Press.

Paust, J. 1989. "Congress and Genocide: They're Not Going to Get Away with It." *Michigan Journal of International Law* 11:91–104.

Piper, C. 1985. "Reservations to Multilateral Treaties: The Goal of Universality." *Iowa Law Review* 71:295–322.

Purdy, L. 1992. *In Their Best Interests? The Case against Equal Rights for Children.* Ithaca: Cornell University Press.

Ramcharan, B. G. 1989. *The Concept and Present Status of the International Protection of Human Rights.* Dordrecht: Kluwer.

Rodley, N. 1979. "Monitoring Human Rights by the U.N. System and Non-governmental Organizations." In *Human Rights and American Foreign Policy*, ed. D. Kommers and G. Loescher. Notre Dame: University of Notre Dame Press.

Schaule Jullens, M. 1991. *International Child Labor Seminar.* Delft: Netherlands Organization for Applied Scientific Research.

Schmidt, M. 1990. "Achieving Much with Little: The Work of the United Nations Centre for Human Rights." *Netherlands Quarterly of Human Rights* 4:371–80.

Scott, C. 1989. "The Interdependence and Permeability of Human Rights Norms: Towards a Partial Fusion of the International Covenants on Human Rights." *Osgoode Hall Law Journal* 27:769–878.

Shue, H. 1980. *Basic Rights: Subsistence, Affluence, and U.S. Foreign Policy.* Princeton: Princeton University Press.

Slack, A. 1988. "Female Circumcision: A Critical Appraisal." *Human Rights Quarterly* 10:437–86.

Steiner, H. 1991. *Diverse Partners: Non-Governmental Organizations in the Human Rights Movement.* Boston: Harvard Law School/Human Rights Internet.

Tolley, H. Jr. 1987. *The U.N. Commission on Human Rights.* Boulder: Westview Press.

——. 1989. "Popular Sovereignty and International Law: ICJ Strategies for Human Rights Standard Setting." *Human Rights Quarterly* 11:561–85.

UN CEDAW (Committee on the Elimination of Discrimination Against Women). 1986a. "Summary Records of the 68th Meeting." CEDAW/C/SR.68, March 12.

——. 1986b. "Summary Records of the 71st Meeting." CEDAW/C/SR.71, March 13.

——. 1986c. "Summary Records of the 76th Meeting." CEDAW/C/SR.76, March 20.

——. 1986d. "Summary Records of the 79th Meeting." CEDAW/C/SR.79, March 19.

——. 1986e. "Summary Records of the 81st Meeting." CEDAW/C/SR.81, March 20.

——. 1987. "Summary Records of the 102nd Meeting." CEDAW/C/SR.102, April 10.

——. 1988a. "Summary Records of the 130th Meeting." CEDAW/C/SR.130, March 4.

——. 1988b. "Summary Records of the 129th Meeting." CEDAW/C/SR.129, March 3.

UN CERD (Committee on the Elimination of Racial Discrimination). 1988. "Summary Records of the 805th to the 814th Meetings, 3–7 August, 1987." CERD/C/SR.805–814, September 26.

——. 1989. "Summary Records of the 815th to the 830th Meetings, 1–12 August, 1987." CERD/C/SR.815–830, vol.1, December 29.

——. 1990. "Provisional Agenda and Annotations: Note by the Secretary-General." CERD/C/198, May 18.

UN CHR (Commission on Human Rights). 1978a. "Question of a Convention on the Rights of the Child: Draft Resolution Presented by Poland." E/CN.4/L.1366, February 7.

——. 1978b. "Summary Record of the 1438th Meeting." E/CN.4/SR.1438, February 13.

——. 1978c. "Summary Record of the 1472nd Meeting." E/CN.4/SR.1472, March 8.

——. 1978d. "Summary Record of the 1471st Meeting." E/CN.4/SR.1471, March 7.

——. 1978e. "Question of a Convention on the Rights of the Child." E/CN.4/NGO/225, February 23.

——. 1978f. "Question of a Convention on the Rights of the Child: Report of the Secretary-General." E/CN.4/1324, December 27.

——. 1979a. "Question of a Convention on the Rights of the Child: Report of the Secretary-General." E/CN.4/1324/Add. 1, February 1.

——. 1979b. "Question of a Convention on the Rights of the Child: Report of the Secretary-General." E/CN.4/1324/Corr. 1, February 27.

——. 1979c. "Question of a Convention on the Rights of the Child: Report of the Secretary-General." E/CN.4/1324/Add. 2, February 14.

——. 1979d. "Question of a Convention on the Rights of the Child: Report of the Secretary-General." E/CN.4/1324/Add. 3, February 28.

——. 1979e. "Question of a Convention on the Rights of the Child: Report of the Secretary-General." E/CN.4/1324/Add. 4, March 5.

——. 1979f. "Question of a Convention on the Rights of the Child: Report of the Working Group on a Draft Convention on the Rights of the Child." E/CN.4/L.1468, March 12.

——. 1980a. "Question of a Convention on the Rights of the Child: Report of the Secretary-General." E/CN.4/1324/Add. 5, January 22.

——. 1980b. "Question of a Convention on the Rights of the Child: Report of the Working Group on a Draft Convention on the Rights of the Child." E/CN.4/L.1542, March 10.

——. 1980c. "Question of a Convention on the Rights of the Child." E/CN.4/1349, January 17.

——. 1981. "Question of a Convention on the Rights of the Child: Report of the Working Group on a Draft Convention on the Rights of the Child." E/CN.4/L.1575, February 17.

——. 1982. "Question of a Convention on the Rights of the Child: Report of the Working Group on a Draft Convention on the Rights of the Child." E/CN.4/1982/30/Add. 1:47–78.

——. 1983. "Question of a Convention on the Rights of the Child: Report of the Working Group on a Draft Convention on the Rights of the Child." E/CN.4/1983/62, March 8.

——. 1984. "Question of a Convention on the Rights of the Child: Report of the Working Group on a Draft Convention on the Rights of the Child." E/CN.4/1984/71, February 23.

——. 1985a. "Question of a Convention on the Rights of the Child: Report of the Working Group on a Draft Convention on the Rights of the Child." E/CN.4/1985/64, April 3.

——. 1985b. "Question of a Convention on the Rights of the Child: Statement of NGOs." E/CN.4/1985/NGO/41, February 25.

——. 1986a. "Question of a Convention on the Rights of the Child: Report of the Working Group on a Draft Convention on the Rights of the Child." E/CN.4/1986/39, March 13.

——. 1986b. "Report of the Working Group on Traditional Practices Affecting the Health of Women and Children." E/CN.4/1986/42, February 4.

——. 1987. "Question of a Convention on the Rights of the Child: Report of the Working Group on a Draft Convention on the Rights of the Child." E/CN.4/1987/25, March 9.

——. 1988. "Question of a Convention on the Rights of the Child: Report of the Working Group on a Draft Convention on the Rights of the Child." E/CN.4/1988/28, April 6.

——. 1989a. "Technical Review of the Text of the Draft Convention on the Rights of the Child." E/CN.4/1989/WG.1/CRP.1, October 15, 1988.

——. 1989b. "Question of a Convention on the Rights of the Child: Report of the Working Group on a Draft Convention on the Rights of the Child." E/CN.4/1989/48, March 2.

——. 1989c. "Summary Record of the First Part of the 55th Meeting." E/CN.4/1989/SR.55, March 8.

——. 1989d. "Summary Record of the Second Part of the 55th Meeting." E/CN.4/1989/SR.55/Add. 1, March 8.

——. 1989e. "Status of the Convention Against Torture and Other Cruel, Inhuman or Degrading Treatment or Punishment: Report of the Secretary-General." E/CN.4/1989/17, December 8, 1988.

——. 1989f. "Status of the Convention Against Torture and Other Cruel, Inhuman or Degrading Treatment or Punishment: Report of the Secretary-General." E/CN.4/1990/15, December 11.

——. 1989g. "Summary Record of the 54th Meeting." E/CN.4/1989/SR.54, March 8.

——. 1990. "Effective Functioning of Bodies Established Pursuant to United Nations Human Rights Instruments." E/CN.4/1990/39, January 31.

——. 1991. "Consolidated Guidelines for the Initial Part of the Reports of States Parties." HRI/1991/1, February 27.

UN CRC (Committee on the Rights of the Child). 1990. "Determination of the

Duration of the Meetings of the Committee on the Rights of the Child in Accordance with Article 43, Paragraph 10, of the Convention: Note by the Secretary-General." CRC/SP/3, December 12.

———. 1991a. "Status of the Convention on the Rights of the Child: Note by the Secretary-General." CRC/SP/4, March 26.

———. 1991b. "Summary Record of the 14th Meeting." CRC/C/1991/SR.14, January 6, 1992.

———. 1991c. "Interim Report Adopted by the Committee at its 27th Meeting." CRC/C/7, November 7.

———. 1991d. "Provisional Rules of Procedure." CRC/C/4, November 14.

———. 1991e. "General Guidelines Regarding the Form and Content of Initial Reports to be Submitted by States Parties under Article 44, Paragraph 1 (a) of the Convention." CRC/C/5, October 30.

———. 1991f. "Summary Record of the 2nd Meeting." CRC/C/1991/SR.2, October 23.

———. 1991g. "Summary Record of the 23rd Meeting." CRC/C/1991/SR.23, October 21.

———. 1991h. "Summary Record of the 24th Meeting." CRC/C/1991/SR.24, January 31, 1992.

———. 1991i. "Summary Record of the 3rd Meeting." CRC/C/1991/SR.3, October 7.

———. 1991j. "Summary Record of the 7th Meeting." CRC/C/1991/SR.7, October 7.

———. 1991k. "Summary Record of the 2nd Meeting of the States Parties." CRC/SP/SR.2, March 5.

———. 1991l. "Summary Record of the 10th Meeting." CRC/C/1991/SR.10, October 9.

———. 1991m. "Summary Record of the 11th Meeting." CRC/C/1991/SR.11, January 28, 1992.

———. 1991n. "Summary Record of the 17th Meeting." CRC/C/1991/SR.17, October 16, 1992.

———. 1991o. "List of Participating Organizations: Note by the Secretary-General." CRC/C/6, November 14.

———. 1991p. "Summary Record of the 15th Meeting." CRC/C/1991/SR.15, October 14.

———. 1991q. "Summary Record of the 16th Meeting." CRC/C/1991/SR.16, February 11, 1992.

———. 1991r. "Summary Record of the 6th Meeting." CRC/C/1991/SR.6, November 1.

———. 1991s. "Consideration of Reports Submitted by States Parties under Article 44 of the Convention." CRC/C/3, August 9.

———. 1991t. "Summary Record of the 9th Meeting." CRC/C/1991/SR.9, October 8.

———. 1991u. "Summary Record of the 13th Meeting." CRC/C/1991/SR.13, October 14.

———. 1991v. "Election of the Ten Members of the Committee on the Rights of the Child in Accordance with Article 43 of the Convention." CRC/SP/2, January 16.

———. 1991w. "Election of the Ten Members of the Committee on the Rights of the Child in Accordance with Article 43 of the Convention." CRC/SP/2/Add. 1, February 4.

——. 1991x. "Election of the Ten Members of the Committee on the Rights of the Child in Accordance with Article 43 of the Convention." CRC/SP/2/Add. 2, February 14.

——. 1991y. "Election of the Ten Members of the Committee on the Rights of the Child in Accordance with Article 43 of the Convention." CRC/SP/2/Add. 3, February 20.

——. 1991z. "Election of the Ten Members of the Committee on the Rights of the Child in Accordance with Article 43 of the Convention." CRC/SP/2/Corr. 1, February 22.

——. 1991aa. "Initial Reports of States Parties Due in 1992: Note by the Secretary-General." CRC/C/3, August 9.

——. 1992a. "Report on the Second Session." CRC/C/10, October 19.

——. 1992b. "Election, in Accordance with Article 43 of the Convention on the Rights of the Child, of Five Members of the Committee on the Rights of the Child, to Replace Those Whose Terms Are Due to Expire on 28 February 1993." CRC/SP/9, December 23.

——. 1992c. "Summary Record of the 28th Meeting." CRC/C/SR.28, October 16.

——. 1992d. "Determination of the Duration of the Meetings of the Committee on the Rights of the Child in Accordance with Article 43, Paragraph 10, of the Convention: Note by the Secretary-General." CRC/SP/7, August 21.

——. 1992e. "Initial Reports of States Parties Due in 1993: Note by the Secretary-General." CRC/C/8/Rev. 1, December 2.

——. 1992f. "Initial Reports of States Parties Due in 1994: Note by the Secretary-General." CRC/C/11, December 2.

——. 1992g. "States Parties to the Convention on the Rights of the Child and Status of the Submission of Reports under Article 44 of the Convention: Note by the Secretary-General." CRC/C/12, December 2.

——. 1992h. "Initial Reports of States Parties Due in 1992: Sweden." CRC/C/3/Add. 1, September 23.

——. 1992i. "Initial Reports of States Parties Due in 1992: Sudan." CRC/C/3/Add. 3, December 16.

——. 1992j. "Initial Reports of States Parties Due in 1992: Russian Federation." CRC/C/3/Add. 5, October 22.

——. 1992k. "Initial Reports of States Parties Due in 1992: Egypt." CRC/C/3/Add. 6, December 11.

——. 1992l. "Summary Record of the 29th Meeting." CRC/C/SR.29, October 2.

——. 1992m. "Summary Record of the 34th Meeting." CRC/C/SR.34, December 17.

——. 1992n. "Summary Record of the 35th Meeting." CRC/C/SR.35, October 7.

——. 1992o. "Summary Record of the 36th Meeting." CRC/C/SR.36, October 2.

——. 1992p. "Summary Record of the 38th Meeting." CRC/C/SR.38, January 22, 1993.

———. 1992q. "Summary Record of the 39th Meeting." CRC/C/SR.39, October 12.

———. 1992r. "Summary Record of the 41st Meeting." CRC/C/SR.41, October 14.

———. 1993a. "Report on the Third Session." CRC/C/16, March 5.

———. 1993b. "Election, in Accordance with Article 43 of the Convention on the Rights of the Child, of Five Members of the Committee on the Rights of the Child, to Replace Those Whose Terms Are Due to Expire on 28 February 1993." CRC/SP/9/Add. 1, February 3.

———. 1993c. "Election, in Accordance with Article 43 of the Convention on the Rights of the Child, of Five Members of the Committee on the Rights of the Child, to Replace Those Whose Terms Are Due to Expire on 28 February 1993." CRC/SP/9/Add. 2, February 12.

———. 1993d. "Election, in Accordance with Article 43 of the Convention on the Rights of the Child, of Five Members of the Committee on the Rights of the Child, to Replace Those Whose Terms Are Due to Expire on 28 February 1993." CRC/SP/9/Add. 3, February 16.

———. 1993e. "Election, in Accordance with Article 43 of the Convention on the Rights of the Child, of Five Members of the Committee on the Rights of the Child, to Replace Those Whose Terms Are Due to Expire on 28 February 1993." CRC/SP/9/Add. 4, February 22.

———. 1993f. "Initial Reports of the States Parties Due in 1992: Costa Rica." CRC/C/3/Add. 8, February 19.

———. 1993g. "Initial Reports of the States Parties Due in 1992: Indonesia." CRC/C/3/Add. 10, January 14.

———. 1993h. "Concluding Observations of the Committee on the Rights of the Child on Reports Submitted by States Parties under Article 44 of the Convention: Note by the Secretary-General." CRC/C/15, February 15.

———. 1993i. "Concluding Observations of the Committee on the Rights of the Child: Bolivia." CRC/C/15/Add. 1, February 18.

———. 1993j. "Concluding Observations of the Committee on the Rights of the Child: Sweden." CRC/C/15/Add. 2, February 18.

———. 1993k. "Concluding Observations of the Committee on the Rights of the Child: Russian Federation." CRC/C/15/Add. 4, February 18.

———. 1993l. "Concluding Observations of the Committee on the Rights of the Child: Egypt." CRC/C/15/Add. 5, February 18.

———. 1993m. "Concluding Observations of the Committee on the Rights of the Child: Sudan." CRC/C/15/Add. 6, February 18.

———. 1993n. "Concluding Observations of the Committee on the Rights of the Child: Viet Nam." CRC/C/15/Add. 3, February 18.

———. 1993o. "Summary Record of the 42nd Meeting." CRC/C/SR.42, March 3.

———. 1993p. "Summary Record of the 47th Meeting." CRC/C/SR.47, January 18.

———. 1993q. "Summary Record of the 52nd Meeting." CRC/C/SR.52, January 22.

———. 1993r. "Summary Record of the 54th Meeting." CRC/C/SR.54, January 21.

UN ECOSOC (Economic and Social Council). 1980. "Question of a Convention on the Rights of the Child: Comments by ILO." E/CN.4/WG.1/WP.1/1, November.

——. 1984. "Question of a Convention on the Rights of the Child: Comments by ILO." E/CN.4/1984/WG.1/WP.1 December.

——. 1987a. "Question of a Convention on the Rights of the Child: Written Statement Submitted by the World Young Women's Christian Association." E/CN.4/1987/NGO/27.

——. 1987b. "Question of a Convention on the Rights of the Child: Written Statement Submitted by Defense for Children International." E/CN.4/1987/NGO/39.

——. 1988. "Consolidation of Human Rights Machinery." E/CN.4/1988/NGO/36, February 9.

——. 1990a. "Situation and Developments Regarding the Logistical and Human Rights Resources Support for the Activities of the Centre for Human Rights in the Field of Human Rights: Report of the Secretary-General." E/1990/50, April 24.

——. 1990b. "Eradication of the Exploitation of Child Labour, and of Debt Bondage: Comments of Governments." E/CN.4/Sub.2/AC.2/1990/5, May 30; Add. 1, June 11; Add. 2, June 18; Add. 3, June 19; Add. 4, July 10.

——. 1990c. "Eradication of the Exploitation of Child Labour, and of Debt Bondage: Comments of Nongovernmental Organizations." E/CN.4/Sub.2/AC.2/1990/6, May 21; Add. 1, June 18; Add. 2, August 8.

——. 1990d. "Report of the Sub-commission on Prevention of Discrimination and Protection of Minorities on Its Forty-Second Session." E/CN.4/1991/2, E/CN.4/Sub.2/1990/59, October.

——. 1991a. "An Analytical Summary of Comments Received by the Secretary-General on the Draft Programme of Action for Prevention of Sale of Children, Child Prostitution, and Child Pornography." E/CN.4/1991/50, January 28.

——. 1991b. "Sale of Children: Report Submitted by Mr. Vitit Muntarbhorn, Special Rapporteur Appointed in Accordance with Resolution 1990/68 of the Commission on Human Rights." E/CN.4/1991/51, January 28.

UN GA (General Assembly). 1984. "Report of the Committee on the Elimination of Discrimination Against Women: Third Session." A/39/45, Supp. 45.

——. 1985a. "Reporting Obligations of States Parties to United Nations Conventions on Human Rights: Report of the Secretary-General." A/40/600, September 26.

——. 1985b. "Reporting Obligations of States Parties to United Nations Conventions on Human Rights: Report of the Secretary-General." A/40/600/Add. 1, October 1.

——. 1986a. "Status of the Convention on the Elimination of All Forms of Discrimination Against Women." A/41/608, October 7.

——. 1986b. "Status of the Convention on the Elimination of All Forms of Discrimination Against Women." A/41/608/Add. 1, October 23.

——. 1986c. "Report of the Committee on the Elimination of Discrimination Against Women: Fifth Session." A/41/45.

——. 1987. "Report of the Committee on the Elimination of Discrimination Against Women: Sixth Session." A/42/38, Supp. 38.

——. 1988a. "Report of the Committee on the Elimination of Racial Discrimination." A/43/18.

——. 1988b. "Report of the Committee on the Elimination of Discrimination Against Women: Seventh Session." A/43/38, Supp. 38.

——. 1989a. "Reporting Obligations of the States Parties to the United Nations Instruments on Human Rights." A/44/98, February 3.

——. 1989b. "Effective Implementation of International Instruments on Human Rights, Including Reporting Obligations under International Instruments on Human Rights." A/44/668, November 8.

——. 1989c. "Provisional Verbatim Record of the Sixty-First Meeting." A/44/PV.61, November 20.

——. 1990a. "Ceremony for the Presentation of the Declaration and Plan of Action Adopted by World Leaders at the World Summit for Children." A/45/625, October 18.

——. 1990b. "Effective Implementation of United Nations Instruments on Human Rights and Effective Functioning of Bodies Established Pursuant to Such Instruments: Note by the Secretary-General." A/45/636, October 30.

——. 1990c. "Report of the Open-Ended Working Group on the Drafting of an International Convention on the Protection of the Rights of All Migrant Workers and Members of Their Families." A/C.3/45/1, June 21.

——. 1990d. "Personnel Questions: Report of the Secretary-General on the Composition of the Secretariat." A/45/541, October 9.

——. 1990e. "Report of the Committee on the Elimination of Discrimination Against Women: Ninth Session." A/45/38, Supp. 38.

——. 1990f. "Report of the Committee on the Elimination of Discrimination Against Women: Eighth Session." A/44/38, 1990.

——. 1990g. "Effective Implementation of United Nations Instruments and Effective Functioning of Bodies Established Pursuant to Such Instruments: Report of the Secretary-General." A/45/707, November.

——. 1990h. "United Nations Fund for Victims of Torture: Report of the Secretary-General." A/45/633, October.

——. 1990i. "Report of the Committee on the Elimination of Racial Discrimination." A/44/18, Supp. 18.

——. 1990j. "Report of the Committee on the Elimination of Racial Discrimination." A/45/18.

——. 1992a. "Personnel Questions: Report of the Secretary-General on the Composition of the Secretariat." A/47/416, October 7.

——. 1992b. "Effective Implementation of International Instruments on Human Rights, Including Reporting Obligations under International Instruments on Human Rights." A/47/628, November 10.

—— C.3 (Third Committee). 1989a. "Summary Record of the 38th Meeting." A/C.3/44/SR.38, November 10.

———. 1989 b. "Summary Record of the 36th Meeting." A/C.3/44/SR.36, November 8.

———. 1989 c. "Summary Record of the 37th Meeting." A/C.3/44/SR.37, November 9.

———. 1989 d. "Summary Record of the 40th Meeting." A/C.3/44/SR.40, November 13.

———. 1989 e. "Summary Record of the 41st Meeting." A/C.3/44/SR.41, November 14.

———. 1989 f. "Summary Record of the 44th Meeting." A/C.3/44/SR.44, November 15.

———. 1989 g. "Summary Record of the 45th Meeting." A/C.3/44/SR.45, November 16.

———. 1989 h. "Summary Record of the 39th Meeting." A/C.3/44/SR.39, November 13.

———. 1990 a. "Summary Record of the 37th Meeting." A/C.3/44/SR.37, November 19.

UN GA C.5 (Fifth Committee). 1989. "Proposed Programme Budget for the Biennium 1990–1991: Adoption of a Convention on the Rights of the Child." A/C.5/44/28, November 15.

UNICEF (United Nations Children's Fund). 1991. *The State of the World's Children 1991.* New York: Oxford University Press.

———. 1992. *The State of the World's Children 1992.* New York: Oxford University Press.

———. 1993. *The State of the World's Children 1993.* New York: Oxford University Press.

UNITAR (United Nations Institute for Training and Research). 1991. *Manual on Human Rights Reporting.* New York: United Nations.

UN LS (Legislative Series). 1985. "Review of the Multilateral Treaty-Making Process." ST/LEG/SER/B/21. Sales No. E/F.83.V.8.

———. 1993. "Multilateral Treaties Deposited with the Secretary General: Status as at December 31, 1992." ST/LEG/SER/E/11.

United Nations. 1991. "Report of an International Consultation on AIDS and Human Rights: Geneva, 26–28 July 1989." HR/PUB/90/2.

van Boven, T. 1979. "United Nations and Human Rights: A Critical Appraisal." In *UN Law—Fundamental Rights: Two Topics in International Law,* ed. A. Cassese. The Netherlands: Sijthoff and Noordhoff.

———. 1989. "The Future Codification of Human Rights: Status of Deliberations—A Critical Analysis." *Human Rights Law Journal* 10:1–11.

———. 1991. "The International System of Human Rights: An Overview." In *Manual on Human Rights Reporting.* New York: United Nations Institute for Training and Research.

———. 1992. "The Role of the United Nations Secretariat." In *The United Nations and Human Rights: A Critical Appraisal,* ed. P. Alston. Oxford: Clarendon Press.

Veerman, P. 1991. *The Rights of the Child and the Changing Image of Childhood.* Dordrecht: Martinus Nijhoff Publishers.

Verhellen, E. 1992. "Changes in the Images of the Child." In *The Ideologies of Children's Rights,* ed. M. Freeman and P. Veerman. Dordrecht: Martinus Nijhoff Publishers.

Weiner, M. 1991. *The Child and the State in India: Child Labor and Education Policy in Comparative Perspective.* Princeton: Princeton University Press.

Weissbrodt, D. 1984. "The Contribution of International Nongovernmental Organizations to the Protection of Human Rights." In *Human Rights in International Law: II,* ed. T. Meron. London: Oxford University Press.

——. 1988. "Human Rights: An Historical Perspective." In *Human Rights,* ed. P. Davies. London: Routledge.

Wiseberg, L., and H. Scoble. 1979. "Monitoring Human Rights Violations: The Role of Nongovernmental Organizations." In *Human Rights and American Foreign Policy,* ed. D. Kommers and G. Loescher. Notre Dame: University of Notre Dame Press.

Wolf, J. 1992. "The Concept of the 'Best Interest' in Terms of the UN Convention on the Rights of the Child." In *The Ideologies of Children's Rights,* ed. M. Freeman and P. Veerman. Dordrecht: Martinus Nijhoff Publishers.

Wolfson, S. 1992. "Children's Rights: The Theoretical Underpinning of the 'Best Interests of the Child.'" In *The Ideologies of Children's Rights,* ed. M. Freeman and P. Veerman. Dordrecht: Martinus Nijhoff Publishers.

World Conference (World Conference on Human Rights). 1993. "Final Statement of the World Conference on Human Rights, 1993: Vienna Declaration and Programme of Action." June.

333

IN THE HUMAN RIGHTS IN
INTERNATIONAL PERSPECTIVE SERIES

~

VOLUME 1

*Human Rights and Peace:
International and National Dimensions*

By David P. Forsythe

~

VOLUME 2

Human Rights in the New Europe: Problems and Progress

Edited by David P. Forsythe

~

VOLUME 3

*The Convention on the Rights of the Child: United Nations
Lawmaking on Human Rights*

Lawrence J. LeBlanc